1967

JONATHAN SWIFT
AND THE AGE OF COMPROMISE

JONATHAN SWIFT
AND THE AGE OF COMPROMISE

by

KATHLEEN WILLIAMS

University of Kansas Press
Lawrence, 1965

PRINTED IN THE U.S.A. BY
THE UNIVERSITY OF KANSAS PRESS
LAWRENCE, KANSAS

PREFACE

The purpose of this study is to put forward an interpretation of Swift's work based entirely on the writings themselves and on their relation to ideas, attitudes, and literary methods current in his own day. It arises from the belief that one cause of the frequent misunderstanding of the major satires is that they have been considered in isolation from the political tracts, the letters, the sermons, the sets of maxims, and even in isolation from one another. As a result, the older interpretations of *Gulliver's Travels,* for instance, are totally contrary to attitudes Swift expresses elsewhere throughout his work. The "Voyage to the Houyhnhnms" is the crucial point in any critical estimate of Swift, and it has long seemed to me virtually impossible that so convinced an opponent of Deism could suggest as even desirable, whether or not attainable, a mode of life in which Deist principles are so obviously embodied as in that of the rational horses.

It is perfectly possible, I believe, to interpret *Gulliver's Travels, A Tale of a Tub,* and indeed all Swift's work, satisfactorily, by following his guidance as a responsible satirist in each individual work, and this is what the last two chapters of this study set out to do. Swift has not failed in his task of making his meaning clear to the candid reader. But because of the long history of preconceptions and misinterpretations it is difficult for us to come unprejudiced to the reading of his work. Despite the efforts of modern biographers, old memories of Swift the hater and destroyer of mankind still lurk at the back of our minds, and infinite damage has been done to the great satires by the popular image of Swift and the more lurid interpretations of his friendship with Vanessa and with Stella. Swift, it is too readily supposed, came to grief in his life through an excessive devotion to reason and an unbalanced loathing of the human body. Consequently, we expect to find the same extremism and the same disgust as part of the meaning of his work, and until these extraneous considerations are forgotten our minds are not open to the real effect of his satire. I have not therefore been concerned, in the chapters which follow, to give any consideration to the details of Swift's life. Many of these are too much a matter of conjecture to be other than misleading in relation to the moral satires, and I have done no more than suggest, on the evidence of what he actually wrote in the letters and elsewhere, certain personal tendencies which may have reinforced his conscious opinions on various matters of vital importance in his own day. But my chief concern is with the conscious opinions themselves, and with their embodiment in the major works.

Swift's characteristic ways of thinking and of writing are intimately related to the conditions of his time. His ideas are, for the most part, traditional, those of his Christian classical heritage, but his ways of reaching them, holding to them, and expressing them in words are intensely individual—individual and yet conditioned by the difficulties of an age in which the tradition to which he owed allegiance was under steady attack from various sides. When we look at the works themselves we see not idealistic extremism but practical and fruitful compromise: not a devotion to reason but a conviction that reason is not enough; not a scorn of the bodily nature of man but the certainty, frequently reiterated and shaping the very form and manner of his satire, that only through mind and body, through feeling as well as thought, can man live humanly and well. That extremism of various kinds existed in Swift's age cannot be doubted; but in his own work what is visible is a steady, careful weighing of extremes so that the traditional balance may still, however precariously, be kept. In this study of Swift I have attempted to show, by considering his work as a whole and in relation to certain contemporary attitudes, this process in action, and finally to examine, in the light of it, the three major satires. Only by such a re-examination, I believe, can false preconceptions be removed and the essential unity of Swift's work, and still more important, its balance, sanity, and humane wisdom, be convincingly demonstrated.

In recent years much work of the first importance has been done in the field of Swift studies, and I should like to pay here a debt of gratitude to the many scholars whose books and articles I have found stimulating and informative. Specific obligations are listed in the notes, but there are debts of a more general and pervasive nature which cannot be so listed; and, because my concern here has been primarily with the relation of Swift's thought to that of his contemporaries and immediate predecessors, I have left unmentioned many valuable studies, in other aspects of Swift's work, from which I have profited. I hope that this general acknowledgment will serve to convey my appreciation.

I am glad to give more particular thanks to Professor Irvin Ehrenpreis of Indiana University; to the Rev. W. Moelwyn Merchant of the University College of South Wales and Monmouthshire; and to Professor Alan D. McKillop of the Rice Institute, for whose valuable suggestions I am most grateful. I am indebted to the Editor of the University of Kansas Press for the help and guidance he has so readily given me. I wish also to thank the Editors of the *Journal of English Literary History,* who have kindly permitted me to make use of material which first appeared in that journal. I am obliged to the Oxford University Press for permission to quote from *The Poems of Jonathan Swift* and *Swift's Journal to Stella,* edited by Harold Williams; *A Tale of a Tub,* edited by A. C. Guthkelch and D. Nichol Smith; Louis A. Landa, *Swift and the Church of Ireland;* Rae Blanchard, *The Englishman: A Political Journal by Richard Steele; The Fable of the Bees,* edited by F. B. Kaye; and *Boswell's Life of Johnson,* edited by G. Birkbeck Hill. My extensive quotations from *The Prose Works of Jonathan Swift* are made by permission of Sir Basil Blackwell and Professor Herbert Davis.

—K. W.

CONTENTS

Illustrations

Chapter I

THE NEED FOR COMPROMISE

Jonathan Swift has perhaps always been to some degree an enigmatic figure. For generations of readers, his character and the details of his private life have provided a fascinating and probably insoluble problem. Legend and controversy have proliferated about the figure of the "mad parson," the "ribald priest and perjured lover," and they are with us still. In his own lifetime, opinions differed as to Swift's character and intentions, and as opinions differed, passions rose. Swift was always capable of arousing extremes of affection or dislike, and he seems, moreover, to have been one of those rare and striking persons whose slightest actions or sayings have a vividness which makes them significant. Avidly seized upon by his biographers, these assume a legendary or prophetic quality, and are made the key to his whole personality and work. "I shall be like that tree, I shall die at the top," "and not die here in a rage, like a poisoned rat in a hole"—such comments as these, some not quite serious, all natural and humane enough when read in their context and in relation to the circumstances in which their author found himself at the time, have inspired detailed descriptions of a tortured, self-centered misanthrope. Or, on the other hand, the mood of self-confidence displayed in Bishop Kennett's brilliant, malicious sketch of Swift showing off a little in the Queen's antechamber at Windsor can be seen as expressing his overbearing arrogance. A man like this, doomed to legendary significance, can be allowed no ordinary flippancy, no careless exaggeration or ingenious wit, in his private life or letters. He is forced into a consistency which properly belongs only to the creatures of our imagination, and of the many Jonathan Swifts offered us by the biographers not a few have been of that order. Yet when we read the letters and the *Journal to Stella* we meet a man who is after all very like ourselves: ambitious, self-doubting, sometimes despondent and sometimes assertive and cheerful, and all these only in the common degree, although he has been ill served by that capacity for the memor-

1

able phrase which has transfixed into permanence so many of his passing thoughts or moods.

Of course it is true that, apart from his personal qualities, the circumstances of Swift's life do invite interpretation, and are of the kind about which mystery and speculation easily grow. His own reticence about his relations with Esther Johnson and Hester Vanhomrigh soon set people searching for explanations, and around the whole subject of Swift's possible marriage, and why it took place or alternatively why it did not take place, an almost impenetrable thicket of report and hearsay and mere guesswork quickly grew up. Modern scholarship has thinned the growth, separating what is known and proved from what has been assumed or invented, and it would seem that Swift's situation, though unusual, is not unprecedented, and that it is not necessarily explicable only in terms of the sensational. But what is known and proved is remarkably little. From his correspondence and his political writings we can reconstruct whole periods of Swift's day-to-day life in detail; we know much of his opinions on public affairs, his anger at public mismanagement, his hopes and fears and his affection for the friends who shared them. But there are regions of his life to which we have no access, regions from which his dearest friends were deliberately shut out. From our knowledge of the *Journal to Stella* and of the prayers during her sickness we are probably more fully aware of the depth of Swift's affection for her than Pope and Bolingbroke and his other English friends appear, from the tone of their comments, to have been, but of what lay behind that unusual friendship we are ignorant still. Swift is always reticent in such matters; even in letters to Esther Johnson and Hester Vanhomrigh themselves there is concealment, whether behind the comforting pretense of the little language or behind the lists of unexplained episodes "from the time of spilling the coffee to drinking of coffee, from Dunstable to Dublin."

Under such circumstances there is temptation, perhaps, to look for more mystery than is really suggested by the few available facts, and though modern methods have checked the old-fashioned scandalmongering of which Swift was so often a victim, there is still an urge to explain both his writings and his life by medical or psychological means. From "the learned Dr. Beddoes" whom Sir Walter Scott refutes in his *Memoirs of Jonathan Swift* to the present day, there is a variety of such explanations to choose from. Some psychiatrists have applied the name "Lilliputian hallucinations" to neurotic fantasies about dwarfs, and Swift has been posthumously psychoanalyzed largely through an examination of the voyages to Lilliput and Brobdingnag, supported by reference to some of the more improbable stories of his life;[1] and while no doubt from the point of view of the psychoanalyst these studies are useful and interesting they have the danger to the layman interested in Swift's life and work, of appearing to exaggerate the oddities of both. Clearly, Swift's writings, like most of our greatest literature, make much use of subconscious material, and great writers, though probably no more odd than the rest of us, leave more evidence of their oddity to posterity than most people would disclose outside the analyst's consulting room. Clearly, too, Swift was not that rare creature, the normal man, but to readers of his work what is important is the power and conviction that result when subconscious material is used for conscious ends. To probe into the possible neurotic origins of the images which arise from below the threshold of consciousness can only be misleading to the ordinary reader. The present chapter is not intended, therefore, as in any way a biographical study or an interpretation of Swift's life. There are admirable modern biographies which have told us all we can know unless new facts come to light, and the purpose of this chapter is merely to suggest that certain personal tendencies, of which Swift was himself usually conscious, affected his writing in various recognizable ways.

Swift's enemies in his lifetime, and those who have written of him with dislike since his death, have laid much stress upon the dictatorial manner which his friends seem not to have resented or to have regarded as anything but a superficial foible. Indeed the deliberative assertiveness of Swift's public manner only half conceals the inner uncertainties more fully revealed in the *Journal to Stella,* the letters, and the prayers, for Swift's was an apprehensive nature, always waiting upon disaster. He seems to have recognized

3

this tendency in himself, and to have related it to his early life, and to the natural expectation that the future would follow the pattern of the past. It is noticeable that the fragment of formal biography that he left in manuscript, "Anecdotes of the Family of Swift,"[2] is essentially a record of disappointments, beginning even before his birth. Of the marriage of his father, Jonathan, and Abigail Erick, he remarks that it "was on both sides very indiscreet; for his wife brought her husband little or no fortune, and his death happening so suddenly before he could make a sufficient establishment for his family, his son (not then born) hath often been heard to say, that he felt the consequences of that marriage not only through the whole course of his education, but during the greatest part of his life." In so brief and selective an account of his youth, he finds it worth while to tell the curious story of his removal by his nurse, at the age of a year, from Dublin to Whitehaven, where he remained for almost three years; and certainly such an upheaval might well have shaken the confidence of so young a child. The account continues with further disappointments: the "ill-treatment of his nearest relations," which helped to bring about his being "stopped of his degree for dullness and insufficiency," his illness, the failure of the mission to King William on which he was sent by Sir William Temple, the meanness and dissimulation which robbed him of the promised prebend of Canterbury or Westminster, of the secretaryship to the Earl of Berkeley, and finally of the deanery of Derry. Similar disappointments dogged him, as we know, through the rest of his life, and it is hardly surprising that he should have written to Bolingbroke in 1729, "I remember, when I was a little boy, I felt a great fish at the end of my line which I drew up almost on the ground, but it dropped in, and the disappointment vexes me to this very day, and I believe it was the type of all my future disappointments."[3]

Such a nature is capable of great and sudden elation, but of equally sudden alarm when it seems that, after all, there is to be no permanent escape from disappointment; and the charm, and much of the value, of the *Journal to Stella* lie in its intimate portrayal of the sensitive and volatile nature usually so carefully concealed in public. We see how easily he could be made downcast and fearful by some slight happening, or by a dream even; "I was dreaming the most melancholy things in the world of poor Stella," he writes on December 1, 1710, "and was grieving and crying all night."[4] The dreams he mentions are all intimations of misfortune, for his mind turned naturally to apprehension and in any sudden event his first reaction was to fear the worst. On the letter which brought him news, from Pope and Arbuthnot, of the death of John Gay, he wrote: "On my dear friend Mr. Gay's death; received December 15, but not read till the 20th, by an impulse foreboding some misfortune."[5] And to Sheridan in 1726: "I have had two months of great uneasiness at the ill account of Mrs. Johnson's health, and as it is usual, feared the worst that was possible, and doubted all the good accounts that were sent me."[6] There are other indications of his ready fears of the loss of friends, and his wretchedness when the dreaded parting came about. The death of friends was a disaster feared more than any, and it was these losses, not the repeated failure of his hopes of preferment, which were the most desperately felt "disappointments" of Swift's life. In February 1735-6 he was writing to Mrs. Whiteway, on her son's death, "I was born to a million of disappointments; I had set my heart very much upon that young man, but I find he has no business in so corrupt a world."[7] The illness of his dearest friends hung fearfully upon his spirits, "for I do not yet find that years have begun to harden me,"[8] he wrote to Pope in January 1730-1. Separation was only less terrible; of all Swift's letters one of the most moving in its humanity and vulnerability is that written to Arbuthnot, perhaps the most dearly loved of his English friends: "Writing to you much would make me stark mad; judge his condition who has nothing to keep him from being miserable but endeavouring to forget those for whom he has the greatest value, love, and friendship."[9] The origins of Swift's fearfulness, his dread of desertion and loss, can only be guessed at, but the form it took was a not ignoble one.

Swift's habit of mind, then, would seem to be that of a man quickly oppressed by circumstances and by others' opinions of him, and he recognized, resented, and fought against the depression so easily induced in him by events beyond his own control. As he remarks in "Thoughts on Various Subjects," "Small causes are sufficient to make a man uneasy, when great ones are not in the way: for want of a block he will stumble at a straw."[10] Perhaps it was this incessant mental activity, seizing upon the slightest causes of uneasiness when it was not exercised upon some creative work, which was the "conjured spirit" of his mind "that would do mischief if I would not give it employment,"[11]

> that fatal bend of mind,
> Still to unhappy restless thoughts inclin'd,[12]

as he calls it in the poem "Occasioned by Sir William Temple's Late Illness and Recovery." A similar remark occurs in an early letter to Thomas Swift, in 1693: "I protest I cannot much pity your present circumstances, which keep your mind and your body in motion, and myself was never very miserable while my thoughts were in a ferment, for I imagine a dead calm to be the troublesomest part of our voyage through the world."[13] The activities of the conjured spirit of alarm, and Swift's irritated efforts to subdue it, are plain enough in the *Journal*. In April 1711 he tells Stella that he has dined with St. John, Prior, and Erasmus Lewis, and that St. John seemed "terribly down and melancholy," and at once his fears are ready: "perhaps something is gone wrong; perhaps there is nothing in it. God bless my own dearest MD, and all is well."[14] Two days later, he is writing to tell Stella how he has fought his fear of having offended, and has scotched his apprehensions by a direct attack on St. John:

One thing I warned him of, Never to appear cold to me, for I would not be treated like a school-boy; that I had felt too much of that in my life already (meaning from Sir William Temple); that I expected every great minister, who honoured me with his acquaintance, if he heard or saw any thing to my disadvantage, would let me know it in plain words, and not put me in pain to guess by the change or coldness of his countenance or behaviour; for it was what I would hardly bear from a crowned head.[15]

His unease brings to his mind the early days with Temple, when dependence had been inescapable, but this time he has escaped from his sense of oppression and fear: "Don't you remember how I used to be in pain when Sir William Temple would look cold and out of humour for three or four days, and I used to suspect a hundred reasons? I have pluckt up my spirit since then, faith; he spoiled a fine gentleman."[16] The note of humorous bravado is unmistakable; it suggests that the independence of Swift's attitude to St. John and other high-placed or high-ranking friends was a necessity for him, a deliberate effort to escape the pain of apprehension and the fear that he was somehow at fault. High-handedness was Swift's way of asserting himself positively over circumstance, assuming some sort of control over the events outside and those within his own mind, particularly the recurring sense of disaster. And the passages where he laughs at his own "proud stomach" in the *Journal* would suggest that he knew what he was doing. Too much can be made of the confession to Pope, in a joint letter to him and to Bolingbroke in April 1729, that all his endeavors, from a boy, to distinguish himself were for want of a great title and fortune, "that I might be used like a Lord by those who have an opinion of my parts—whether right or wrong, it is no great matter, and so the reputation of wit or great learning does the office of a blue ribbon, or of a coach and six horses." Far from being a serious confession of disappointed ambition and consequent embitterment, this is a humorous assumption of such ambition, adopted in order to lead up, by way of a friendly hit at lordship as exemplified by Bolingbroke, to an urbane and well-turned compliment to Pope himself:

To be remembered for ever on the account of our friendship, is what would exceedingly please me; but yet I never loved to make a visit, or to be seen walking with my betters, because they get all the eyes and civilities from me. I no sooner writ this than I corrected myself, and remembered Sir Fulke Greville's epitaph, Here lies, etc, who was friend to Sir Philip Sidney. And therefore I most heartily thank you for your desire that I would record our friendship in verse, which, if I can succeed in, I will never desire to write one more line in poetry while I live.[17]

Swift's ambitions were not of so commonplace a kind, and his despondency during the first years of exile in Dublin was caused less by the loss of power and of being "used like a Lord"—though the intensity of his social, political, and literary undertakings in London must have subdued the "conjured spirit" and made him happier than he had ever been—than by the loss of that secure circle of affectionate and understanding friends for which he was never to find a thoroughly satisfactory substitute.

The letters, then, suggest—as do Swift's perplexed relations with Stella and Vanessa, whatever the detailed truth may be—a certain lack of confidence in himself and the probable course of his life. It is as though there always existed, for Swift, an emptiness, a state of despondency in which life became meaningless. He feared it because he knew how readily it opened to engulf him when his mind had no better employment than apprehension, and he took all possible means to prevent despondency, if only by "la bagatelle." This is not to say that he was particularly unbalanced; thousands of people live in such a state of insecurity, which is very easily caused. Dr. Johnson, whose likeness to the author he so much disliked has been frequently remarked upon ever since Boswell's shocked comment that his opinion of human nature was "worse than Swift," is perhaps the best-documented case of this type of character among literary men, and it did not lead to unbroken despair or to insane egoism any more than in Swift. Neither of them was habitually melancholic or misanthropic, and much of Swift's life and work, and much of his correspondence, until the very last years, is decidedly cheerful. It is misleading to lay too much stress on such isolated remarks as the definition of life as "a ridiculous tragedy, which is the worst kind of composition,"[18] or the claim that *Gulliver's Travels* is intended to vex, not to divert, the world. Both passages are written in response to letters from Pope. The first adjusts "the common saying of life being a farce" to formulate a definition more in keeping with Pope's situation; his constant illness was at that time particularly acute, and Swift's response to illness, pain, or death among his friends was the quite common one of baffled wretchedness which the phrase "ridiculous tragedy" implies. The tragedy of life consists, for Swift, in the loss of friends; he defines life as a tragedy in a letter of condolence to Mrs. Moore on the loss of her daughter: "For life is a tragedy, wherein we sit as spectators awhile, and then act our own part in it."[19] The second of these famous comments is an attempt to show Pope and the other Scriblerians that

8

Gulliver's Travels will not be the light topical satire on scientific and antiquarian oddities that they obviously expect, but a work of greater seriousness and scope. Against this may be set his letter to Charles Wogan in 1732, in which during an account of contemporary satire he explains, "You see Pope, Gay, and I, use all our endeavours to make folks merry and wise,"[20] and against his moments of apprehension and despondency can be put his description of himself as "a perfect Stranger to the Spleen"[21] and the many comments of his friends upon his high spirits and good humor, even late in his life. Probably his own remark to Chetwode in 1723 is the best summing-up of his nature: "I always expect tomorrow will be worse, but I enjoy today as well as I can."[22] Swift's pessimism was ingrained; but it was the kind of pessimism that, because it expects the worst, is always ready to make the most of things as they are. This is the attitude constantly found in his writing—not the attitude of a seriously disordered mind. Swift's work cannot be explained as merely the result of mental disturbance; the old explanation of *Gulliver's Travels* as being the splenetic outburst of a man with a grudge against life really explains nothing, and has no relation to the facts of his life or character, or indeed to the work itself. Swift has left us his own warnings against such simplicity of interpretation. One such warning is given in his famous letter of September 29, 1725, to Pope, where he appears anxious to insist that his *Travels* is not to be interpreted as an outburst of the "Fiercenesse, Rage, Wrath, and Inhumanitie" of Timon. The insistence is humorously expressed, for Swift could laugh at his own seriousness, but it is insistence none the less. After referring to his definition of man as *"animal rationis capax"* he continues: "Upon this great foundation of misanthropy, though not in Timon's manner, the whole building of my *Travels* is erected; and I never will have peace of mind till all honest men are of my opinion. By consequence you are to embrace it immediately, and procure that all who deserve my esteem may do so too. The matter is so clear that it will admit of no dispute; nay, I will hold a hundred pounds that you and I agree in the point."[23] After the publication of *Gulliver's Travels,* Swift wrote a parody of the attacks made on him as a malicious, embittered misanthrope—

attacks based on an overliteral interpretation of his habitual presentation of the moral in terms of the physical, on a reading of allegory as if it were a straightforward narrative. In this poem, the "Panegyric on the Reverend Dean Swift," he attributes to himself, so he tells Lord Bathurst, qualities in the direct reverse of his character:[24]

> Since you alone of all the Race
> Disclaim the Human Name, and Face,
> And with the Virtues pant to wear
> (May Heav'n Indulgent hear your Pray'r!)
> The Proof of your high Origine,
> The Horse's Countenance Divine.[25]

Swift's writings are shaped, as he was anxious to make his friends understand, by a deliberate and considered attitude towards the nature of man and of the world man has made for himself. But, as he would himself have been the first to agree, it is rarely possible to separate a man's rational conclusions from those irrational convictions which are a part of his character, and in Swift's case as in so many others it is doubtless true that the general direction of his attitude was inherent in his nature, however completely it was worked out in intellectual terms. For instance, the "middle way" which Swift advocates in so many aspects of social and personal life is both a reasoned conclusion and, probably, a necessity of his temper, and it may be that the indirection of his satiric methods is due both to the complexity of what he has to express—for the Augustan middle way is not a simple thing—and to a strong personal sense of the complication of life, making him withdraw from too positive a position. In so far as it is a part of this indirection, a way of dealing with complexity, the "mask" or mouthpiece[26] so often employed by Swift may also illustrate the coincidence of deliberate method and personal bias, but again its significance must not be overstressed, for its use is by no means habitual in Swift, and it is unlikely, therefore, that it was necessary to him as a disguise for timidity or self-consciousness. Nor is he singular in his adoption of such a technique, for some sort of assumed personality is often a necessity for a satirist, and among Swift's contemporaries Dryden, Pope, Addison, and

10

sometimes Defoe adopt in their satiric writings a personality which differs slightly or, on occasion, markedly, from their everyday selves. By this method an opinion can be expressed with the necessary emphasis or exaggeration, or an absurdity can be parodied. But it is true that this use of the mouthpiece is very simple, compared with Swift's usual practice. The difference is not that the mouthpiece itself is in Swift more fully developed or consistent, but that the handling of it is far more elaborate; it is not, normally, a simple disguise but a satiric tool of great adaptability, part of Swift's habitually crablike approach to his subject. The word "mask" is, indeed, a little misleading in Swift's case. There are a few simple disguises, like the "Person of Quality" of "A Letter to a Young Gentleman Lately Entered into Holy Orders," which offers an escape from Swift's official personality as a Churchman of some rank, and enables him to express his own opinions more freely, as from the layman's point of view. But more typical of Swift is the character used not like a mask, to conceal, but like a puppet, to express openly through its antics the opinions of its master. He does not hide behind his mouthpiece, but is constantly in view, manipulating it, laughing at it, keeping us conscious that it exists only as it is created and used by him. This is the satirist's technique; Fielding, when he came to write novels, handled his characters in the same way. Himself a satirist, he retained the satirist's need to keep himself directly in touch with his readers, and he speaks not through but by means of his characters. For Swift, the need is imperative; in his most important satires the mouthpieces are themselves ironically treated, so that we feel ourselves to be in touch not so much with a convincing creation as with the mind which simultaneously creates and criticizes it. Nor are the mouthpieces developed consistently as characters, for such a method allows only of comparatively simple satiric effects, and Swift's aims are complex and inclusive. It would be hazardous, therefore, to suppose that Swift normally uses masks because of some lack of confidence in himself, as a means of concealment which will allow him to write more freely because less self-consciously; in effect they do not hide, but reveal. But they constitute one of his chief methods of indirection, and

11

one may perhaps suggest that the mind which most fully expresses itself in the complicatedly ironical treatment of Lemuel Gulliver is a mind too deeply conscious of the difficult and many-sided nature of experience to present any simple, confident answers to its problems. The early poems, again, though often interesting in their content and their choice of imagery, are clumsy and ineffectual, and it is only when he ceases to express himself directly and develops his characteristic irony and urbanity that Swift can organize his emotions and ideas into a successful poem. Perhaps the "little language" in which the more intimate passages of the *Journal to Stella* are written, or the evasiveness of the letters to Hester Vanhomrigh and of "Cadenus and Vanessa" (also intended for Hester alone) are further examples of the greater comfort and ease of expression that Swift found in obliquity. Possibly, though he doubtless evolved his various techniques of indirection as necessary satiric devices, their peculiar value to him, and the ingenuity and brilliance of his use of them, are to be explained partly in terms of a temperamental need.

But the plainest examples of how in Swift personal reactions can effectively reinforce rational positions occur in the most powerful symbols of *Gulliver's Travels,* the Struldbrugs of Book III and the Yahoos of Book IV. The episode of the Struldbrugs is written for a purpose which, in the context of the book, one can define in intellectual terms, but the vivid horror of Gulliver's account, which so excellently reinforces the intellectual and moral meaning, surely comes from the horror in Swift's own mind which he tried so strenuously to avoid. From many of his comments it is evident that Swift feared his recurrent illness of deafness and giddiness would develop into madness in later life, and though the miseries of his last years have given this recurrent fear, in retrospect, an exaggerated and melodramatic significance of prophecy, it was real and natural enough, considering the state of medical knowledge in his day and the fact that his uncle did die insane. In any case the fear of lunacy was, however unfounded, one of the forms which Swift's apprehensiveness took from time to time, one aspect of the void of despair always ready to receive him when high spirits and activity failed. The Struldbrugs ex-

12

press an intellectual conviction of the limitations of man's nature and a desire to combat newer and less stern conceptions, but conviction is backed by a natural pessimism, and an upsurge of obsessive fear for his own future, which brings home the lesson with an unforgettable pathos and force. The Yahoos, whose function in Book IV is as precise as that of the Struldbrugs in Book III, are similarly brought to vivid life by a hatred of the unreasoning and the meaningless, another side of Swift's fear of madness, which powerfully reinforces those traditional views of the nature of man to which his conscious allegiance was given.

Occasionally conscious allegiance is at odds with personal tendencies, and the curious tensions of parts of *A Tale of a Tub* may perhaps be attributable to such a situation, but even in such cases, where reluctance to accept what rationally must be accepted wells up in the tone of voice or the kind of image, personal feeling is made to contribute to the whole effect. This again is not an unusual state of affairs, except perhaps in the degree to which Swift masters and makes artistic use of such tensions between feeling and intellectual conviction, but it was particularly to be expected at the time in which he lived and wrote. The *Essay on Man* is one of the most difficult and most fascinating of the poems of Swift's friend Pope largely because, as well as the deliberate attempt at reconciliation between the old traditional view of the universe and the different view of a scientific age—whether by means of intellectual argument or by imagery and positioning of material—there is an occasional inability on the part of the poet to accept his own conclusions.

> Who sees with equal eye, as God of all,
> A hero perish, or a sparrow fall,
> Atoms or systems into ruin hurl'd,
> And now a bubble burst, and now a world.
>
> Like bubbles on the sea of Matter born,
> They rise, they break, and to that sea return.[27]

In such lines as these, Pope contemplates the cold inhuman majesty of that Newtonian universe which he must accept as true but which cannot, really, be reconciled with the old order. A compact universe swung from heaven by a golden chain has given place to a vast emptiness in which worlds as ephemeral as bubbles rise into brief existence, only to break and to be replaced, under the equal eye of a God now infinitely remote, by the same inevitable process. The chill magnificence of Pope's images and the resigned dignity of his cadences reveal his underlying knowledge of the hopelessness of his self-imposed task, his underlying aversion to that picture of man and his world which he has chosen to celebrate. Pope's *Essay* is one of the most ambitious examples— all the more honest and impressive for its partial failure—of the Augustan attempt to keep the old in accepting what must be accepted of the new. Their gallant effort was complicated by the subconscious or half-conscious loyalties which sometimes disrupted conscious decisions, but none the less it is in terms of the deliberate effort that the work of these men must be discussed. For in recent years as our knowledge of the early eighteenth century, its ideas and preoccupations, has increased, so the poetry and prose of the period has been seen as less assured, more troubled and tentative. For the "peace of the Augustans" has been substituted an age of difficult and conscious adjustment, an age of effort.

The reign of Queen Anne and that of her successor constituted a period of transition from the great ferment of the seventeenth century to the relative stability which characterized the age of Johnson. During the first quarter of the eighteenth century there was a great settling down and sorting out of values. A new outlook was developing and the intellectual world had to be reorganized in accordance with it. The great developments brought about by the intellectual, political, and social revolutions of the preceding half century had to be absorbed; the useless part of the old had to be discarded, the false and dangerous part of the new had to be curbed.[28]

Similarly the writers of the time are now seen as the spokesmen of a period whose hallmark is not a complacent acceptance of what is new but an attempt, exemplified by Pope's *Essay on Man,* to blend what is useful in the new attitudes with what is indispensable in the old. The effort involved, of course, not only assimilation and reconciliation but attack; aspects either of the new thought or of the old, which appeared wrong or absurd, and so hampered the process of adjustment, must be fought. The Scrib-

14

lerus Club, more inclusive than the Addison circle with its emphasis on political tolerance and social urbanity, is a particularly good example of this. The aim of the Club was a serious one, to ridicule ways of thought, whether ancient or modern, which seemed extravagant and unrealistic; and this task of reconciliation, of achieving a balance between conflicting errors, was one which Swift attempted on a wider scale in his own satires.

Our recent emphasis on the difficult and transitional nature of the early years of the eighteenth century has had its effect on our interpretation of the methods, as well as of the material, of the writers of the time. Several critics—for example, Dr. Leavis and Professor Maynard Mack—have shown the complexities which underlie the smooth Augustan surface of the poetry of Pope; Dr. Herbert Davis has pointed out the richness of Swift's seventeenth century style in *A Tale of a Tub,* and shown that it is "in the direct line of Wit."[29] Swift often uses the witty style as part of his satiric method, parodying the soaring of a mind which, losing its direction in the mazes of metaphysical conjecture, falls into anticlimax as the dead Bird of Paradise falls to the ground. The "Tritical Essay on the Faculties of the Mind" is a simple, though neat, example of this, but the *Tale* is more ingenious in its adaptation of a seventeenth century style to suggest busy, meaningless mental activity of any kind and of any period. A comparison of a famous passage from the *Tale* with an almost equally famous one from *The Anatomy of Melancholy* will show how perfectly the manner is captured and turned to satiric point. Here is Burton's passage, from the Third Member of the Second Section of the Second Partition, "Air rectified. With a digression of the Air" (the complicated and happily digressive structure of the *Anatomy* itself relates pointedly to the *Tale*):

As a long-winged hawk, when he is first whistled off the fist, mounts aloft, and for his pleasure fetcheth many a circuit in the air, still soaring higher and higher till he be come to his full pitch, and in the end when the game is sprung, comes down amain, and stoops upon a sudden: so will I, having now come at last into these ample fields of air, wherein I may freely expatiate and exercise myself for my recreation, awhile rove, wander round about the world, mount aloft to those ethereal orbs and celestial spheres, and

15

so descend to my former elements again. In which progress I will first see whether that relation of the friar of Oxford be true, concerning those northern parts under the Pole (if I meet *obiter* with the Wandering Jew, Elias Artifex, or Lucian's Icaromenippus, they shall be my guides). . . .

This is Swift's version of Burton's pleasurable anticipation of fruitful conjecture, with the footless Bird of Paradise, unable to come to earth until it drops dead upon the wing, substituted for Burton's purposeful hawk:

AND, whereas the mind of Man, when he gives the Spur and Bridle to his Thoughts, doth never stop, but naturally sallies out into both extreams of High and Low, of Good and Evil; His first Flight of Fancy, commonly transports Him to Idea's of what is most Perfect, finished, and exalted; till having soared out of his own Reach and Sight, not well perceiving how near the Frontiers of Height and Depth, border upon each other; with the same Course and Wing, he falls down plum into the lowest Bottom of Things; like one who travels the East into the West; or like a strait Line drawn by its own Length into a Circle. Whether a Tincture of Malice in our Natures, makes us fond of furnishing every bright Idea with its Reverse; Or, whether Reason reflecting upon the Sum of Things, can, like the Sun, serve only to enlighten one half of the Globe, leaving the other half, by Necessity, under Shade and Darkness: Or, whether Fancy, flying up to the imagination of what is Highest and Best, becomes over-short, and spent, and weary, and suddenly falls like a dead Bird of Paradise, to the Ground. Or, whether after all these Metaphysical Conjectures, I have not entirely missed the true Reason; The Proposition, however, which hath stood me in so much Circumstance, is altogether true. . . .[30]

The kind of image used, the loosely linked clauses, the way in which ideas are related to other ideas by arbitrary mental association—all these are as much a part of the satire as is the content of the passage, and that he can use this involuted style, itself "like a strait Line drawn by its own Length into a Circle," so convincingly and at the same time ironically, with no more exaggeration than is required to make his point, is a further indication of the divided allegiance of the day. Indeed complexity, in some shape, remains a feature of Swift's manner to the end; he could never have expressed himself in the simple clarities of the Enlightenment.

The leading figures of the early eighteenth century were very much aware of their task of adaptation, Swift as much as any;

and in him, with his extraordinary sensitivity to the effect of the tone of voice in writing, style is frequently the embodiment of a particular way of thinking which is being set before us for our contemplation. The breathless, aimless eagerness of manner in so much of *A Tale of a Tub* brings before us the dangers of uncontrolled speculation, a spider-like spinning of systems and theories from our own entrails, whether the systems be on the model of Aristotle or of Descartes. But Swift, with his restless energy, the inexhaustible inventiveness which produced the *Tale* itself and the fabulous voyages of Gulliver, knew only too well the seductiveness of undisciplined speculation, and his delight in it, as well as his disapproval of it, is made to contribute to satiric effect. In Swift's work, the views expressed can no more be considered without reference to the manner of their expression than they can be in any other successful writer, nor can they be divorced from personal experience and personal feeling.

But in reading authors of this period, one should attempt to relate them to the uncertainties, and the efforts towards certainty, of their time. They cannot be explained in terms of the age of Donne, or of Milton, or of Samuel Johnson; we can only try to see what they clung to and what they discarded in the attitudes of their predecessors and those of their contemporaries who pointed forward to another kind of certainty. Their opinions, and their ways of embodying those opinions in words, are both conditioned by the mental upheavals of that physically peaceful age, when questions of religious, philosophical, social, and political importance had somehow to be worked out until at least a temporary and practical solution could be reached. Most people agreed that the internal physical peace of the country must not be broken again: the threat of France, and the constant menace of the exiled court of James at Saint-Germain, provided a spur to the efforts of Queen Anne's subjects to reach a settlement of outstanding problems. In politics Robert Harley, who became Swift's dearly loved friend, was trying hard early in the century to form the nucleus of a group which would bring moderates of both parties into power, and Addison, also a friend of Swift, was campaigning,

17

with elegance and good humor, for a reasonable tolerance in all the public activities of mankind.

But behind political and social problems, and threatening always to intensify them, were the deeper problems of religion, morals, and philosophy; differences in the interpretation of the nature and function of man, and of man's relationship to the universe and its creator. In all these problems Swift was actively and often passionately concerned, and his writings are shaped by a deliberate and considered attitude towards them. Where his conclusions are tentative, and where his solutions are compromises, it is because such conclusions and such solutions seem to him the only ones practicable in an age of "sorting out of values," though it may well be that the inconclusiveness of an age of transition is reinforced by a personal lack of trust and confidence. The satires are the work of a most individual mind and character, but it was a mind involved in the particular problems of his day, and only where the personal and the public coincide do Swift's private problems concern us. So, although it is doubtless true that the complication and difficulty of Swift's satire is the result of complication and difficulty in the man himself as well as in the material he strove to order, his personal predicament is of importance to the reader only in so far as it reinforces with emotional emphasis the methods and ideas consciously adopted in his work. It is not through his relations with Stella or Varina or Vanessa, but through his relations with the moral, philosophic, and political thinking of the age, that we can approach most nearly to the meanings of this most indirect of satirists.

Chapter II

THE ORDERING MIND

Among the tasks with which the more traditional thinkers of the late seventeenth century were faced, perhaps the most difficult and the most pressing was that of maintaining the responsibility of man in various spheres, his power to shape circumstances. Swift no doubt felt the problem to be especially urgent, because his own personal need to assert his control over circumstances and over his own mind was markedly strong. Only thus could he hope to rise above his natural apprehensiveness, or overcome the dread of madness, and it is perhaps a sense of personal urgency which gives so sharp an edge to his pronouncements upon various ways of thought that might rob man of his human responsibility. Again a personal predicament vitalizes an intellectual position; but in any case the neoclassic tradition which Swift inherited had always stressed the importance of the ordering mind of man. Alone among the creatures, man was honored and burdened with the task of imposing unity on the multitudinous world, of finding some approximation to the order and meaning intended by the Divine Mind itself. For early and confident classicists like Sidney, and for Milton later, the process was related in its lesser way to the creative power of God, and though further philosophic developments prevented such a comparison in the Augustan period, the strenuous assertion of order, the interpretation of the flux of experience, remained up to Dr. Johnson's day an essential part of literary and also of moral activity. But the task, always an heroic one, became overpoweringly difficult in the situation in which the neoclassic tradition found itself at the turn of the century. Dryden's poetry and prose provide an epitome of the turmoil of the age: he inherits the high Renaissance classicism of the Elizabethans, with whom he has a certain temperamental affinity, but he is faced with the formidable influence of Hobbes and of the scientific movement at the moment of their greatest power. Dryden, with his lucid quick intelligence and his sensitiveness to the current of ideas in his time, was very well aware of his position

betwixt two Ages cast,
The first of this, and hindmost of the last,[1]

and aware too that the primacy of the ordering mind, in the universe and in the microcosm man, could only be maintained by a certain amount of temporizing with the new world. Thus in the Preface to *Annus Mirabilis* he defines the process of poetic creation in Hobbes's terms, but without yielding the most important point, the positive, shaping activity of the poet.[2] In Dryden's definition the poet retains the responsibility which had in some form belonged to him since Sidney's formulation of English neoclassic theory; he shapes and selects among the thronging associations which the senses pass into his mind. Dryden's accounts of how poetry is conceived and written stress above all the interpreting power of the mind over its material; it interprets by ordering, by relating its materials to form a unity. To a mind so devoted to the neoclassic ideal of order, a philosophy which suggests that man's life or his poetry was at the mercy of chance occurrences, of atoms or association, was horrifying, particularly since Dryden's mind, like that of his "cousin Swift," was a full one; and without confidence in "the providence of wit" he could scarcely control the thronging images. His lines to Sir Robert Howard show clearly the connection which still tenuously existed between the creating mind of man and the creative power which had produced and still sustained the universe:

> Or is it Fortune's work, that in your head
> The curious Net that is for fancies spread,
> Lets through its Meshes every meaner thought
> While rich Idea's there are only caught?
> Sure that's not all; this is a piece too fair
> To be the child of Chance, and not of Care.
> No Atoms casually together hurl'd
> Could e're produce so beautifull a world.
> Nor dare I such a doctrine here admit,
> As would destroy the providence of wit.[3]

Dryden searched for meaning and order in poetry, religion, politics, faced always with a materialism which carried more authority than the Lucretianism which had threatened his predecessors. Sidney and Spenser had both been forced to defend the meaning of the universe against the atomic philosophy of the ancients and against certain eccentric moderns like Giordano Bruno, but they had been supplied with adequate weapons. Spenser's world was unified by his all-embracing Christian Neo-platonism, and by the habit of mind which saw, in all the things of this world, aspects of their divine original, the "soveraine light, From whose pure beams al perfect beauty springs."[4] Material things, since for Spenser they all embody the Ideas to a greater or less degree, are themselves already latent symbols of those Ideas, and thus he is armed against the materialism which threatened to rob man's world of meaning, and can allow the partial truth of Lucretianism only to show it as itself a part of the meaning of the universe, not a denial of that meaning. Chance and change are themselves part of the developing purpose of God; variety is only another aspect of unity. In the strength of this certainty Spenser can deal even with that mutability and apparent decay which recent observation of the heavens had brought so powerfully before the Elizabethan mind, and can put into the mouth of Nature the sovereign goddess, vicegerent of God, the confident verdict:

> I well consider all that ye have sayd,
>   And find that all things stedfastnes doe hate
>   And changed be: yet being rightly wayd
>   They are not changed from their first estate;
>   But by their change their being doe dilate:
>   And turning to themselves at length againe,
>   Doe work their owne perfection so by fate:
>   Then over them Change doth not rule and raigne;
> But they raigne over change, and doe their states maintaine.[5]

As Pope was to put it later in his own less convinced and less convincing version of the same argument,

> All Nature is but Art unknown to thee,
> All Chance, Direction which thou canst not see.[6]

Spenser's confidence was not achieved without effort, for his intense consciousness of mutability, of the beauty and pathos of what changes and dies, complicated his task, but for the more de-

21

tached and intellectual Sidney it would seem to have been easier. In *Arcadia* the materialist doctrines of Cecropia, the wicked queen, present only a slight challenge to the absolute integrity of Pamela, and one which she is able contemptuously to refute by the exercise of an exalted reason. Cecropia's insidious suggestion that the universe is mindless, and that God is only the invention of human fear, is countered by Pamela's "For that is chaunceable which happeneth; and if it happen, there was a time before it hapned, when it might not have happened: or els it did not happen; and so of chaunceable, not eternall, as now being, then not being. And as absurd it is to thinke that if it had a beginning, his beginning was derived from Chaunce: for Chaunce could never make all thinges of nothing." Perfect order, beauty, constancy cannot be the result of chance; in fact, "This worlde therefore cannot otherwise consist but by a minde of Wisdome, which governes it."[7] And Sidney's *Apologie for Poetrie* remains the noblest neoclassic expression of confidence in that power in the mind of man which is the counterpart in human terms of the divine wisdom, man's "exalted wit" which in a fallen world can yet gain some knowledge of the original creation of the "heavenly maker."

Sidney's trust is in reason, the characteristic neoclassic way to the discovery of meaning in the world, and a way which long retained its prestige. But the reason that had served him so well was less serviceable to the Augustans, since it was falling from its high estate; nor of course could Spenser's Neoplatonism be used with much conviction. Dryden can still quote the Italian Neoplatonist Bellori; in the "Parallel of Poetry and Painting" he quotes his theory of the nature of art in some detail—a purely Neoplatonic theory. Dryden is clearly aware of the relation of Bellori's ideas to his own classicism, but his approval of them is rather shamefaced: "In these pompous expressions, or such as these, the Italian has given you his Idea of a Painter; and though I cannot much commend the style, I needs must say, there is somewhat in the matter."[8] Pope, again, uses an emasculated version of Spenser's Platonic view of the nature of the universe in the *Essay on Man,* in a gallant attempt to blend the old and the

22

new, but admirable poem though it is the *Essay* indicates the grave limitations, for the Augustan age, of Platonism as a way of upholding meaning in the world.

The neoclassic love of order is necessarily cut off, in an age of clear and distinct ideas when all is "reduced to sense," from the Platonism which once had done so much to nourish it. "All those sublime thoughts which tower above the clouds," said Locke, "and reach as high as heaven itself, take their rise and footing here: in all that good extent wherein the mind wanders, in those remote speculations, it may seem to be elevated with, it stirs not one jot beyond the ideas which sense or reflection have offered for its contemplation."[9] The Platonic Ideas, and the theories of art and nature which Renaissance classicists derived in part from them, could scarcely survive unscathed in the new atmosphere, and during the eighteenth century neoclassicism is gradually separated, by the movement of modern thought, from the Ideas and the Aristotelian Universals which gave it life. For Hobbes, "There is nothing universal but names,"[10] and for Locke "general and universal belong not to the real existence of things, but are the inventions and creatures of the understanding, made by it for its own use."[11] Dryden, though he never surrendered his conviction that Providence is the unity behind "wild nature," and that similarly in man the providence of wit asserts itself over the confusion of the senses, is not at all certain how to prove his case. He is certain enough about the truth of Nature, order, unity, but ready to temporize about the way to find that truth, whether in poetry, politics, or religion. To keep the essentials clear it was necessary, now, to be adaptable in matters of proof or of technique. For Dryden and for many of his contemporaries it was often useful to be "inclined to scepticism in philosophy."

Swift's situation in the neoclassic tradition was in some ways akin to Dryden's. His fragmentary "Thoughts on Freethinking" shows an insistence similar to Dryden's on the power of the mind to select from and shape the thoughts which flow in upon it. He tells us that "a prelate of the kingdom of Ireland" remarked to him "that the difference betwixt a madman and one in his wits, in what related to speech, consisted in this; that the former spoke out whatever came into his mind, and just in the confused manner as his imagination presented the ideas: The latter only expressed such thoughts as his judgment directed him to choose, leaving the rest to die away in his memory."[12] Swift appears to find the distinction an important one; perhaps he welcomed it as a proof—though on another level than that of the creative poet, with which Dryden is concerned—of the positive action of the mind upon its experience.[13] The terms in which the remarks of the Irish prelate are put forward are substantially those of Hobbes, but the total effect is different from that of Hobbes's account: what is stressed is not that "external bodies in motion press on the internal motions and produce phantasms or immediate appearances, and these are prolonged by memory and imagination which is decaying sense,"[14] but that though all men are presented by the imagination with a mass of confused ideas the sane man has complete power over the ideas which come—will he, nill he—into his mind. Hobbes's account gives the impression of a mechanism, in spite of all the presence of judgment in his scheme, for judgment is of the same lineage as fancy—"Time and education beget experience; experience begets memory; memory begets judgment and fancy" —and judgment's role seems in itself to be mechanical and elementary: "For memory is the world, though not really, yet so as in a looking-glass, in which the judgment, the severer sister, busieth herself in a grave and rigid examination of all the parts of nature, and in registering by letters their order, causes, uses, differences, and resemblances."[15]

Swift, or the Irish prelate, selects verbs which express more than tabulation: "such thoughts as his judgment directed him to choose, leaving the rest to die away in his memory." Swift's mind is less flexible, perhaps more responsible, than Dryden's, but the slight adjustment he makes here is related to Dryden's agile adaptability. Both inherit the old admiration for a simple, ordered unity; neither can assert its truth with the confidence of Sidney. Dryden, however, retains enough of the old spirit to spend his life trying to attain in practice what he cannot prove in theory; Swift, whose practicality is one of his most obvious characteristics, accepts the task as impossible, sets it aside, and tries instead to balance the conflicts of his time, to fashion a semblance of order from chaos, though it cannot be the grandly simple truth of the older classicism. Simplicity can now be gained only by leaving out what has its own often unwelcome validity. An inclusive compromise is the only way open of imposing the order of mind upon that chaotic circumstance which, even in the most ordinary affairs of human life, was so vivid and overwhelming to Swift.

The early, Pindaric, poems are often reminiscent of Dryden in their desire for simplicity of truth and their dislike of mechanistic theories of the universe. Dryden's unyielding opposition to the notion of a world consisting of "Atoms casually together hurl'd" is echoed by Swift's lines in the "Ode to the Athenian Society," where he mocks in the awkward Pindarics of his youth the "Modish System of reducing all to sense":

> 'Tis but to say, that what we daily meet,
>   And by a fond mistake
> Perhaps imagine to be wondrous Wit
> And think, alas, to be by mortals writ,
> Is but a Crowd of Atoms justling in a heap.[16]

Inferior though these lines are to the strength and elegance of Dryden's poem "To Sir Robert Howard," they treat of the same parallel between the providence of wit in a writer and the providence which formed the world, and the theme is continued through the poem in a series of clashing contrasts. Mind gives life and meaning to material substance:

> For when the animating Mind is fled,
>   (Which Nature never can retain,
>   Nor e'er call back again)
> The Body, tho' Gigantick, lyes all Cold and Dead.[17]

Wit and order may be overwhelmed by the blind hordes of barbarism, the Gothic swarms "From Ignorance's Universal North." Intelligence, life, unity, and order are so constantly and effectively opposed here to chaos, blindness, death, and the whole conception is so fully worked out, that it seems to be more than an elaborate and ingenious compliment to the Athenian Society, and to show Swift's interest in this vital problem of the day and his conscious-

25

ness of the issues involved. Truth, in these early poems, is described as changeless and eternal, as the "First of God's darling attributes," and as independent of "giddy circumstance of time or place."[18] Truth is not to be found on earth,

> For this inferior world is but Heaven's dusky shade,
> By dark reverted rays from its reflection made;
> Whence the weak shapes wild and imperfect pass,
> Like sun-beams shot at too far distance from a glass.[19]

These lines are from the "Ode to Dr. William Sancroft," who was committed to the Tower by James II as one of the Seven Bishops and who later, under William and Mary, became a nonjuror. Sancroft's fixity of principle allows Swift to present him here as himself the world's best pattern of eternal truth, showing that he is so by his fixed and single mind; he stands firm while opinion eddies about him, and represents all that the church holds of its primitive purity. To Swift he is "holy Sancroft," "primitive Sancroft." The images in the early poems are often variations on the theme of the one steady light unseen or broken by mortal frailty, and the figure of the fixed star of truth, or the sun of wit which lesser minds break and scatter, is as insistent as it is in the poetry of Dryden.[20]

These early odes suggest, indeed, an attitude rooted in the conceptions of the classical Renaissance, and the old insistence on the unity which gives meaning to the multiplicity of this world is still very noticeable. But already Swift is uneasily convinced that the eternal and single truth exists only in a world far removed from ours, and that it is something very difficult for man to attain even by the greatest assertion of the shaping mind. As he grew older, and the tendencies of the age still further split the rays of universal truth into "scattered beams," even this insecure hold on the confidence of Renaissance neoclassicism was loosened. In all Swift's later work we are conscious less of a desirable unity than of the chaotic conditions of life which make that unity impossible to reach. This is true of Swift's contemporaries as well; most of the greatest writers of the Augustan age strive to achieve unity on a smaller, less ambitious scale than that of Spenser or

Sidney, to organize small areas of existing experience through the balance and control typified by the antithetical heroic couplet, rather than to unify the whole of experience by relating all human affairs to a central truth. Spenser's *Faerie Queene* is his interpretation of life in terms of the true Nature of classic theory; no such work, with the exception of Pope's magnificent failure, the *Essay on Man,* was written in the Augustan period. Success would have been next to impossible in an age when Nature, in the old sense of the true intention of the universe to be sought by reason, was being lost to view behind the growing philosophical importance of what would once have been called "sublunary" or in Dryden's term "wild" nature, the purposeless mutable world of the senses. Later in the century Samuel Johnson showed his awareness of the two meanings of the word, and of the increasing contemporary interest in what an earlier generation would have considered the lesser meaning, in the terms he uses to justify Shakespeare's use of the form of tragicomedy. In strict neoclassic theory this was a nauseous hybrid which mingled two disparate forms, but Johnson remarks that tragicomedies are "compositions of a distinct kind; exhibiting the real state of sublunary nature." That is, they deal not with the world of clarity and permanence traditionally situated above the moon, but with our actual disorderly world "which partakes of good and evil, joy and sorrow, mingled with endless variety of proportion and innumerable modes of combination."[21]

For Dryden too, though he was of an earlier and in some ways more confident generation than Swift's, the task of attaining a simple unity was, in the conditions of his time, dispiritingly difficult, and in his work one can see something of where the difficulty lay—in the limiting of that very faculty which should attain unity, reason itself. The alteration in the content of this keyword of the neoclassic tradition has been recognized as being responsible for much of the philosophical confusion and controversy of the period, and it could be used at this time in a number of senses, varying from a logical process to an approximation to intuitive reason, from Locke's perception of the agreement and disagreement of ideas to the intuition of Descartes. Swift himself uses the word in more senses than one,[22] and sets those senses against one another, trying out meanings as though in the hope of finding the one that is applicable.

Reason was the watchword of more than one conception of the nature of man, the state, and the universe, during this period of change. Dryden gravely considers the central problem in the opening lines of *Religio Laici:*

> Dim, as the borrowed beams of Moon and Stars
> To lonely, weary, wandring Travellers
> Is Reason to the Soul: And as on high
> Those rowling Fires discover but the Sky
> Not light us here; so Reason's glimmering Ray
> Was lent, not to assure our doubtfull way,
> But guide us upward to a better Day.
> And as those nightly Tapers disappear
> When Day's bright Lord ascends our Hemisphere;
> So pale grows Reason at Religion's sight;
> So dyes, and so dissolves in Supernatural Light.

Reason was not now capable, as had been the exalted wit of Sidney, of penetrating the highest truths which the heavenly maker intended to be available to man; it now had its own sphere and must stay within it, limiting itself to the logical conclusions it could come to in the world of material fact; to Hobbes it was, as Swift put it, like "casting up accounts," to Locke a chain of linked ideas. It could have little to say beyond the material sphere, and that little was often destructive, aiming, behind a screen of deference to orthodoxy, at the foundations of Christianity or even of religion altogether.

Too great an insistence on reason as explaining the ultimate nature of the universe thus became suspect as showing a tendency to Deism, or conversely Deist example showed the potential destructiveness of a dependence on reason, and so the orthodox were robbed of one of their chief weapons. Deism was felt as a greater practical danger than atheism—though Deists were often loosely termed atheists—because it was more insidious, and instead of shocking the public into opposition by denying a God, proposed to divest religion of superstition and enthusiasm and show it in its native simplicity. The reason of man could find its way unaided to a religion of reason; Dryden, defending orthodoxy in

Religio Laici, turns promptly to attack Deism and its claim to found a natural religion on natural reason:

> Thus Man by his own strength to Heaven wou'd soar:
> And wou'd not be Obliged to God for more.
> Vain, wretched Creature, how art thou misled
> To think thy Wit these God-like notions bred!
> These Truths are not the product of thy Mind,
> But dropt from Heaven, and of a Nobler kind.

In fact, "'Tis Revelation what thou thinkst Discourse," or why did not discourse of reason discover a natural religion for the giant wits of the great ancients?

> Canst Thou, by Reason, more of God-head know
> Than Plutarch, Seneca, or Cicero?[23]

Reason, if taken beyond its proper bounds as by the presumptuous followers of Deism, becomes pride, and blinds rather than enlightens. Pope's attempt to justify the nature of the universe is carried out in the teeth of proud reason, as opposed to the "simple Reason" of the Golden Age when

> The worker from the work distinct was known,
> And simple Reason never sought but one:
> Ere Wit oblique had broke that steddy light,
> Man, like his Maker, saw that all was right.

Pope's consciousness that reason, broken now by the prism of "Wit oblique," is no longer the way to faith is further suggested in that notoriously unconvincing couplet,

> And spite of Pride, in erring Reason's spite,
> One truth is clear, WHATEVER IS, IS RIGHT.[24]

Insistence on a drastic limitation of the activities of reason is frequent in the *Essay* and is an essential part of Pope's theme; only by this means can he assert the goodness of God's purpose, for it is "in Pride, in reas'ning Pride" that our error lies. Reason is a hindrance at least as much as it is a help; it is best to presume not God to scan, to admit that we are only darkly wise and that too much reliance on our reason is foolish presumption. Pope is conscious like Dryden that the traditional view of reason as operat-

29

ing within the firm outlines laid down by revealed truth is being destroyed, and that modern reason believes itself capable of operating upon revealed truth itself. So he, like Dryden and also like Swift, emphasizes the old distinction between the realms of faith and reason which Deism would not recognize.

The only way to assert the unity and singleness of truth with the grandeur of simplicity and without the niggling objections of proud reason would have been to ignore this kind of reason altogether and to revert to an older meaning, finding some approximation to the simple reason of Pope's Golden Age, which had not separated itself from religious faith. But this was scarcely practicable for a generation unwillingly convinced by and partly committed to the new definition. The Cambridge Platonists, a little earlier, had returned to the old ways of unifying and giving meaning to experience, but to Swift an unconcealed Platonism could only seem fantastical. Pope in the *Essay on Man* makes a covert use of Neoplatonic tradition, and Platonism is one element in the eclectic moral scheme of Lord Shaftesbury; but the general impression made by the *Characteristicks,* and even by Pope's *Essay,* was of an alarming tendency away from orthodoxy and towards natural religion. To so passionate a churchman as Swift, naturally seeing the past in the light of present dangers, the Platonism of the "latitude men" must have seemed, like that of their admirer Shaftesbury, too closely allied to the insidious menace of Deism to be acceptable, and their trust in reason could only be suspect, however orthodox their aims. So in his version of Anthony Collins's *Discourse* "the famous Dr. Henry More" is one of the many writers cited by Collins in support of freethinking, and Swift is cut off from a way of thought which might have led him to that essential and unified truth which he, as much as Dryden or the Platonists themselves, desired and needed. For the strength of the Cambridge group was in their awareness of the tendencies of empirical and materialist thought, and in their deliberate efforts to relate these tendencies to a more inclusive truth as Spenser had done with the less dangerous materialism of the ancients. Their opposition to the contemporary narrowing of the term "reason" was consistent and deliberate, and they asserted strongly the active power of the mind. What was true and important for them was not the universe of "grave, solid, and substantial senseless matter," but the divine reality of which this world is only a rough copy, and the active mind of man, which have a direct relationship to one another. Cudworth, for instance, believed that it is only by our participation in divine and perfect mind that we begin to think. They believed in a religious reason, which includes moral activity, a will to right action, as well as logical activity, and which can have knowledge of God; but this is not the limited faculty of contemporary thought, indeed it should not, according to John Smith, be called a faculty "but far rather a light." "Wherefore," said Cudworth, "mere speculation, and dry mathematical reason, in minds unpurified, and having a contrary interest of carnality, and a heavy load of infidelity and distrust sinking them down, cannot alone beget an unshaken confidence and assurance of so high a truth as this, the existence of one perfect understanding Being, the original of all things."[25]

Reason and religion are thus kept in a close relationship, and the Cambridge Platonists envisage no divorce between revelation and reason. "Reason is not a shallow thing: it is the first participation from God; therefore he that observes Reason, observes God."[26] But the Platonists' insistence on the candle of the Lord, the light of reason, was met with misgivings by many of their contemporaries. Tuckney, in his protesting letters to Whichcote, suggests that his friend too much emphasizes the right reason of heathen philosophy, "a *recta ratio* much talked of, which I cannot tell where to find,"[27] and in the heyday of the Deist controversy the Cambridge light of reason, seeming so reminiscent of Lord Herbert of Cherbury's stoical "common notions," would carry still more alarming overtones. John Toland, whose *Christianity Not Mysterious* was burned by order of the Irish Parliament, calls reason the candle lodged by God in every man.

Despite a natural tendency towards "simple reason" and single truth, Swift does not regard the relation of reason to truth with the serene confidence shown in John Smith's "Truth needs not at any time fly from reason, there being an eternal amity between them."[28] In Swift's day amity existed only between reason and a certain radical simplification of truth which left out much that he believed to be essential for the maintaining of Christian values and of that respect for morality which only the authority of revealed religion could inculcate. Several of the entries in his "Thoughts on Religion" are concerned with the relation of reason to religious belief, and seem to have been written with Deism in mind. They show that respect for reason which one would expect from Swift, with his allegiance to the attitudes of an older world, but they show also the suspicion of reason which is a result of the conditions of his day. The first entry is, "I am in all opinions to believe according to my own impartial reason; which I am bound to inform and improve, as far as my capacity and opportunities will permit," and the fourth, "To say a man is bound to believe is neither truth nor sense." These stout statements could have been made by a Cambridge Platonist; Chillingworth maintained that no man could or should be compelled to believe a doctrine repugnant to his reason. But the difference between Chillingworth and Swift soon becomes apparent; it is visible in the very next entry, with its uncomfortable suggestion of force: "You may force men, by interest or punishment, to say or swear they believe, and to act as if they believed: You can go no further."

What is lacking in the "Thoughts" is the confidence, so strong in the Platonists, that there is no fundamental doctrine of religion that is, in fact, repugnant to reason, that reason is the strongest support of faith and must be freely exercised. In the entries which follow, Swift further considers the status of reason, in relation to certain contemporary dangers, and the effect is of a qualification of the view first posited: "Every man, as a member of the commonwealth, ought to be content with the possession of his own opinion in private, without perplexing his neighbour or disturbing the public," and "Violent zeal for truth hath an hundred to one odds to be either petulancy, ambition, or pride." While the ninth entry runs:

To remove opinions fundamental in religion is impossible, and the attempt wicked, whether those opinions be true or false; unless your avowed design be to abolish that religion altogether. So, for instance, in the famous doctrine of Christ's divinity, which hath been universally received by all bodies of Christians, since the condemnation of Arianism under Constantine and his successors: Wherefore the proceedings of the Socinians are both vain and unwarrantable; because they will be never able to advance their own opinion, or meet any other success than breeding doubts and disturbances in the world. *Qui ratione sua disturbant moenia mundi.*[29]

Such comments indicate uneasiness, as though the free exercise of reason were being gradually related to Deism and Socinianism. The application of reason to religion suggests in this age the "show of logic" of the Deist Anthony Collins, the Arian William Whiston, and their kind. It was the Deists who made reason the measure of all things, supposing that what it could not demonstrate must necessarily be false. In "Mr. Collins's Discourse of Freethinking" Swift makes Collins say that "Dr. South describes the incarnation of Christ, as an astonishing mystery, impossible to be conceived by man's reason; *ergo,* it is contradictory to itself, and to reason, and ought to be exploded by all freethinkers."[30] A bold return to older conceptions of reason's nature and scope could only have led to dangerous misunderstanding. "They who wou'd prove Religion by Reason," says Dryden in the Preface to *Religio Laici,* "do but weaken the cause which they endeavour to support: 'tis to take away the pillars from our Faith, and to prop it only with a twig." They do, in fact, play into the Deists' hands; John Toland, blandly laying one of his infamous traps in the Preface to *Christianity Not Mysterious,* puts the position with his usual subtlety:

No Atheist or Infidel of any kind can justly be angry with me for measuring Swords with them, and attacking them only with the Weapons they prescribe me. The true Christian can no more be offended when he finds me imploy Reason, not to enervate or perplex, but to confirm and elucidate Revelation; unless he is apprehensive I should render it too clear to my self, or too familiar to others, which are Absurdities no Body will own. I hope to make it appear, that the Use of Reason is not so dangerous in Religion as it is commonly represented, and that too by such as mightily extol it, when it seems to favour 'em, yet vouchsafe it not a hearing when it makes against them, but oppose its own Authority to it self. These are high Privileges indeed, and the surest Means of having always the better of the Dispute that could possibly be devis'd.[31]

In such circumstances John Locke's limited version of the place of reason, that its task is to vouchsafe the authenticity of revealed truth by judging "of the truth of its being a revelation, and of the signification of the words wherein it is delivered"[32] must have seemed to many people as well as to Swift and Dryden to be safer than more ambitious claims. So Swift in common with many of his contemporaries calls to his aid the traditional distinction between the sphere of reason and the divine truths of faith which, though they cannot contradict reason, are incomprehensible to it. In the seventeenth century this old distinction, made in an age when the truth of revelation was virtually unquestioned and seized upon by Bacon as a protection of scientific truth, is turned to new use against those whose proud reason would attack faith itself.

The heart of the matter is reached in one of the later "Thoughts on Religion," which indicates that Swift saw reason as a potential threat to faith: "I am not answerable to God for the doubts that arise in my own breast, since they are the consequence of that reason which he hath planted in me, if I take care to conceal those doubts from others, if I use my best endeavours to subdue them, and if they have no influence on the conduct of my life."[33] It seems at least possible that the first person here applies literally to Swift himself, since it follows an entry which is clearly personal, referring to "myself, in the capacity of a clergyman," and again there may be a personal fear and hope in this passage from "Thoughts on Various Subjects": "I am apt to think, that in the Day of Judgment there will be small Allowance given to the Wise for their want of Morals, or to the Ignorant for their Want of Faith; because, both are without Excuse. This renders the Advantages equal of Ignorance and Knowledge. But some Scruples in the Wise, and some Vices in the Ignorant, will perhaps be forgiven upon the Strength of Temptation to each."[34] He probably had some doubts and scruples lying upon his conscience, and it was "that reason which he hath planted in me" which he saw as responsible for them. Certainly if the choice had been presented to him he would have chosen faith and the subduing of reason; the "Thoughts on Religion," the prayers, the letters leave no doubt of the importance of his faith to Swift. Doubt he regards as a fault, even if sometimes an unavoidable one; the tenth of the "Thoughts on Religion" is "The want of belief is a defect that ought to be concealed when it cannot be overcome."[35] To surrender to it, even to glory in it and try to infect others with it, as the freethinkers do, is far worse than to publish doctrines of rebellion and sedition and should be similarly "liable to the severest punishments the law can inflict."[36]

The reason so flaunted by the Deists and other freethinkers is, in Pope's term, "reas'ning Pride," which tries to do more than it should and exercises itself upon those aspects of Christianity—the "mysteries" and particularly the doctrine of the Trinity—before which it ought to subdue itself.[37] Toland asserted that "Reason is the only Foundation of all Certitude; and that nothing reveal'd, whether as to its Manner or Existence, is more exempted from its Disquisitions, than the Ordinary Phenomena of Nature,"[38] but in Swift's belief some other faculty than reason as we know it will be required, at the day of resurrection, to understand the mysteries which God will then fully reveal to us. The mysteries are certainly not according to reason in Locke's definition: "According to reason are such propositions, whose truth we can discover by examining those ideas we have from sensation and reflection."[39] As for the "common Reason" we now possess, indeed, Swift regards the mysteries as directly contrary to it, and those who exercise common reason upon such matters are, really, unreasonable.[40] Only in such paradoxes could the position be fairly put; it is significant that Ralph Venning, in 1657, published his views on such problems as these in a work accurately named *Orthodox Paradoxes Theoretical and Experimental, or a Believer Clearing Truth by Seeming Contradictions,* and that one of his paradoxes is that the believer "believes that which reason cannot comprehend, yet that there is reason enough why he should believe it."[41] The Christian view was now necessarily expressed in more or less paradoxical terms, and both Pope and Swift in their different ways accepted the necessity.

The sermon "On the Trinity" is a good example of Swift's use of the word "reason" in several senses, on the play between which the whole argument depends. There is the common reason of man, a faculty of the intellect which has its own proper if limited sphere—"It must be allowed, that every Man is bound to follow the Rules and Directions of that Measure of Reason which God hath given him"—but which is corrupt if it exercises itself upon those mysteries which it should humbly accept. "For Instance: if I should be commanded by an Angel from Heaven to believe it is Midnight at Noon-day; Yet I could not believe him. So, if I were directly told in Scripture, that Three are One, and One is Three, I could not conceive or believe it in the natural common Sense of that Expression, but must suppose something dark or mystical was meant, which it pleased God to conceal from me, and from all the World." Man's reason is simply not capable of grasping these mysteries of which the Trinity is the least comprehensible, and it is not the mysteries which are at fault, but human reason. We must yield to the authority of the Scriptures, and to believe upon this assurance without ever enquiring further "can be contrary to no Man's Reason, although the Knowledge of it is hid from him."[42] The "Young Gentleman, Lately enter'd into Holy Orders" is advised not to meddle with the mysteries during his sermons: "I do not find that you are anywhere directed in the Canons, or Articles, to attempt explaining the Mysteries of the Christian Religion. And, indeed, since Providence intended there should be Mysteries; I do not see how it can be agreeable to Piety, Orthodoxy, or good Sense, to go about such a Work."[43] The arguments and explanations of the divines only provide ammunition for the Deist denial.

Reason's place in the consideration of revealed truth is shown again in the "Further Thoughts on Religion," where Swift remarks that "The Scripture-system of man's creation, is what all Christians are bound to believe, and seems most agreeable of all others to probability and reason." The reason here invoked is a limited faculty enough, and is commonly appealed to in the sermons of Dr. South and other Anglican divines; the elaboration of Swift's opening statement shows that the probability and reasonableness of the scriptural account of man's creation and fall lie in its truth to experience. It is convincing because it accounts for the degenerate nature of man, an observed and experienced fact, and it is not considered as an event probable or improbable in itself. It is reasonable to accept the account not only because it is revealed by an infallible God but because it is true to life: the nature of animals is constant, "But men degenerate every day, merely by the folly, the perverseness, the avarice, the tyranny, the pride, the treachery, or inhumanity of their own kind."[44] As with Pascal, if the Fall is a mystery it does at least explain the mystery of man.

Reason is often mentioned by Swift as a faculty which must prove itself sound by its truth to experience and its practical results. In *Sentiments of a Church of England Man* he remarks that reason which produces bad effects in the common conduct of life must be in error. "According to Hobbes's Comparison of Reasoning with casting up Accounts; whoever finds a Mistake in the Sum total, must allow himself out; although, after repeated Tryals, he may not see in which Article he hath misreckoned."[45] That "free" thinking leads to "free" action—that is, to immorality—is one of his chief objections to Deism. If our reason leads us to undesirable practical ends and ends counter to the word of God, it must somehow be wrong, though we may not be able to see where our mistake has occurred.

The sermon "On the Trinity," also, deals with reason considered in this sense, as a faculty concerned with practical morality. Commenting upon the importance laid upon faith, both in the Old Testament and in the New, Swift remarks that this importance "is highly reasonable; for, Faith is an entire Dependence upon the Truth, the Power, the Justice, and the Mercy of God; which Dependence will certainly incline us to obey him in all Things. So, that the great Excellency of Faith, consisteth in the Consequence it hath upon our Actions." It is highly reasonable to be guided by faith, because it produces better practical results, and it is unreasonable to rely on reason as a guide to virtuous conduct "Because he who hath no Faith, cannot, by the Strength of his own Reason or Endeavours, so easily resist Temptations, as the other who depends upon God's Assistance in the overcoming his Frailties, and is sure to be rewarded for ever in Heaven for his Victory over them."[46] This is neatly argued, but it has a different tone

37

either from the Cambridge Platonists' confident belief in reason as the will to right action, or from Pascal's "Soumission est usage de la raison, en quoi consiste le vraye Christianisme." Swift's appeal to practical results is typical of that defensive attitude which alone seemed to offer a precarious safety. Reason, considered as an intellectual or as a moral faculty, is bedeviled by the threat of freethinking, of the self-sufficiency which cuts itself off from the past of Christian neoclassicism and ignores traditional experience instead of organizing it into a unity as reason had once been able to do. The tone of these references to reason has less even than Dryden's limited confidence in the "glimmering Ray" which can "guide us upward to a better Day." The neoclassic pursuit of the unity of truth through the exalted reason has become complicated to the point of impossibility, and the Truth, the Other Nature, or the Reason, which while it existed in perfection beyond this world could yet be sought and found by man in whom it dwelt, is now cut off from him. The contrast between perfect Reason and the reason of man is seen in this same sermon "On the Trinity": "Reason itself is true and just, but the Reason of every particular Man is weak and wavering, perpetually swayed and turned by his Interests, his Passions, and his Vices."[47] Reason, like the truth of the "Ode to Sancroft" of which it is another aspect, is not now to be found by the aspiring wit of man; indeed the intelligible cannot be found embodied in this world as it was found by Spenser and Sidney and Cudworth. The spiritual may be the most rational, as Whichcote had asserted, but for Swift it is rational in a way beyond the wit of man to see. Between truth and the reason of man there can be no identity, only a compromise which withstands the mechanism of Hobbes but takes care not to fall into the Deist error which the Cambridge Platonists even, and certainly Shaftesbury, seemed scarcely to avoid. The fall of reason from a source of certainty to a source of doubts and scruples, which Blake saw so clearly, had already taken place, "And Urizen who was Faith and Certainty is changed to Doubt."

Swift's early odes already suggest, though in more tentative form, the conclusions of his maturity. The address to truth which has been quoted from the "Ode to Dr. William Sancroft" stresses

38

above all the contrast between eternal truth and the falsity of sublunary life:

> Truth is eternal, and the Son of Heav'n,
>> Bright effluence of th' immortal ray,
> Chief cherub, and chief lamp of that high sacred Seven,
> Which guard the Throne by night, and are its light by day:
>> First of God's darling attributes,
>>> Thou daily seest Him face to face,
> Nor does thy essence fix'd depend on giddy circumstance
>>> Of time or place,
> Two foolish guides in ev'ry sublunary dance:
>> How shall we find Thee then in dark disputes?
>> How shall we search Thee in a battle gain'd,
>> Or a weak argument by force maintain'd?
>> In dagger-contests, and th' artillery of words,
>> (For swords are madmen's tongues, and tongues are madmen's swords)
>>> Contriv'd to tire all patience out,
>>> And not to satisfy the doubt.

Even through the poverty of the verse, the nostalgic note, the
regret for a vanished unity, is perceptible; and the old-fashioned
contrast between sublunary confusion and the calm perfection of
the higher spheres is continued in the second verse, with its
Platonic echoes merging into the perplexities of modern science:

> For this inferior world is but Heaven's dusky shade,
> By dark reverted rays from its reflection made;
>> Whence the weak shapes wild and imperfect pass,
> Like sun-beams shot at too far distance from a glass;
>> Which all the mimic forms express,
> Tho' in strange uncouth postures, and uncomely dress;
>> So when Cartesian artists try
>>> To solve appearances of sight
>>> In its reception to the eye,
> And catch the living landscape thro' a scanty light,
>> The figures all inverted shew,
>>> And colours of a faded hue. . . .
>> Such are the ways ill-guided mortals go
>> To judge of things above by things below.
> Disjointing shapes as in the fairy-land of dreams,
>> Or images that sink in streams;
>> No wonder, then, we talk amiss
>> Of truth, and what, or where it is.[48]

39

The world is here described in traditional Platonic fashion, as an imperfect copy of the heaven where alone truth resides, but this sense of limitation is given greater urgency by the topical reference to the experiments by which the "Cartesian artists" explore the perceptions of the senses; already for Swift, as years later in *Gulliver's Travels,* the world of scientific experiment expresses more vividly than the common world the confusion of mankind. Not only is our world a broken and twisted version of the truth, but man now seems less capable than once he had been of penetrating beyond it to what is eternally valid. Inescapable distortions accompany his efforts towards truth. The data on which reason depends are supplied to it by the senses,[49] yet our senses, it seems, are far from reliable. The confusion of sublunary change and "giddy circumstance" is intensified by the disturbing suggestions of contemporary science; the new science of optics, for example, was producing far more complicated instances of illusion than the ancient example of the stick seen through water.[50] Our own limitations are such that it is difficult for us to recognize even the imperfect copies of truth which surround us: we are caught in uncertainties, in "the fairy-land of dreams," surrounded by what Hobbes calls the apparitions or phantasms which our senses make us think really exist in the world outside us. This, he says, is the great deception of sense.

Later in the same poem, Swift again makes use of an image which blends the old and the new, in his own version of an example which the philosophers of the seventeenth and eighteenth centuries adopted to illustrate the deceptiveness of the senses—the example of the sun which to our sense perceptions appears smaller and closer than it is. Swift uses, instead of the sun, the fixed stars, and thus gives a familiar illustration deeper significance by linking it with an old symbol of eternal truth above the moon:[51]

> Nothing is fix'd that mortals see or know,
> Unless, perhaps, some stars above be so;
>   And those, alas, do shew
> Like all transcendent excellence below;
>   In both, false mediums cheat our sight,
> And far exalted objects lessen by their height.[52]

Perhaps even those few examples of fixity that man thinks he sees beyond his own narrow world, even "the incorruptible life of the celestiall bodies," are only a cheat. It is Spenser's problem of mutability, intensified by the uncertainties of the age, the arguments of philosophers, and the experiments of scientists.

Much as Swift valued the ordering mind which gives meaning to the confusion of existence, he seems to have been deeply conscious of the difficulties which in man, limited as he is by physical accident, attend the functioning of mind and cut him off from the single truth. Man is cheated by false mediums, and his efforts to bring order into a multifarious world can only be imperfect, since he is necessarily to some degree in a state of deception, and cannot wholly escape from his fairyland of dreams. The theme of deception, found everywhere in Swift's later work, has its beginnings here. Reason is indeed true and just, but "the Reason of every particular Man is weak and wavering," partly through his own individual fault but only partly.

In his comments on reason and its powers, Swift's natural attitude seems to be to regard it as both an intellectual and an ethical faculty, and of course the two aspects of reason, speculative and moral, which are brought into rather hesitant relationship in his justification of faith in the sermon "On the Trinity" had always been present in Christian and neoclassic tradition. Swift inherited the traditional view of reason as a single faculty which is exercised in both the intellectual and the moral sphere, and as being in both spheres an assertion of mind over wild nature. But the current degeneration in the meaning of the word made it difficult to see how this was so, and his efforts to relate the two aspects are groping and unconvincing. Modern reason, the "mere speculation and dry mathematical reason" of Cudworth, functioning logically upon a distorted impression furnished by the senses, was difficult to interpret in the old way. In his endeavor to answer the vital questions of his day—how far reason is capable of succeeding in the search for divine truth; how far reason is a sufficient principle of moral conduct—Swift can never equate reason and the highest moral truth with the sureness of Whichcote's "To go against Reason is to go against God."[53] Reason, as it appeared in his day,

41

could be itself a source of intellectual doubt and hence of moral danger: "I am not answerable to God for the doubts that arise in my own breast, since they are the consequence of that reason which he hath planted in me, if I take care to conceal those doubts from others, if I use my best endeavours to subdue them, and if they have no influence on the conduct of my life."[54]

Chapter III
REASON AND VIRTUE

For Swift, the consideration of reason as a moral force takes the traditional shape of the relation of reason to the passions and senses. The reconciliation of mind and body possible to the Neoplatonist Spenser was not, of course, possible for Swift in the age of dualism, and he adopts the more orthodox view of Christian classicism, that reason is the controller of the passions. Here again considerable dexterity and flexibility of mind were required if the wisdom of the past was to be upheld, for this was an age when for some thinkers reason alone, and for some feeling alone, was the source of the good life. Those who, like Swift and Pope, regarded either extreme as a dangerous simplification, attempted to follow a middle course more in accord with their inherited view of the nature of man, and to guide themselves safely between opposed dangers. Swift's task was to maintain the power of mind over the chaos of passions and senses, but to point out that it was a strictly limited power. To assert that the passions could be eliminated or quenched by the power of reason would be to take up a position nearer to the Stoics than to the fathers of the Church, and as well as being unorthodox it would be unrealistic. Swift, like Dryden, knew well enough that there were aspects of modern thought that he must accept, and the power of self-love, no less than the weakening of reason, had become a part of the consciousness of his age. It could not be simply ignored. His conception of reason as a moral faculty can be fairly summed up in these quotations from two of his sets of "Thoughts," or maxims:

Although reason were intended by providence to govern our passions, yet it seems that, in two points of the greatest moment to the being and continuance of the world, God hath intended our passions to prevail over reason. The first is, the propagation of the species, since no wise man ever married from the dictates of reason. The other is, the love of life, which, from the dictates of reason, every man would despise, and wish it at an end, or that it never had a beginning.[1]

The motives of the best actions will not bear too strict an inquiry. It is allow'd, that the cause of most actions, good or bad, may be resolved into the love of ourselves: but the self-love of some men, inclines them to please

43

others; and the self-love of others is wholly employ'd in pleasing themselves. This makes the great distinction between virtue and vice. Religion is the best Motive of all Actions, yet Religion is allow'd to be the highest instance of self-love.[2]

These "Thoughts," "fugitive ideas and impressions" kept in a commonplace book, are good indications of the subjects which Swift turned over in his mind and the problems he tried to solve, and he is clearly attempting here to come to some working compromise in grappling with one of the most difficult questions of the time. His tentative conclusion seems to be that to oppose reason as the good principle to the passions as wholly bad is unrealistic. Reason is probably intended by God to rule over our passions generally, but there are exceptions to this general arrangement, passions which God himself must approve, since without them life would cease. Moreover, the passions can be on occasion not only permissible but positively beneficial. It is impossible to make a doctrinaire division between good reason and evil passion, when religion itself can be seen as the highest instance of self-love, as well as being "highly reasonable." Such passions as the love of fame, which can scarcely be reconciled with reason, may contribute to virtue and perhaps may be placed in our nature for that very end:

The humour of exploding many things under the names of trifles, fopperies, and only imaginary goods, is a very false proof either of wisdom or magnanimity, and a great check to virtuous actions. For instance, with regard to fame: there is in most people a reluctance and unwillingness to be forgotten. We observe even among the vulgar, how fond they are to have an inscription over their grave. It requires but little philosophy to discover and observe that there is no intrinsic value in all this; however, if it be founded in our nature, as an incitement to virtue, it ought not to be ridiculed.

Or again, the passions may be regarded as an essential part of our nature, necessary to enliven our minds: "In a Glass-House, the Workmen often fling in a small Quantity of fresh Coals, which seems to disturb the Fire, but very much enlivens it. This may allude to a gentle stirring of the Passions, that the Mind may not languish."[3] Pope's solution of the problem is the same when he considers, in *An Essay on Man,* the function of that most formidable of the passions, self-love:

> Two Principles in human nature reign;
> Self-love, to urge, and Reason, to restrain,

and again

> On life's vast ocean diversely we sail,
> Reason the card, but Passion is the gale.[4]

Among divines, Bishop Butler makes substantially the same point: the passions and affections are necessary spurs to actions in creatures like ourselves, who are imperfect and interdependent, "who naturally and, from the condition we are placed in, necessarily depend upon each other. With respect to such creatures, it would be found of as bad consequence to eradicate all natural affections, as to be entirely governed by them. This would almost sink us to the condition of brutes; and that would leave us without a sufficient principle of action."[5]

Swift's position, indeed, is not by any means peculiar to himself; it was shared by many contemporaries as well as by Butler and Pope. But it is only one of several conflicting contemporary interpretations of the nature of man, and the tone of Swift's "Thoughts" suggests that it was original at least in the Johnsonian sense that he had thought it out for himself, as the only feasible defense against the extreme positions taken up by the more dangerous thinkers of the day. Like Dryden in the then connected field of literary theory he partially accepts certain modern conclusions in order to keep a firm grasp on the essentials. He allows the power of the passions, including the self-love of Hobbes and his followers, to enable him to avoid the extremes of their position, and, on the other hand, the extremes of the rationalists. The danger, to a Christian society, of the ideal of Stoic apathy seems to have been as vivid to both Butler and Pope as the danger of a brutish surrender to the passions, and some lines in *An Essay on Man* seek to justify the passions by attacking this chilly pagan ideal of virtue:

> In lazy Apathy let Stoics boast
> Their Virtue fix'd; 'tis fix'd as in a frost;

Contracted all, retiring to the breast;
But strength of mind is Exercise, not Rest:
The rising tempest puts in act the soul,
Parts it may ravage, but preserves the whole.[6]

The insistence on a strenuous and positive virtue is in the tradition of Spenser, Sidney, and Milton, but in contemporary circumstances too heavy a stress on reason would obliterate rather than support such virtue; the "sufficient principle of action" lies in the passions. Reason alone cannot produce the exertion of mind necessary to a fighting virtue. Nor can it, as both Butler and Pope make plain, produce that social usefulness which was an important value in eighteenth century eyes; goodness in a context of social and political activity is stressed throughout Pope's later poetry, and the passions were necessary to produce it.

For Swift too, Stoic apathy appeared as an ideal still strong enough to be threatening, for the pagan Stoicism of history was revived in the self-sufficiency which to certain minds formed a satisfying answer to the religious and philosophical uncertainties of the age. Stoicism was related, in the minds of many of Swift's contemporaries, with Deism, not without cause, since Stoicism seems to have been at least one of the influences which helped to shape natural religion. The descent is clear in the "common notions" of Lord Herbert and sporadically visible in the eclectic system of Shaftesbury. "Right reason" in this period, the *recta ratio* of the Stoics, carried a connotation of Deism, or at best of the school of Samuel Clarke and William Wollaston, with their stress on the "fitness of things." In the *Argument against Abolishing Christianity* right reason is equated with freethinking, or Deism, and is praised by Swift's mouthpiece as being a remarkable eradicator of false notions such as virtue and conscience. When Swift uses the term in his own voice, he is careful to set it in a Christian and non-Stoic context. For instance, in the sermon "On Mutual Subjection," right reason works from the assumption that our talents are lent us by God, and that we have no means of knowing how our apparently less gifted fellows may contribute to God's purpose, and so it comes to the conclusion that pride is not permissible.

46

For, if God hath pleased to entrust me with a Talent, not for my own Sake, but for the Service of others, and at the same time hath left me full of Wants and Necessities which others must supply; I can then have no Cause to set any extraordinary Value upon myself, or to despise my Brother, because he hath not the same talents which were lent to me. His Being may probably be as useful to the Publick as mine; and therefore, by the Rule of right Reason, I am in no sort preferable to him.[7]

In another of his few surviving sermons, "Upon the Excellency of Christianity," Swift sets out to disprove the lofty virtue of the ancients. This was a common practice among Churchmen, and could be carried to absurd extremes. Swift was very conscious of the disrepute into which this habit could bring the views of the church among the classically educated gentlemen of the day, and in the "Letter to a Young Gentleman" he, in the assumed character of a well-disposed layman, refers to "the common unsufferable Cant, of taking all Occasions to disparage the Heathen Philosophers," and points out that some of them had attained a considerable level of moral achievement. "Even that divine Precept of loving our Enemies, is at large insisted on by Plato; who puts it, as I remember, into the Mouth of Socrates." None the less "The System of Morality to be gathered out of the Writings, or Sayings of those antient Sages, falls undoubtedly very short of that delivered in the Gospel; and wants, besides, the Divine Sanction which our Saviour gave to his."[8] Swift was himself an admirer of the ancients, and in his sermon he explains that he does not propose to detract from their wisdom. What he intends is to engage, upon their own ground, with those who "highly exalt the wisdom of those Gentile sages, thereby obliquely to glance at, and traduce Divine Revelation, and more especially that of the gospel; for the consequence they would have us draw, is this: that, since those antient philosophers rose to a greater pitch of wisdom and virtue than was ever known among Christians, and all this purely upon the strength of their own reason and liberty of thinking; therefore it must follow, that either all Revelation is false, or what is worse, that it hath depraved the nature of man, and left him worse than it found him."[9]

The superior virtue of the ancients was of course a favorite theme of the Deists and all who advocated "the strength of their

47

own reason and liberty of thinking." Certain ancient philosophies were now a danger to traditional acceptances in two ways; the serenity and virtue to which they sometimes led were used by the freethinkers as a stick to beat Christian revelation, and moreover they amalgamated with and supported the still more dangerous philosophies of the later seventeenth century. The atomism and sensationalism of Epicurus lived again in the philosophies of Descartes and of Hobbes; at the other extreme Stoicism seemed to merge into the self-sufficiency of the Deists and of all thorough-going rationalists. The task of combating Epicurus and Zeno was therefore a strictly contemporary one which had to be undertaken if traditional values were to be maintained. Similarly Spenser and Dryden had been perturbed by Lucretius as a classical writer who gave authoritative support to those forces in their respective times which tended to undermine the providence of wit. In "Upon the Excellency of Christianity" Zeno and Epicurus are especially singled out for their inadequacy. Stoicism has its "allay of pride," while Epicureanism destroys those fixed eternal values which are the centre of neoclassic thought, for "Epicurus had no notion of justice but as it was profitable; and his placing happiness in pleasure, with all the advantages he could expound it by, was liable to very great exception."[10] The ancients, bolstering up the worst excesses of modernity, could destroy rather than uphold the in-clusive values of Christian neoclassicism, whose aim was to order and shape the flux of experience, and not to simplify it out of existence. Epicurus is the type of all who deny the possibility of imposing the order of mind on experience; the Stoics the type of all who set up an arid inhuman order by the oversimple method of denying all but mind. Swift's opinion of the Stoic solution is best and most pithily summed up in the "Thoughts on Various Subjects": "The Stoical Scheme of supplying our Wants, by lopping off our Desires; is like cutting off our Feet when we want Shoes."[11] Swift was himself, by nature and tradition, anxious to achieve order and unity, and the confusion and variety that faced him no doubt intensified that desire, but nature, tradition, and the confusion of the times also made him very conscious of the difficulty of his task, and very sure that if order could be achieved only by denying part of man's inheritance, by "cutting off our Feet" rather than recognizing our needs, it was not worth achieving. The answer to his problems did not lie in simplification, but in a process of compromise and delicate adjustment that constitutes one aspect of the "spirited rearguard in the retreat of Renaissance humanism before the march of science"[12] which Augustan literature, at its most typical, exemplifies.

Swift's way of coming to some kind of working solution among the conflicting theories of his day, a way of strenuous and continuing adjustment, means that it is possible to find many points of contact, in attitudes and ideas, between him and contemporary philosophical writers, or writers of an earlier generation who were still influential in his lifetime. On the other hand, because of the very nature of the task of compromise which he set himself, it is impossible to identify him completely with any of the extremist views of his day. There are certain positions, pre-eminently those of Shaftesbury, Toland, Collins, and Deists in general, to which he is consistently opposed, but to combat them he will take whatever comes usefully to hand from other thinkers with whom he certainly is not in complete agreement. Like Dryden, he finds a modified scepticism a useful tool, though neither writer could be classified as a sceptic. The terms in which Dryden writes of scepticism are very general and tentative. To be "inclined to scepticism in philosophy" is not to approve of the Pyrrhonists, who as a formal sect were not very reputable. Such writers as Joseph Glanvill were anxious to disclaim the label of sceptic or Pyrrhonist which the more militant rationalists were so quick to pin upon any who expressed doubt in the power of reason, and anxious, too, to differentiate sharply between philosophy and religion, since a thoroughgoing Pyrrhonism would scarcely be reconcilable with Christianity. Glanvill, who was himself a clergyman and who used scepticism in his complex dealings with Cartesianism and scholasticism, makes a careful distinction in *Scepsis Scientifica:* "Though I confess, that in Philosophy I'm a Seeker; yet cannot believe that a Sceptick in Philosophy must be one in Divinity. Gospel-light began in its Zenith; and, as some say the Sun, was created in its Meridian strength and lustre. But the beginnings of Philosophy were in a Crepusculous obscurity; and It's not yet scarce past the Dawn."[13]

Sir Thomas Browne's "In philosophy where Truth seems double-fac'd, there is no man more Paradoxical than myself: but in Divinity I love to keep the Road" shows a similar turn of mind. But provided that the formalities were observed, there were many in the seventeenth and early eighteenth centuries who found scepticism, in this general and respectable sense of a doubt of the ability of human reason to reach certainty, useful enough as a clue to lead them through the various dogmatic and conflicting views of the age.[14] To suspend judgment and base one's actions on probabilities must often have seemed the only possible course. Montaigne,[15] most genial of sceptics, whose *Apologie of Raymond Sebond* has been called the classic standard exposition of modern sceptical thought, would seem to have been a favorite of Swift's, to judge from the bantering tone in which Bolingbroke refers, in a letter to him, to "your old prating friend Montaigne."[16] There is a covert suggestion in the letter that Swift had taken some ideas from him, and certainly Montaigne's ironic, undogmatic manner, "always making room for another idea, and implying always a third for provisional, adjudicating irony,"[17] is like Swift's in many of his works. Both search among ideas, rather than assert ideas, feeling their way among a multiplicity of conflicting and assertive doctrines. True, the tone of Swift's work is usually different from that of Montaigne's, for in him one senses a personal insecurity and a desire for certainty which prevents the attainment of Montaigne's detached serenity; for Swift the search is a thing of urgency, and he cannot exist calmly in the life of suspense. But the method is often similar, even if the temper is different; and such conclusions as Swift comes to in the common affairs of life are, like Montaigne's, tentative ones often based on probability and existing custom, or as Montaigne himself puts it, referring to the Pyrrhonists in the *Apologie of Raymond Sebond:* "Touching the actions of life, in that they are after the common sort, they are lent and applied to naturall inclinations, to the impulsion and constraint of passions, to the constitutions of lawes, and customes, and

50

to the tradition of arts: For God would not have us know these things, but onely use them."[18]

The opinion that Montaigne expresses in the *Apologie* is that a sceptical attitude towards the achievements of man's reason is, in fact, a healthy moral and religious position, and that the reasoning pride of man can best be combated by such an attitude. "The meanes I use to suppresse this frenzy, and which seemeth the fittest for my purpose, is to crush, and trample this humane pride and fiercenesse under foot, to make them feele the emptinesse, vacuitie, and no worth of man: and violently to pull out of their hands, the silly weapons of their reason; to make them stoope, and bite and snarle at the ground, under the authority and reverence of God's Majesty."[19] Glanvill too bases his argument for the agreement of reason and religion on the paradox that reason supports religion by showing us how little capable we are of reasoning even upon lesser matters than the mysteries of God. Reason defends the mysteries of truth and religion by demonstrating

That the Divine Nature is infinite, and our Conceptions very shallow and finite; that 'tis therefore very unreasonable in us to indeavour to pry into the Secrets of his Being, and Actions; and to think that we can measure and comprehend them: That we know not the Essence and Ways of acting of the most ordinary and obvious Things of Nature, and therefore must not expect throughly to understand the deeper Things of God; That God hath revealed those Holy Mysteries unto us; and that 'tis the highest reason in the World to believe, That what he saith is true, though we do not know how these things are.[20]

To trample human pride underfoot, or in Glanvill's more moderate terms to show that man's conceptions are very shallow and finite, was to support the claims of faith, and the sceptic insistence that man can come to no final conclusions, and that reason can only be used "to enquire and debate, and not to stay and choose," left the way open to faith. As Bishop Huet said, the sceptic doctrine "is very proper to captivate Men's Minds to the Obedience of Faith and Religion," and the Christian fathers, including St. Augustine, had pointed to the weakness of human understanding.[21] Swift has a comment, in the sermon "Upon the Excellency of Christianity," which suggests that the restless intellect, forced to

51

recognize its own insufficiency, is laid open to revelation. The fruitless reasoning of the ancient philosophers at the time of Christ resulted in "not only an acknowledgment of the weakness of all human wisdom, but likewise an open passage hereby made, for the letting in those beams of light, which the glorious sunshine of the gospel then brought into the world."[22] Dryden was only one of many who found that the restlessness of the endless sceptic quest tossed him into the arms of the Church:

> My thoughtless youth was wing'd with vain desires,
> My manhood, long misled by wand'ring fires,
> Follow'd false lights; and when their glimps was gone,
> My pride struck out new sparkles of her own.
> Such was I, such by nature still I am,.
> Be Thine the glory and be mine the shame.
> Good life be now my task: my doubts are done,
> (What more could fright my faith, than Three in One?)

Dryden found his single truth at last in the Roman Catholic Church, "Entire, one solid shining Diamond," and his description of it is significantly in terms of the unity which he, and the tradition to which he belonged, had always sought:

> One is the Church, and must be to be true:
> One central principle of unity.
> As undivided, so from errors free,
> As one in faith, so one in sanctity.

And his prayer now is that God, who has provided "For erring judgments an unerring Guide," will teach him

> to believe Thee thus conceal'd,
> And search no farther than Thy self reveal'd.[23]

The ancient sceptic tradition, duly modified to a world which had been granted a divine revelation, was indeed a useful ally against the proud, destructive reason, the erring judgment which undermined faith. Huet points out that the aim of the modern sceptics like himself is not to achieve Ataraxie, or indifference, but to avoid obstinacy and arrogance, and to prepare the mind to receive divine faith. Shaftesbury's Philocles, who is converted to theism by Theocles in *The Moralists,* is an example of a sceptic who never exalts reason above faith, and is completely obedient to his spiritual guides. The modern sceptics used many of the illustrations which had served ancient philosophers to show the faultiness both of reason and of the data, passed through the senses, on which reason had to work. The stick seen as crooked in water, the varying apparent size of the sun and stars, the yellowness of all objects "to those that have the Jaundice," all these venerable examples appear in the sceptics of the seventeenth century, in such lists as that given by Bishop Huet, by Sir Walter Raleigh in *The Sceptick,* and by Glanvill in his essay *Against Confidence in Philosophy, and Matters of Speculation.*[24] But Glanvill, like Swift, can add to these ancient examples from modern inventions. The magnifying glass shows us that we are even less sure of the realities about us than we had supposed:

From this narrowness of our Senses it is, that we have been so long ignorant of a World of Animals that are with us, and about us, which now at last the Glasses, that in part cure this imperfection, have discover'd; and no doubt, there is yet a great variety of living Creatures that our best Instruments are too gross to disclose: There is Prodigious fineness, and subtilty in the works of Nature, which are too thin for our Senses, with all the advantages Art can lend them. . . . So that we cannot have other than short and confused apprehensions of those works of Nature: And I sometimes fear, that we scarce yet see anything as it is.

In short, "Our Senses extremely deceive us in their reports, and informations; I mean, they give occasion to our minds to deceive themselves"—or in Swift's more striking phrase, we are in "a fairy-land of dreams"; we live each in our own world of appearances, with no certainty that things seem to others as they do to us. We can be certain only that we do not see things as they really are; "The World of God, no doubt, is an other thing, than the World of Sense is; and we can judg[e] but little of its amplitude and glory by the imperfect Idea we have of it."[25]

It is this kind of thinking, part of the atmosphere of uncertainty, that lies behind Swift's recurring theme of the self-deceit of man, and Glanvill like Swift has no confident answer to the problem. We must do the best we can, reducing self-deceit as much as possible but knowing that we must always be, to some extent,

53

limited by it. Glanvill recognizes a dual reason; reason in itself, "Reason in the Object," is sound and unchanging, but *our* reason, the act "which connects Propositions and deduceth Conclusions," the faculty of understanding, "is very much weakened and impaired; It sees but little, and that very dully, through a Glass darkly." Thus we cannot clearly see "those Principles of Truth which are written upon our Souls; or any Conclusions that are deduced from them: These are the same that they ever were, though we discern them not so clearly as the Innocent State did."[26] Or, to quote Swift's similar idea in the sermon "On the Trinity," "Reason itself is true and just, but the Reason of every particular Man is weak and wavering, perpetually swayed and turned by his Interests, his Passions, and his Vices." Swift is not the only man of his age who can be described as a rationalist with no faith in reason, and can write such apparent contradictory sentences as (by the supposed Friend of Anthony Collins) "To this it may be objected, that the bulk of mankind is as well qualified for flying as thinking," and (in a "Letter to a Young Gentleman") "A plain convincing Reason may possibly operate upon the Mind both of a learned and ignorant Hearer, as long as they live." Men's corrupt reason cannot, as the freethinkers suppose, carry them to truth, but they are able to recognize the reasonable truths of religion and morality when they are set fairly before them, for these are "the same that they ever were." Reason is man's only natural guide, but to use it well we must know its weakness, and the difficulties which beset it. In the words of Locke, which are set on the title-page of Huet's *The Weakness of Human Understanding,* "'Tis of great Use to the Sailor to know the Length of his Line, though he cannot with it fathom all the Depths of the Ocean." And at times it is most reasonable to subdue reason, or as Pascal (himself a judicious admirer of Montaigne's use of scepticism in the cause of religion) put it, "Il n'y a rien de si conforme à la raison que le desaveu de la raison dans les choses qui sont de foy." One of Ralph Venning's *Orthodox Paradoxes* makes, somewhat less succinctly, the same point:

[The Christian] believes that reason is not equal in all men, nor perfect in any men; but so weak, fickle, and unconstant in the most of men; that he

The Reverend
Dr. J. Swift D. St. P. D.

From an engraving by George Vertue, reproduced in *The Works of J. S., D. D., D. S. P. D.*, Dublin, 1735. Courtesy of the British Museum.

Gulliver in Brobdingnag and in Houy-hnhnm-land, from *Voyages de Gulliver*, Seconde Edition, Paris, 1727. Courtesy of the British Museum.

believes there is no reason why any man should lean to his own understanding, and that there is none or little reason why any man should impose on another, he being so seldom and so little while consistent with himself, who was as confident, and upon thought-reason, as confident of the opinion wherein he was, as he is of the opinion wherein he is.[27]

Glanvill, who has an unbounded admiration for "the Grand Secretary of Nature, the miraculous Descartes," is most pleased with the Cartesian method because it is "a Scepticism, that's the only way to Science," and because Descartes "intends his Principles but for Hypotheses, and never pretends that things are really or necessarily, as he hath supposed them: but that they may be admitted pertinently to save the Phaenomena, and are convenient supposals for the use of life,"[28] in the true sceptic manner. We are advised to follow the Cartesian method, suspending the giving our assent to an apparent truth, however plausible, "till we have examin'd them by a free, and unpossest Reason; and to admit nothing but what we clearly, and distinctly perceive," but he has little hope of our success. "This is the great Rule, in the excellent method of Des-Cartes; but the practice of it requires such a clear, sedate, and intent mind, as is to be found but in a very few rare tempers; and even in them, prejudices will creep in, and spoil the perfection of their Knowledge. . . . Yea, 'tis a hard matter for the best and freest minds to deliver themselves from the Prejudices of Phancy . . . these all arise, either from the false Images of Sense, and the undue compositions, and wrong inferences that we raise from them,"[29] or from the influence of our affections upon our minds. Glanvill's eagerness, as an admirer of the Royal Society, to discredit the Aristotelians, leads him to a less qualified description of Descartes than one might expect from a devotee of sceptic method; Descartes himself has to be forced rather violently into the sceptic mould so that an appearance of consistency can be preserved. Huet, Bishop of Avranches, has no such difficulties. In *The Weakness of Human Understanding* he points out that Descartes, though he began from the necessity of doubt, built up a system none the less, and he severely censures such rationalism as doomed to failure, for "human Understanding depressed to Earth by Confinement to a terrestrial Body, and confessing that hereby

55

the Way to Truth is precluded from it, will more surely avoid
Lapses and Errors by remaining in its Ignorance, and the Doubt
which attends Ignorance, than by vain Attempts to break through
the Obstructions, and instead of a Juno embrace Nothing in the
End but a Cloud."[30] Descartes's sceptical method of enquiry is
thus distinguished from the dogmatic explanations which he too
hastily formulated.

In both Glanvill and Huet, the great hindrance to the achievement of knowledge through clear and distinct perceptions is
summed up in the word "prejudices," the term used, in an age of
Cartesian dualism, for "the Opinions our minds are possessed
with," and they are less confident than Descartes that these opinions can be uprooted. In this Swift was at one with them. The
word was frequently used in the philosophy of his day, and became a comprehensive term for all those notions which obscure
the "free and unpossest Reason." Such things arise from the senses
and affections, whose deceits our weak reason is not able to pene-
trate, and include, in Glanvill's terms, "the translation of our own
passions to things without us; as we judg Light and Heat, and
Cold, to be formally in the Sun, Fire, and Air; when as indeed
they are but our own perceptions"—that is, the confusion of primary and secondary qualities in the objects we perceive—"and the
fallacies of our Imaginations, whose unwarrantable compositions,
and applications, do very frequently abuse us."[31]

Prejudices, in fact, are a part of our physical nature, and are
associated with imagination (apprehension of absent corporal objects, and so closely related to the senses) and passions, as well as
with the mistaken impressions we pick up in the haphazard irrational business of daily life, especially in childhood. Prejudices
are part of the giddy circumstance of sublunary life as opposed to
the conceptions of "right ratiocination."[32] The Cartesian Malebranche, whose work Swift possessed, makes explicit the connection between prejudices and the impressions made on us by our
senses, passions, and instincts. All that comes to us through the
body—*"par le corps, ou à l'occasion du corps"*—obscures the eternal truth of reason; it is union with the body which weakens the
God-given reason. "Le principe général de nos préjugés c'est que

56

nous ne distinguons pas entre *connaître* et *sentir,* et qu'au lieu de juger des choses par les *idées* qui les représentent, nous en jugeons par les *sentiments* que nous en avons."[33] Huet, likewise, in his reference to the understanding as being pressed down to earth by confinement to a terrestrial body, stresses the limitation our physical nature imposes upon reason, and thus the distrust of man's rational powers can appeal to the traditional view of the dual nature of man, half beast, half intellectual being, and of the degeneracy which is a result of the Fall.

Among Christian thinkers, indeed, there had been for centuries a reciprocal action between the sceptic distrust of human reason and the Biblical theme of the Fall of man, and there is a Christian scepticism which is a statement in philosophical terms of the doctrine of original sin, the theological and the philosophical revealing themselves as two aspects of the same attitude. Glanvill expresses the traditional belief that in the state of innocence man's intellect was infinitely more powerful than now, was not disturbed by the passions, which then "kept their place as servants of the higher power," and was better served by the senses. In *The Vanity of Dogmatizing* he enlarges upon this in a manner which later seemed to him fantastical, and which was replaced in *Scepsis Scientifica* by a sober passage more in keeping with the standards of the Royal Society to whom the later version of the work was addressed. The earlier passage makes the hazardous guess that Adam's senses were not, like ours, deceived; he could, without a Galileo's tube, see much of the glory of the heavens: "Adam needed no spectacles." But the passage in which he writes of the ruin caused in us by the Fall remains substantially unchanged in *Scepsis Scientifica:* "And yet this is the miserable disorder, into which we are laps'd: the lower Powers are gotten uppermost; and we see like men on our heads as Plato observ'd of old, that on the right hand, which indeed is on the left. The Woman in us, still prosecutes a deceit, like that begun in the Garden: and our Understandings are wedded to an Eve, as fatal as the Mother of our miseries."[34] This familiar elaboration of the old description of man as *"arbor inversa,"* an inverted tree rooted in air, not in earth, or as Glanvill puts it in *An Apology for Philosophy,* an "inversed

57

plant," is the basis of Swift's *jeu d'esprit,* the "Meditation upon a Broomstick," written in the style of Mr. Boyle: "But a Broomstick, perhaps you will say, is an Emblem of a Tree standing on its Head; and pray what is Man, but a topsy-turvy Creature? His Animal Faculties perpetually mounted on his Rational; his Head where his Heels should be, groveling on the Earth."[35] And it is also, more seriously, the cause of madness in *A Tale of a Tub* that vapours ascend from the lower faculties to overshadow the brain, "a Man's Fancy gets astride of his Reason" and "Imagination is at Cuffs with the Senses, and common Understanding, as well as common Sense, is Kickt out of Doors."[36] *A Discourse of the Mechanical Operation of the Spirit* is founded upon the same distinction between mind and body, part of that human degeneracy which "the Scripture-system of man's creation" best accounts for.

Of course by no means all writers who accepted the Cartesian dualism related it to the Fall. The moralists and philosophers of the time, though so many of them use the term "prejudices" with its implication of the distortions of sense and passion, differ in their notions of how far prejudices can be torn from the mind, leaving reason free to operate. Descartes and his follower Malebranche, and the rationalists, whether Christian or Deist, had considerable confidence in the ultimate power of reason; the more sceptical, and the more pessimistic, stressed the impossibility of escape from prejudice. "Our Understandings are wedded to an Eve, as fatal as the Mother of our miseries." Swift's position is alongside the more sceptical and pessimistic. His temperament, his experience as a practical politician and, perhaps more important, as a practical and earnest clergyman with a considerable knowledge of ordinary human nature, led him to the opinion that man must divest himself of such prejudices as he can, but that we cannot entirely wake from our fairyland of dreams. The word "prejudice" is often used in *A Tale of a Tub,* and is a favorite of the "modern" author, himself one of the objects of Swift's satire. In Section VIII the author gives an account of the "renowned sect of Aeolists," and congratulates himself on having done justice to a society of men usually so misrepresented, and he closes with his customary naïve pride: "For, I think it one of the greatest, and best of humane Actions, to remove Prejudices, and place Things in their truest and fairest Light; which I therefore boldly undertake without any Regards of my own, beside the Conscience, the Honour, and the Thanks."[37] In the Apology prefixed to the *Tale* in 1710 the word occurs again during Swift's account of his intentions in writing a book which had met with so much disapproval. Speaking of himself as a young man he says that "by the Assistance of some Thinking, and much Conversation, he had endeavour'd to Strip himself of as many real Prejudices as he could," but the term "real" suggests that he felt some things commonly called prejudices were not real ones, and indeed he goes on: "I say real ones, because under the Notion of Prejudices, he knew to what dangerous Heights some Men have proceeded."[38] One such man, no doubt, is John Toland, for whom much of revelation was "prejudice," since it could not be justified by reason. "To be confident of any thing without conceiving it," he wrote, "is no real Faith or Persuasion, but a rash Presumption, and an obstinate Prejudice."[39] Since *A Tale of a Tub* was so misinterpreted, and was even said to be influenced by Toland, it was important that Swift should dissociate himself from those who saw man's nature in terms of this simple dualism. The hint in the *Tale* is developed years later in *Gulliver's Travels*, when Gulliver comments with amusement and some condescension on the prejudices of the King of Brobdingnag, shown in his horror at his guest's account of the effects of gunpowder. Here it is Gulliver who is really in the grip of prejudice, the mere irrational "opinion" of political expediency; what he regards as prejudice is in fact the proper humane feeling of a well-regulated man. The word has become a cant term, dangerous because it can be used to destroy all decency and humanity in the name of reason, and even to attack religious belief. It is associated with Deism in *The Sentiments of a Church of England Man*, and in *Examiner* No. 22, where there is an ironic reference to "the Slavery of believing by Education and Prejudice," and in No. 26, where the Earl of Rochester is sorrowfully rebuked: "But then, his best Friends must own that he is neither Deist nor Socinian: He hath never conversed with Toland, to open and en-

large his Thoughts, and dispel the Prejudices of Education."[40]
Again there is much play with the word in *An Argument against
Abolishing Christianity,* with the same association with Deism:

> It is further objected against the Gospel System, that it obliges Men to
> the Belief of Things too difficult for Free-Thinkers, and such who have
> shook off the Prejudices that usually cling to a confin'd Education.
>
> It is likewise proposed, as a great Advantage to the Publick, that if we
> once discard the System of the Gospel, all Religion will, of Course, be
> banished for ever; and consequently along with it, those grievous Prejudices
> of Education; which, under the Names of Virtue, Conscience, Honour,
> Justice, and the like, are so apt to disturb the Peace of human Minds; and
> the Notions whereof are so hard to be eradicated by right Reason, or
> Free-thinking, sometimes during the whole Course of our Lives.[41]

And Gulliver's error is summed up succinctly in one of the
"Thoughts on Various Subjects": "Some Men, under the Notions
of weeding out Prejudices; eradicate Religion, Virtue, and common Honesty."[42] In this matter Swift is nearer to the sceptics than
to the rationalists. For him, we are so far in the grip of inescapable deceit that we may easily mistake what prejudice is; like
Gulliver we may take for prejudice the good as well as the bad,
impulses of our bodily nature. A man deceived may easily mistake
in what he is deceived: a simple dualism is not enough to pene-
trate the fatal deceit "begun in the garden."

In indicating certain parallels between Swift's attitude and that
of writers who make use of the sceptic tradition, I have not intended to suggest any debt to those writers unless perhaps to
Montaigne. Such ideas were in the air; and for anyone except a
professional philosopher it was a matter of choosing from all
kinds of sources the conceptions most useful for oneself. Indeed
the date of the *Sentiments of the Weakness of Human Understanding* would preclude any significant debt in the case of Bishop
Huet, and Glanvill would not have been personally acceptable to
Swift as a "latitude man" and an excited admirer of the Royal
Society and of that arch system-maker, Descartes. In one of his
early letters he refers to *Scepsis Scientifica* as a "fustian piece of
abominable curious virtuoso stuff"—"fustian" presumably because
of Glanvill's tortuous and highly figurative style, which is often

reminiscent of the more metaphysical flights of the author of *A Tale of a Tub,* or the whirling metaphors of the "Tritical Essay on the Faculties of the Mind." And certainly the homage paid to the Royal Society and its endeavors in *Scepsis Scientifica,* in Swift's eyes, would justify the phrase "curious virtuoso stuff." Glanvill's sceptical pessimism about the potentialities of human reason is bound up with his justification of the Cartesian system and the efforts of the virtuosi, which Swift rather unfairly saw as so much more system-making. Unlike Glanvill, he did not regard either Descartes or the Royal Society as having an attitude of sceptical humility towards their own mental constructions. To him they were a set of "world-makers" or mere presumptuous "projectors"; for though Swift could do rough justice to the work of Francis Bacon, he is less than fair to Bacon's more modern successors the members of the Royal Society, whom he saw only as a threat to humane values. Yet, though the use to which Glanvill's scepticism is often put is antipathetic to Swift, the scepticism itself has much in common with his attitude, and its tendencies and purpose can be more clearly seen in the works of these contemporary philosophers than in his own more complex writing. One might say that had Glanvill followed the sceptic attitude to conclusions more properly to be deduced from it, as did the Bishop of Avranches, he like Swift would have regarded Descartes's efforts as vanity, embracing nothing in the end but a cloud. Of course Swift cannot be described as a sceptic or a Pyrrhonist: there was no distinct school of sceptic philosophers in the seventeenth century, and if there had been he would have disapproved of them. To doubt all things was no longer possible, for truth had been revealed to us once and for all in the Bible, and Swift's reference to the sceptics as a distinct philosophical sect, in the *Four Last Years of the Queen,* shows plainly enough that he would—as is only to be expected—condemn a sceptical attitude towards revealed religion, which is not, as he puts it, in the category of "speculative opinions."[43] It is a mark of the wrongheadedness of the author of *An Argument against Abolishing Christianity* that he regards Christianity as a "system" which "after the Fate of other Systems is generally antiquated and exploded."[44] If Glanvill could reject the name of

61

sceptic, and criticize certain aspects of sceptical thinking, there is no doubt that Swift would have gone further in his criticisms. At that time as in later ages, the term "sceptic" was widely applied to unbelievers. To be frankly and fully a sceptic would be to reject all certainty and with it the Christian faith, remaining uncommitted in a state of suspense. The comment in Swift's "Thoughts on Various Subjects" which immediately precedes that on the Stoics, presumably refers to the sceptic school: "It is a miserable Thing to Live in Suspence; it is the Life of a Spider."[45]

Some kind of certainty was a necessity to a man for whom chaos always lay in wait as it did for Swift. But a modified and limited scepticism leading not to system-making or to endless suspense but to religious faith, in Montaigne's fashion, could be a refuge not only from rationalism but from the extremes of scepticism itself, from such a complete acceptance of uncertainty and suspense, such an insidious persuasion to atheism, as is suggested in these words of Bernard Mandeville:

> It is very true, that our Senses sometimes deceive us, that our Reasons are false, and our Judgment errs. This I confess is a mortifying Reflection; but still the greatest Certainty we can receive must come from them; for when once we begin to doubt of our Reason, and our Senses, we are longer sure of nothing, an immediate Revelation from God not excepted; for how shall we trust to a Revelation, when we cannot depend either on the Senses by which we receive it, nor our Reason, the only Touchstone, by which we can assure our selves of its being Divine?[46]

Such threats to revealed Religion had to be grappled with, and when the premises of the argument are commonly accepted there is little to be done but to turn the enemy's weapons against him. Pascal, in *Entretien avec Saci,* saw clearly that Montaigne's scepticism, directed against *"la superbe raison,"* had its uses when contrasted with the self-sufficiency of Epictetus, though the view of man it expresses is only partially true and must be completed by the inclusive view given by Christian revelation, as indeed Montaigne himself had pointed out. So Swift in his turn, like others before him, both churchmen and laymen, took up certain attitudes to be found also in sceptic writers, in his own efforts to find some sort of guide through contemporary confusion which would suit his personal needs. In doing so, he did not break new ground; it is not his ideas, but the embodiment of them in words and in the strange creatures of his imagination, that is original: yet his methods as a writer do themselves depend upon the complicated, shifting relationships of prevailing ideas that he needs to express. The brilliance of his writing, the perfect congruity of method and idea, makes more vigorous and telling than those of his contemporaries his attack on the rationalistic pride which, whether intentionally or not, could only result in the undermining of religion and morality.

Chapter IV
THE TREASURE OF BASENESS IN MAN

In the writing of Swift and his contemporaries it is impossible to separate sharply the consideration of reason as an intellectual faculty and as a moral force. Any examination of Swift's distrust of reason as a way to truth must inevitably become an examination of his view of the moral nature of man, since for him the way to truth is the way to virtue, though it is a way very difficult to find. Distrust of reason is linked with a traditional acceptance of man as a fallen creature in whom since the deceit begun in the garden the "lower powers are gotten uppermost." Our reason is weak because our virtue is weak, and the clouding of our intellect is consequent upon the loss of innocence; a curtain has fallen between us and the truth which once we knew. The modern evidence of the deceit in which we live has only revealed to us more clearly our inestimable loss. Deists and extreme rationalists tacitly ignored the doctrine of original sin, and among the more Latitudinarian churchmen too the idea was in some disrepute; the degenerate nature of man constituted but a small part of their teaching. But Swift could not ignore this doctrine, because apart from being "what Christians are bound to believe," it seemed to him to be supported by what he had experienced, both in other men and in himself. The exclamation from his "Thoughts on Religion"— "Miserable mortals! Can we contribute to the honour and Glory of God?"[1]—is far from the complacency widespread even among sincere churchmen of the period. It is the cry of a man who not only understands, as a matter of theory, that humanity is in a state of sin, but knows and feels that he himself is sinful, a miserable mortal at infinite distance from the glory of God. It is personal experience which leads him to accept the biblical account of the creation and fall of man, as not only part of a body of revealed truth, but as something psychologically convincing, "most agreeable of all others to probability and reason" because it explains what we know of ourselves. He writes again of original sin, though in a lighter tone, in a letter to Deane Swift in 1735, giving an account of his own state of mind and body in a charmingly turned allegory of the "poor little house of clay" which he inhabits: "I might have had my lease on much better terms, if it had not been the fault of my great-grandfather. He and his wife, with the advice of a bad neighbour, robbed an orchard belonging to the Lord of the Manor, and so forfeited their grand privileges; to my sorrow I am sure, but, however, I must do as well as I can."[2]

For all its simplicity, this little story has a serious air. Swift is writing in the gently humorous tone that is so frequent in his letters, especially those to friends younger than himself, and that makes them such a delight to read. But it is the rueful humor of a resigned and matter-of-fact acceptance of the limitation of man's state, "but, however, I must do as well as I can." With a similar humorous resignation he had sent his advice to the innocent and mercurial Thomas Sheridan ten years before: "Therefore sit down and be quiet, and mind your business as you should do, and contract your friendships, and expect no more from man than such an animal is capable of."[3] And to Pope in the same year: "I tell you after all, that I do not hate mankind: it is *vous autres* who hate them, because you would have them reasonable animals, and are angry for being disappointed."[4] A sense of personal weakness, and of the sinfulness of even so loved and respected a person as Stella, is visible too in the prayers written during her illness. It is mercy and forgiveness that he asks for her even in the midst of his own grief, since the best of mankind is at so great a distance from goodness and truth. Indeed it is his sense of his own, and all men's, sinfulness that—among other things—makes Swift so great a satirist. We accept his picture of mankind because we recognize that he includes himself as one of the miserable mortals; he too is the animal, man. Despite his assumption of an unconcerned tone for satiric purposes, Swift is the least detached of satirists; like Gulliver he is condemning in the Yahoos a part of his nature. "For a man who is thoroughly acquainted with his own heart, does already know more evil of himself, than anybody else can tell him."[5] High standards, and an unflinching honesty which made him conscious that he could not fulfil them, reinforce in Swift a sense of sin which contemporaries like Shaftesbury and Bolingbroke so conspicuously lack. What gives such force to the Yahoos and Struldbrugs of *Gulliver's Travels,* and such intensity to the private "Thoughts" and prayers, is a certainty of personal wrongness, a knowledge of baseness through facing it and dreading it in himself. Swift's greatest and most moving satire comes, in this way, from inside, from personal experience. As dean and as man he drove himself hard, and with his rigorous personal standards came, of course, tension, the effort to live up to them and the remorse of not always doing so. The unresolved tensions which contribute so much to his disturbing power as a writer are there too in his life; there is always in Swift something of the frustrated perfectionist of the odes, forcing him to search for some kind of compromise between unattainable goodness and the evil in man until he could "expect no more from man than such an animal is capable of."

For a man so conscious as Swift of innate evil, it was natural to find in La Rochefoucauld a congenial view of mankind. The famous comment in his letter to Pope of November 26, 1725, though couched in the tone of bantering solemnity frequent in his correspondence with Pope and with Bolingbroke, has a core of seriousness. It is a pointer to Swift's real opinion of the nature of man and is to be related to the philosophical and psychological thinking of the time. His admiration for La Rochefoucauld's *Maxims* would seem to have been well known to his London companions, and may have given rise to some friendly argument and amusement. Pope's sweeping announcement that he is "writing a set of maxims in opposition to all Rochefoucauld's principles" has the challenging sound of a piece of deliberate baiting, and Swift's reply is similarly exaggerated: "This I say, because you are so hardy as to tell me of your intentions to write maxims in opposition to Rochefoucauld, who is my favourite, because I found my whole character in him." This is part of the fun, Swift's way of showing that he has seen the joke, but what leads up to it is a considered defense of his own view of man, which has, certainly, something in common with that of La Rochefoucauld:

I tell you after all, that I do not hate mankind: it is *vous autres* who hate them, because you would have them reasonable animals, and are angry for being disappointed. I have always rejected that definition, and made another of my own. I am no more angry with [Walpole] than I was with the kite that last week flew away with one of my chickens; and yet I was pleased when one of my servants shot him two days after. This I say, because you are so hardy as to tell me of your intentions to write maxims in opposition to Rochefoucauld, who is my favourite, because I found my whole character in him.[6]

The passage is definite enough; Swift is claiming that his own low estimate of man's capability for good is both more realistic and more humane than that view which expects more from man "than such an animal is capable of." He expects little, because he believes with La Rochefoucauld that self-love is the spring of man's actions, and so he can contemplate without anger the actions which so disappoint those who expect man to be guided by reason. Swift's comment is not an attack on the unreasoning wickedness of men; it does not proceed from disgust, but from an observation of men's actions and of the workings of their minds which leads him to suppose with La Rochefoucauld that men not only are unreasonable, but cannot help being unreasonable. It is their nature to be so as it is the kite's nature to steal chickens. For both La Rochefoucauld and Swift, to be angry with something so natural and inescapable would be absurd.

This is not to say that either writer believed all men to be equally wicked or selfish creatures, and Swift certainly does not always write of his fellows with the dispassionate calm he here displays. He can be very angry with Walpole, or Wood, or Wharton, or with any man whose self-love seems to lead him to a depravity or a cruelty more pronounced than that of the rest of mankind, for some men's self-love can lead them to behave well, and to please others. It is an attitude which can allow, realistically, for many kinds and degrees of good and bad behavior, and so, Swift is really claiming, it is less likely to result in disappointment and cynicism than is a more rigidly optimistic view. Of course even this adaptable scheme does not free Swift from error in his own judgments of people. Like any man, he could be mistaken, led astray by political prejudices or personal offense as he seems to have been, for instance, in the case of the red-headed Duchess of Somerset whom he pursued with such hatred. But as Dr. Johnson so sensibly points out, a man's errors of behavior do not invalidate the sincerity of his beliefs or the earnestness of his endeavors, and in fact Swift's lapses into persónal rancor are outnumbered by the instances of his tolerance and kindness to those who err simply in the common measure, not cold-bloodedly, in deliberate selfishness, but through the self-love, the prejudices, the passions, which are the basis of our fallen nature and which reason can never uproot. His goodness to his people in Dublin, and to his young protégés in London, is well known, and it is no longer necessary to point out that Swift was, though sometimes brusque, a kindly man. His letters, as well as his actions, often display a fine tolerance; an example is his letter of May 1713 to Richard Steele, who had treated his old friend with a spitefulness strange in so sanguine a man. Perhaps Swift's view that a low opinion of human nature is the best foundation for acceptance of its oddities has something to recommend it, and certainly many good and charitable men have held similar opinions without being misanthropic or considered so by their contemporaries. Fénelon, for instance, found that there were very few worthy men, and expected nothing from his fellows. And the "Verses on the Death of Dr. Swift," based on a maxim of La Rochefoucauld, give an attractive picture of the tolerance which arises from a clear sight of one's own motives and those of others. The opening stanza is a comment which may apply to Swift as well as to his model:

> As Rochefoucault his Maxims drew
> From Nature, I believe 'em true:
> They argue no corrupted Mind
> In him; the Fault is in Mankind.[7]

For all the joking exaggeration of Swift's claim to found his character in La Rochefoucauld, there is a considerable resemblance between them. Details of Swift's thought can often be paralleled in the *Maxims,* but more than that there is a general similarity of outlook. Both recognize the complexity of human nature; man baffles the attempts of reason to classify him without simplification, whether the reason is that of Descartes or of Bolingbroke. For La Rochefoucauld the only clue to the labyrinthine nature of man was self-love, and this alone, he found, could guide the observer through the tortuous behavior of himself and his fellow-men. Similarly others in the seventeenth and eighteenth centuries (including Pope) seized upon the Ruling Passion to explain what reason could not. La Rochefoucauld, it has been said, was an observer, not a reformer or a moralist, and here his likeness to Swift ends, for Swift was passionately concerned in the predicament of man, and the sense we have, as we read, that he feels himself involved in that predicament and bound to do what he can to alleviate it is not to be paralleled in the polished aloofness of the *Maxims*. Perhaps it is this difference that has made La Rochefoucauld and Montaigne acceptable to generations of readers who are made uncomfortable by Swift. Yet Swift's moral and satiric impulse, and La Rochefoucauld's curiosity, lead along the same intellectual path. Both men are obsessed by the idea of making us see the truth about ourselves, though in Swift's case this truth is valued as the first step to improvement. If we believe it possible to be guided entirely by reason, if we persist either in regarding as reasonable actions which arise from disguised self-love, or in denying the possibility that the passions may produce good, then we can never hope to improve even within the limits possible to us. We must know what human nature is made of, in all its limitations and complexity, before we can set to work upon it. In La Rochefoucauld, even this modest moral aim, of knowledge used as a basis for the limited improvement possible to fallen man, seems to be lacking; his purpose in showing us human nature as it is would appear to be simply that of enabling us to accept ourselves and make a working arrangement by which the everyday life of society can be carried on in comparative smoothness.

Both writers therefore, though with a different emphasis because of their difference in temperament and aim, try to strip us of hypocrisy. They cannot strip us of self-love, for that is part of our being, but they can force us to recognize its existence. A comment made on La Rochefoucauld by one of his editors is oddly applicable to Swift: "He sterilises the reader's mind of sentimental impurities."[8] This, as has often been said, is what Swift is always trying to do, to remove impurities, prejudices; but as always in

Swift's case one must hasten to qualify. He wishes to remove prejudices so far as they really are prejudices and so far as they may be removed without harm. His most characteristic satire is not that of exaggeration and caricature but of isolating, stripping, until he has found those limits of man's capability within which it is possible to work for improvement. And like La Rochefoucauld, he regards self-love as the cause of many of our illusions, "the greatest of which is that we can ever escape its domination." The self-love from which passions arise, the senses which provide us with such untrustworthy reports from the outside world, these things complicate incessantly the task of our struggling reason. From whatever point we start, in considering Swift's ideas and attitudes, we are brought back again to the inevitable weakness of reason, to the picture of man lost and baffled, wandering alone enclosed in his own world of dream and deceit. But once we recognize our situation, and do not persuade ourselves that we are reasonable animals, much may be done. For self-love, source of the passions, is not necessarily evil; it is indeed a part of our fallen nature, but it may be used ill or well. So La Rochefoucauld believed: "Nous ne pouvons rien aimer que par rapport à nous, et nous ne faisons que suivre notre goût et notre plaisir quand nous préférons nos amis à nous-même. C'est néanmoins par cette préférence seule que l'amitié peut être vraie et parfaite." Also, "L'intérêt, que l'on accuse de tous nos crimes, mérite souvent d'être loué de nos bonnes actions."[9] In his correspondence Swift makes specific reference to self-love as a motive of action; for example, in a letter of condolence to Mrs. Moore, on the loss of her daughter: "Self-love, as it is the motive to all our actions, so it is the sole cause of our grief. The dear person you lament is by no means an object of pity either in a moral or religious sense."[10]

Of course Swift and La Rochefoucauld were by no means alone in stressing the importance and strength of self-love, but in thinkers of the more progressive and optimistic school self-love tended to lose the content of selfishness or self-concentration which La Rochefoucauld specifically gives it—"l'amour de soi-même et de toutes choses pour soi." In Pope, too, "Modes of Self-love the Passions we may call," and in those passions "Reason the byass

Gulliver in Brobdingnag and in Houyhnhnm-land. Reproduced, by permission
of Sir Harold Williams, from *Voyages du
Capitaine Lemuel Gulliver* . . . , La Haye,
1741.

Gulliver in Brobdingnag and in Houy-
hnhnm-land, from *Travels into Several
Remote Nations of the World, by Lemuel
Gulliver*, London, 1755. Courtesy of the
British Museum.

turns to good from ill,"[11] and so far Swift and La Rochefoucauld, to say nothing of earlier moralists, would doubtless agree with him; but there is nothing in their work to suggest that they would follow him in the grandiose scheme by which self-love, "operating to the social and public good," becomes almost indistinguishable from general benevolence:

> Thus God and Nature link'd the gen'ral frame,
> And bade Self-love and Social be the same.[12]

Here, we may suppose, is visible the influence of Bolingbroke upon the malleable mind of his friend. However far beyond this jaunty optimism the poem as a whole goes (and surely Pope's intense vision of the inescapable miseries and wickedness of man is the inspiration of some of his greatest poetry), there are passages outlining the nominal scheme of the *Essay* which, isolated, treat even "l'amour de soi-même et de toutes choses pour soi" as an admirably contrived part of the nature of man, something to rejoice in, not to treat with the wary acceptance of Swift. "A due use of our reason," says Bolingbroke, "makes social and self-love coincide, or even become in effect the same. The condition wherein we are born and bred, the very condition so much complained of, prepares us for this coincidence, the foundation of human happiness; and our whole nature, appetite, passion, and reason concur to promote it."[13] Here is the calm confident voice of the Enlightenment, but this is not the way that the lot of us miserable mortals appears to Swift, and there are several indications in the letters which he exchanged with Bolingbroke and Pope (they were in the habit of sending joint letters to Swift, who often replied to them jointly) that he profoundly disagreed with Bolingbroke's views of humanity, views which he must have known from conversations before they were committed to writing.

The two men seem never to have been on terms of the closest understanding. It was Oxford who claimed Swift's loyalty and affection, and in the final break between the two ministers he refused all Bolingbroke's offers and, to his great credit, proposed to follow Oxford into retirement and disgrace. Swift admired Bolingbroke's precocious and many-sided brilliance as everybody did, but he was not the man to be dazzled by it, and there may be a note of distrust in his early reference to the Secretary in November 1711: "What truth and sincerity he may have I know not: he is now but thirty-two, and has been Secretary above a year. Is not all this extraordinary?"[14] What seems certain is that Swift never wrote to Bolingbroke with the frankness of his letters to Oxford, still less with the openness and trust that he showed to his deeply loved and respected friend Arbuthnot, on whose understanding he could count because he knew that Arbuthnot shared his fundamental beliefs. His letters to Arbuthnot were few, but only because it gave him pain to remember so dear a friend when he expected that they would never meet again. There was nothing to keep him from being miserable "but endeavouring to forget those for whom he has the greatest value, love, and friendship."[15] There is no mistaking the unity of thinking and feeling which bound these two together, and Arbuthnot, no misanthrope but a kindly, well-balanced, and happy man of "moral and Christian virtues," shared his friend's belief in "that treasure of vileness and baseness, that I always believed to be in the heart of man."[16]

Arbuthnot's poem "Know Yourself," published in 1734, shows an attitude very similar to Swift's in its picture of the dual nature of fallen man, and its criticism of philosophies, particularly Epicureanism and Stoicism, which err in ignoring one side of human nature and so are inadequate guides. Not even Pope, certainly not Bolingbroke, understood Swift as Arbuthnot did, and during the time when Bolingbroke was living at Dawley, in close and continuous touch with Pope, there is present in the correspondence which passed between the three friends a slight strain only partially concealed by exaggerated banter. Swift was doubtless aware that Pope oscillated between his own private vision of things and an intellectual acceptance of the system of thought in which Bolingbroke instructed him with that peculiarly flattering persuasiveness to be seen in action in his letters. In 1735 Swift pointedly expresses his satisfaction at signs of a growing pessimism in Pope: "It pleases me to find that you begin to dislike things in spite of your philosophy; your Muse cannot forbear her hints to that purpose."[17]

The famous letter of November 1725 to Pope, clearly intended for Bolingbroke too, shows a consciousness that even ten years earlier, when they were all more of an age, he had differed from them in some things; and now that they "differ more than ever" he is anxious that they shall not think his disaffection to the world is caused merely by advancing years. Clearly he does not expect them to understand or to agree with him, and Bolingbroke seems to be included among "*vous autres*" who would have mankind reasonable animals. Bolingbroke's letters to Swift constantly return to the question of the nature of man. He dislikes Swift's definition ("*animal rationis capax*") and sneers at La Rochefoucauld, "The founder of your sect, that noble original whom you think it so great an honour to resemble,"[18] as a hypocrite and an embittered, disappointed courtier. There would seem to have been a standing difference of opinion between the two, and it is not surprising that according to Pope and Gay, Bolingbroke disapproved of *Gulliver's Travels:* "Lord [Bolingbroke] is the person who least approves it, blaming it as a design of evil consequence to depreciate human nature, at which it cannot be wondered that he takes most offence, being himself the most accomplished of his species, and so losing more than any other of that praise which is due both to the dignity and virtue of a man."[19] The passage is an ingenious blend of compliment and joke, but it would surely be pointless if there were not an acceptance among the group that Bolingbroke was, like Shaftesbury, a believer in the "dignity and virtue" of man. And in fact the phrase is very apt; Bolingbroke's scheme, though it differs at many points from Shaftesbury's, is similar in its high estimate of man's moral capabilities.

The dislike of Montaigne hinted at in Bolingbroke's letter is based, characteristically, on Montaigne's low estimate of human nature and reason. He accuses Montaigne of having "drawn down human nature as low as he could," and of being among those who "degrade even the human mind and that intelligence and reason wherein we triumph."[20] Certainly Bolingbroke disagreed with Swift's notion of the strength of self-love, particularly in its form of the love of fame, which Swift treats in the "Thoughts on Various Subjects" as a possible incitement to virtue. He seems to sus-

73

pect that Swift was in this too little of a philosopher and too much of a clergyman, so convinced of the depravity of mankind "that you could do no better, nor keep up virtue in the world without calling this passion, or this direction of self-love, in to your aid." Swift's compromise with the passions, his readiness to accept that even directions of self-love not in themselves good may have their uses, is clearly not to Bolingbroke's taste. Man, in his opinion, can do better than this, and he urges Swift to wear a garment of philosophy rather than "that emblematical vestment your surplice,"[21] remarking that the clergy are too ready to sap the foundations of natural religion in order to strengthen their own edifice of revelation.[22] Bolingbroke in fact is impatient at Swift's acceptance of original sin, and seems to have felt that such an allegiance on the part of an intelligent man needed some explanation. One possible answer, he supposes, is that the clergy deliberately depreciate human nature in their own interest. Shaftesbury held a similar opinion, believing that the Church was often an enemy of virtue through its insistence on the evil inherent in the nature of man. "But you will call to mind," says the enlightened Theocles in *The Moralists,* "that even innocently, and without any treacherous design, Virtue is often treated so, by those who would magnify to the utmost the Corruption of Man's Heart; and in exposing, as they pretend, the Falsehood of human Virtue, think to extol Religion."[23]

For Shaftesbury, adverse criticism of mankind in general is evidence either of superstition or of misanthropy, and his Philocles gravely rebukes Palemon for his attacks on the nature of man; one might think him, says Philocles, "a compleat Timon, or Man-hater." But in fact Palemon's view of man, as reported by Philocles, is a perfectly ordinary and traditional one. Man, to him, is a wretched mixture of good and bad, Prometheus's "stoln celestial Fire, mix'd with vile Clay."[24] If this could be interpreted as misanthropy in Timon's manner by people of Shaftesbury's way of thinking, it is small wonder that Swift so earnestly defended himself against any charge of such misanthropy in his letters of November 26 and September 29, 1725: "I tell you after all, that I do not hate mankind," "this great foundation of misanthropy, though not in Timon's manner."[25] This is perhaps written with Shaftesbury in mind; certainly an earlier passage in the letter of September 29 is a deliberate and systematic denial of that "love of the species" which is the keystone of Shaftesbury's moral system and which Bolingbroke too believes to be natural to man: "I have ever hated all nations, professions, and communities, and all my love is toward individuals: for instance, I hate the tribe of lawyers, but I love Counsellor Such-a-one, and Judge Such-a-one; so with physicians—I will not speak of my own trade—soldiers, English, Scottish, French, and the rest. But principally I hate and detest that animal called man, although I heartily love John, Peter, Thomas and so forth."

This is the attitude for which Philocles had been rebuked by the rational and benevolent Theocles in *The Moralists;* "I cou'd love the Individual, but not the Species," he had confessed. "This was too mysterious; too metaphysical an Object for me." It was too mysterious and metaphysical an object for Swift too; he could not agree that "partial Affection, or social Love in part, without regard to a Compleat Society or Whole"[26] was imperfect and inconsistent because he had an opinion of man's nature very different from Shaftesbury's or Bolingbroke's. Theirs depends on abstract theorizing, on a neat moral system which is, in each case, consistent in itself but not related, Swift would feel, to things as they are. Swift's opinion is based on observation of himself and others, and supported by Christian tradition, which he accepts because it seems to explain what he has observed. For him as for the much scorned Palemon of *The Moralists,* man is an ill-starred blend of earth and fire, a "mingled Mass of Good and Bad," as he puts it in one of his later poems, "On Poetry: A Rapsody":

> 'Tis sung Prometheus forming Man
> Thro' all the brutal Species ran,
> Each proper Quality to find
> Adapted to a human Mind,
> A mingled Mass of Good and Bad,
> The worst and best that could be had.[27]

In a sense it is true that Swift was, as he told Bolingbroke, "no philosopher," that is, he found the theories of the new philosophers

75

unrelated to life and men as he knew them, and he preferred tradition, revelation, and his own experience. None the less, his declaration of hatred for all communities and principally for that animal called man is, as he himself insists, not a matter of misanthropy, nor is it caused by disappointment and advancing age. It is the result of an attitude towards mankind as considered and coherent as Shaftesbury's and implacably opposed to it, and so in a sense a "system," "the system upon which I have governed myself many years."[28] An individual member of this mixed and variable race may heartily love another individual, but from the very nature of the facts he cannot sincerely love man as such. Neither is the individual capable of it, nor is the species such as to inspire it. For Shaftesbury and Bolingbroke man is part of a harmonious universe, in which he can live in ease and serenity through his own efforts, just as any animal can, once he has learned the secret of his own nature, and how to fulfil his own potentialities. He is, indeed, an animal who happens to be reasonable, and his problems, though on a higher level, are those of any animal, a matter of adjustment to nature. And "Nature may be known from what we see of the natural State of Creatures, and of Man himself, when unprejudic'd by vitious Education."[29] Swift found man's condition less simple. He did not see man as being at home in the universe: for him as for Shaftesbury's derided Palemon, man is the fatal weakness in the workmanship of nature, a misfit in a world where all other creatures find their appointed place. He has not Shaftesbury's confidence in the moral sense which can bring about a happy and easy co-operation between reason and the passions, or Bolingbroke's belief in the power of reason over self-love. In man it is self-love that rules, and reason, weak and wavering, fights what is usually a losing battle.

Swift's desperate compromise with the power of self-love would not have appealed to Shaftesbury, who is able to dismiss with complacent ease those philosophers who, like Hobbes, "wou'd so explain all the social Passions, and natural Affections, as to denominate 'em of the selfish kind. Thus Civility, Hospitality, Humanity towards Strangers or People in distress, is only a more deliberate Selfishness. An honest Heart is only a more cunning one: and Honesty and Good-Nature, a more deliberate, or better-regulated Self-Love. The Love of Kindred, Children and Posterity, is purely Love of Self, and of one's own immediate Blood."[30] And Shaftesbury says uncompromisingly that although action taken through self-love may sometimes conduce to the good of the species, it is still vicious. An action is not to be commended if self-love is a man's "real Motive in the doing that, to which a natural Affection for his Kind ought by right to have inclin'd him."[31]

The difference in opinion regarding the motives of men's actions was, of course, part of the greater problem of the nature of man, and there were two extreme contemporary views, one supported by thinkers of various kinds of Deistic persuasion, for whom Shaftesbury may conveniently stand as spokesman, and the other put forward by the formidable Thomas Hobbes but treated in greater practical detail, and stubbornly defended, by Bernard Mandeville, follower of Bayle. If Shaftesbury deliberately, in *Characteristicks* and in his preface to Whichcote's sermons, takes issue with Hobbes on the motives of men's actions, Mandeville no less deliberately attacks Shaftesbury, and these two may be taken as examples of the extremists who felt themselves to be in irreconcilable opposition. Mandeville rightly remarks in "A Search into the Nature of Society," that the attentive reader "will soon perceive that two Systems cannot be more opposite than his Lordship's and mine."[32] As Mandeville's editor points out, his author's "whole conception of the rise and nature of society was determined by his belief in the essential egoism of human nature, and Shaftesbury's, by his faith in the actuality of altruism."[33] Shaftesbury, says Mandeville,

Fancies, that as Man is made for Society, so he ought to be born with a kind Affection to the whole, of which he is a part, and a Propensity to seek the Welfare of it. In pursuance of this Supposition, he calls every Action perform'd with regard to the Publick Good, Virtuous; and all Selfishness, wholly excluding such a Regard, Vice. In respect to our Species he looks upon Virtue and Vice as permanent Realties that must ever be the same in all Countries and all Ages, and imagines that a Man of sound Understanding, by following the Rules of good Sense, may not only find out that

77

Pulchrum & Honestum both in Morality and the Works of Art and Nature, but likewise govern himself by his Reason with as much Ease and Readiness as a good Rider manages a well-taught Horse by the Bridle.

Mandeville's objection to this system is given with the contemptuous bluntness characteristic of him. Shaftesbury's notions "are a high Compliment to Human-kind, and capable by the help of a little Enthusiasm of Inspiring us with the most Noble Sentiments concerning the Dignity of our exalted Nature: What Pity it is that they are not true. . . . the Solidity of them is inconsistent with our daily Experience."[34] Again: "To love Virtue for the Beauty of it, and curb one's Appetites because it is most reasonable so to do, are very good Things in Theory; but whoever understands our Nature, and consults the Practice of Human Creatures, would sooner expect from them, that they should abstain from Vice, for Fear of Punishment, and do good, in Hopes of being rewarded for it."[35]

The empirical observation of man's behavior, so characteristic of one line of thought in the seventeenth and eighteenth centuries, convinces Mandeville that theories of the exalted nature of man, and of the comparative ease with which he can attain virtue when once he has understood his own potentialities, are so much noble nonsense. Experience points out to him a fallacy in Shaftesbury's assumption that general benevolence, and a desire for the good of the whole society, is natural to man. In fact, he says, it is his selfishness, not his benevolence, that makes man a successful social animal. He proposes to "convince the Reader, not only that the good and amiable Qualities of Man are not those that make him beyond other Animals a sociable Creature; but moreover that it would be utterly impossible, either to raise any Multitudes into a Populous, Rich, and Flourishing Nation, or when so rais'd, to keep and maintain them in that Condition, without the assistance of what we call Evil both Natural and Moral."[36]

"What we call Evil"—this is the point on which *The Fable of the Bees* turns. Mandeville is there concerned to bring out the irreconcilability of rigorist[37] definitions of virtue and an acceptance of society as it is. In "An Enquiry into the Origin of Moral Virtue" he defines virtue as "every Performance, by which Man, contrary to the impulse of Nature, should endeavour the Benefit of others, or the Conquest of his own Passions out of a Rational Ambition of being good."[38] Virtue, far from being natural to man, is "contrary to the impulse of Nature," a rational conquest of the passions.

The Generality of Moralists and Philosophers have hitherto agreed that there could be no Virtue without Self-denial; but a late Author, who is now much read by Men of Sense, is of a contrary Opinion, and imagines that Men without any Trouble or Violence upon themselves may be naturally Virtuous. He seems to require and expect Goodness in his Species, as we do a sweet Taste in Grapes and China Oranges, of which, if any of them are sour, we boldly pronounce that they are not come to that Perfection their Nature is capable of.[39]

Looking around him, Mandeville found that there was little, in the everyday conduct of man, that could be called virtuous according to his own austere definition; that man was ruled by the principle of self-love, not of self-denial, and that society is a result of that self-love and not of benevolence. As Mandeville's master, Pierre Bayle, had pointed out, what was good for society was not necessarily virtuous, and a rigorous pursuit of reason and self-denial was likely to destroy society altogether as it does in *The Fable of the Bees.*

Shaftesbury's own definition is, in fact, as "rigorous" as Mandeville's, for neither will allow any virtue to an action undertaken through self-love, however beneficial its results may be. Their difference turns upon whether or not this virtue was possible— that is, as Mandeville was fully aware, on the question of what is natural to man. Mandeville is impatient with Shaftesbury's views because they seem to him purely theoretic and unrelated to experience; they oversimplify the situation of modern man living in a complex society. Shaftesbury's solution of the problem is too easy, indeed is not really a solution at all, but an evasion achieved by avoidance of the facts. For Mandeville there is no solution, only the paradox that the good of society is produced by the vices— according to rigoristic definition—of its individual members. In fact, "Private Vices, Publick Benefits." The actions which produce the good of society are the actions which both Mandeville and

79

Shaftesbury would join in calling vicious. As F. B. Kaye points out in the introduction to his edition of *The Fable of the Bees,* Mandeville is really demonstrating that man contributing to the good of society has to be judged according to the results of his actions, while man as an individual must be judged according to the motives of his actions. Shaftesbury's single standard of judgment is inapplicable to the world of men in society, who as Mandeville sets out to prove in such exhaustive detail, are guided by self-love— that self-love which yet has produced so much that is beneficial to society. Execrated as Mandeville was by so many in his day, the dilemma he presented was a real and serious one, and a further example of the moral and philosophic difficulties in which Swift's contemporaries found themselves.

Swift's own position in relation to the sharply opposed systems of Shaftesbury and Mandeville could only be, as always, a compromise. His opinion of human nature divides him clearly from Shaftesbury as from Bolingbroke, and his self-confessed adherence to his "favourite" La Rochefoucauld forms a link between him and Mandeville. But Swift, as churchman and moralist, and of all our satirists one of the most deeply troubled by the ills he writes of, could not be content to set the neat paradoxical problem and satisfy himself with its neatness. He can find only groping and partial solutions, but the need to find a solution is very urgent to him. Compared with the systematic clarity of Shaftesbury's scheme or Mandeville's, Swift's answer can only seem fragmentary and confused, but at least it has the merit of seeming also, like Pope's similar effort at reconciliation in the *Essay on Man,* nearer to the conditions in which man actually finds himself. It is not so easy as Shaftesbury or as Mandeville thought to classify men's motives and condemn or applaud them wholeheartedly. Swift is convinced of the element of truth in Hobbist psychology, but convinced too that it is not the whole truth, and he is ready to accept, without too much probing, actions which lead to good.

The motives of the best actions will not bear too strict an inquiry. It is allowed, that the cause of most actions, good or bad, may be resolved into the love of ourselves; but the self-love of some men, inclines them to please others; and the self-love of others is wholly employed in pleasing them-

80

selves. This makes the great distinction between virtue and vice. Religion is the best motive of all actions, yet religion is allowed to be the highest instance of self-love.[40]

Hobbes, La Rochefoucauld, Mandeville are right, yet man's actions are not to be condemned as vicious because his motives are not based on pure reason, on benevolence, or on self-denial. Actions caused by love of ourselves can still be called good actions or bad; one man's self-love can lead to selfishness, but another man best pleases himself by pleasing his friends. And religion, which Mandeville and Shaftesbury both, after a perfunctory acknowledgment, leave out of their consideration, has to be considered by Swift. It may be possible to reduce religion to self-love, to the fear of punishment and the hope of reward, yet it is certainly impossible to deny that it is the highest of all motives and leads to actions which are plainly good, just as feelings of no intrinsic value or virtue, like the love of fame which is also founded on self-love, can become an incitement to virtue. Thus Swift is able to make his way out of the impasse of Mandevillian thinking, the flat opposition between rigorously defined virtue and human motives, without adopting Shaftesbury's estimate of man which he must have found intolerably unrealistic and, in view of the strength of Deism, more dangerous to revealed religion than Mandeville's opinions could be. As Shaftesbury's writings imply, Hobbes and the churchmen for all their differences often approached one another in the matter of the depravity of man—or, as Bolingbroke would have it, in "a design to depreciate human nature."

The same practical acceptance of the limitations of human goodness is to be found in the sermons. Here Swift, like most of his contemporaries, pays most attention to man's behavior to his fellows; it is the public or social aspects of goodness which especially concern him. This perhaps puts him, with so many churchmen of the time, at a theoretical disadvantage, since he has to fight hostile movements of thought on the ground that they themselves have chosen, that of practical morality. Yet his refusal to concern himself overmuch with theoretical dogma or to use reason in the examination of religion[41] gives him, in practice, strength within a purposely limited field. In the sermons he examines theories of man's nature and conduct in terms of their results; his attitude seems to be that if the Christian scheme can be shown to succeed best in making men behave well to one another, it will not be necessary to prove its validity on theoretical and rational grounds. Once more theories are to be judged from practical results, and once more one may apply the comment in *The Sentiments of a Church of England Man:* a man "may be convinced that he is in an Error, although he does not see where it lies; by the bad Effects of it in the common Conduct of his Life; . . . whoever finds a Mistake in the Sum total, must allow himself out; although, after repeated Tryals, he may not see in which Article he hath misreckoned."[42] So in the sermons Swift is chiefly anxious to instruct his congregation in the practical aid to goodness which religion can give them, and to show that man, with his natural inclination to love of himself and concern for his own interests, needs something firmer than ideas of general benevolence, or honor, or moral honesty, if society is not to become a state of war. If man is ruled by self-love, he will be virtuous only if it can be shown to be in his own interest to be so; self-love can be conquered only by a higher kind of self-love, since "human nature is so constituted, that we can never pursue anything heartily but upon hopes of a reward." As for the notion that virtue is its own reward, this piece of Shaftesburian optimism is dismissed as mere fine talking: "Whereas, if there be any thing in this more than the sound of the words, it is at least too abstracted to become an universal influencing principle in the world, and therefore could not be of general use."[43] Swift makes no appeal to reason or the dignity of man; he would undoubtedly have agreed with Mandeville on one point at least, that "the generous Notions concerning the natural Goodness of Man are hurtful as they tend to mis-lead, and are meerly Chimerical,"[44] and he devotes some time to demonstrating that to depend for goodness on such conceptions as these is worse than useless. The guidance of reason in morality is especially dangerous, because it is so easily swayed by self-interest: "Let any Man but consider, when he hath a Controversy with another, although his Cause be ever so unjust, although the World be against him, how blinded he is by the Love of himself, to believe that Right is Wrong, and Wrong is Right, when it maketh for his own Advantage. Where is then the right Use of his Reason, which he so much boasteth of, and which he would blasphemously set up to controul the Commands of the Almighty?" Only faith can make a good man, and it is for its moral effects that Swift recommends a firm faith to his hearers: "Let no Man think that he can lead as good a moral Life without Faith, as with it; for this Reason, Because he who hath no Faith, cannot, by the Strength of his own Reason or Endeavours, so easily resist Temptations, as the other who depends upon God's Assistance in the overcoming his Frailties, and is sure to be rewarded for ever in Heaven for his Victory over them."[45]

The sermon "Upon the Excellency of Christianity" further examines various substitutes for the control of religion over our moral conduct. The heathen philosophers—to whom Swift no doubt mentally added certain philosophers of his own day—had nothing better to offer than such phrases as that happiness consisted in virtue, or that virtue was its own reward, and worthy to be followed only for itself; these are "vain babbling, and a mere sound of words." Their self-sufficiency—"they trusted in themselves for all things"—was a positive danger, because it expected too much of an imperfect creature; the Stoic virtue was mixed with affectation and pride. Swift's basic objection to all doctrines, ancient or modern, which stress man's moral self-sufficiency is summed up in two phrases from this sermon, referring to the "flagging and fainting of the mind, for want of a support by revelation from God," and to the predicament of even a wise and good man under the heathen dispensation—he was "wholly at the mercy of uncertain chance."[46] Without the support and the hope that revelation gives, sustained moral virtue is impossible, and a man is left in misery amid the meaningless confusion of the world. Searching for a guide through chaos, Swift's conclusion is "that there is no solid, firm Foundation of Virtue, but in a Conscience directed by the Principles of Religion."[47] The guidance of religion is essential because conscience in itself is only the knowledge we have of our own thoughts and actions, and in order to

83

judge these it must have some firm standard to guide it, a standard necessarily quite outside man because of man's capacity for self-deceit. This insistence that conscience is in itself indifferent, needing the external guidance of religion before it can operate morally, sharply distinguishes Swift's view from that of Shaftesbury, for whom conscience is, in itself, a sufficient judge of conduct, relating action to an existing standard of "natural" behavior in man himself. It is described as having "the Reflection in his Mind of any unjust Action or Behaviour, which he knows to be naturally odious and ill-deserving."[48]

For Swift, "moral honesty" has no certain effect upon our conduct because it has nothing to balance against the self-love which is all men's most powerful instinct. "Let it consist with such a Man's Interest and Safety to wrong you, and then it will be impossible you can have any Hold upon him; because there is nothing left to give him a Check, or to put in the Balance against his Profit. For, if he hath nothing to govern himself by, but the Opinion of the World, as long as he can conceal his Injustice from the World, he thinks he is safe."[49] But even if such a man, setting up "for Morality without regard to Religion," succeeds in being just towards his fellows, and so in behaving well in his public capacity, he will have very little incentive to check those personal vices which do not affect his dealings in the way of trade, law, or other public matters. There is nothing to keep him from pride, lust, intemperance, or avarice, which are all part of those dictates of nature which the "meer moral Man" believes he may follow. Honor, again, is no safe guide, since it depends on no absolute value, but on changing fashion and opinion. It is on this very changeableness of man and man's society that Swift's argument for a religious conscience is based. Reason, affection, law, all the possible ways of persuading to virtue, are wavering because of the lack of any firm principle in man himself. His motives change with his circumstances, at the mercy of his self-love, and only religion can steady them.

If the Motives of our Actions be not resolved and determined into the Law of God, they will be precarious and uncertain, and liable to perpetual Changes. I will shew you what I mean, by an Example: Suppose a Man

84

thinks it is his Duty to obey his Parents, because Reason tells him so, because he is obliged by Gratitude, and because the Laws of his Country command him to do so: But, if he stops here, his Parents can have no lasting Security; for an Occasion may happen, wherein it may be extremely his Interest to be disobedient, and where the Laws of the Land can lay no hold upon him: Therefore, before such a Man can safely be trusted, he must proceed farther, and consider, that his Reason is the Gift of God; that God commanded him to be obedient to the Laws, and did moreover in a particular manner enjoin him to be dutiful to his Parents; after which, if he lays a due Weight upon those Considerations, he will probably continue in his Duty to the End of his Life; Because no earthly Interest can ever come in Competition to balance the Danger of offending his Creator, or the Happiness of pleasing him. And of all this his Conscience will certainly inform him, if he hath any Regard to Religion.[50]

Law, and reason, have a part to play in the encouragement of virtue, but only a limited part unless we go beyond them to the one thing that can give them an unquestioned validity, divine command. Only through resolving our own motives into the law of God can we attain that charitable and kindly co-operation with our fellow-men which is so much more admirable than Stoic ideals of "insensibility and indifference," and which the Christian revelation sets forth for us to emulate.

For to Swift, the best and most practical kind of goodness was not pagan virtue but Christian charity. Of course he admired the nobility of the great ancients whom he, in an age of classical education, knew so familiarly; but he has two standards of behavior, that of ancient virtue and that of Christianity, and he is in no doubt as to which is the higher. The same is true of many of his contemporaries; Pope, for instance, uses two standards of moral reference in his satires, and it is noticeable that, when he is most deeply serious, the standard of classical virtue frequently gives way to, or is blended with, overtly Christian reference. When he is concerned not with oddities of behavior or trifling errors but with real evil and true goodness, his imagery is drawn from Bible or prayer-book or from *Paradise Lost,* which as a religious epic presents both the valid standards of behavior:

> Should'ring God's altar a vile image stands. . . .
>
> Or at the ear of Eve, familiar Toad. . . .

85

Lo! thy dread Empire, Chaos! is restor'd;
Light dies before thy uncreating word;
Thy hand, great Anarch! lets the curtain fall,
And universal Darkness buries All.[51]

The great philosophers of the past were to be admired and wondered at because they had achieved so much without the aid of revelation, but none the less "The System of Morality to be gathered out of the Writings, or Sayings of those antient Sages, falls undoubtedly very short of that delivered in the Gospel; and wants, besides, the Divine Sanction which our Saviour gave to his."[52]

It was the want of a divine sanction that Swift saw as the chief misery of the heathen world. Without it, the lonely endeavors of good men were a constant strain; they lacked security and certainty to sustain them when their efforts flagged, and they had no authority over people less enlightened, and less strenuous in the pursuit of virtue, than themselves, so that the bulk of mankind were no better off for the efforts of the few. But in any case even the best of them, understandably, fell far short of the morality of the gospel. They were a minority, necessarily cut off from the rest of mankind, making their own difficult way and depending on their own pride in default of any external guidance. It is not to be wondered at that they did not, under these circumstances, achieve the loving-kindness which Christianity teaches: "The Christian doctrine teacheth us all those dispositions that make us affable and courteous, gentle and kind, without any morose leaven of pride or vanity, which entered into the composition of most Heathen schemes."[53] For those who truly valued the ideals of human conduct which the Gospels express, this was a very real objection to non-Christian morality, ancient or modern; without the support of Christian doctrine, morality could only be achieved by a personal pride which itself leads to sin. Churchmen like Richard Baxter had made much of the virtues of charity and humility which the pagan schemes, relying so strongly on individual endeavor, could not inculcate. Indeed "A great deal of pride was taken for a virtue, and men were instructed and exhorted to be proud."

Christian charity is, then, for Swift the highest standard of human behavior, and the best suited to a community of erring, troubled creatures like ourselves. The same standard appears in his letters to Arbuthnot, joined with, yet differentiated from, the standard of classical virtue which it surpasses. In the correspondence that passed between these two there is complete openness and sincerity; one feels that with Arbuthnot there is no need for the tone of bantering jocularity in which Swift so often writes to his other acquaintances. To Arbuthnot he writes openly in terms of the classic and Christian virtue which he has found more fully embodied in his wise and kindly friend than in anyone else. In November 1734 he tells Arbuthnot: "I do not know among mankind any person more prepared to depart from us than yourself, not even the Bishop of Marseilles, if he be still alive; for among all your qualities that have procured you the love and esteem of the world, I ever most valued your moral and Christian virtues, which were not the product of years or sickness, but of reason and religion, as I can witness after above five-and-twenty years' acquaintance."[54] Arbuthnot possesses both the virtue of reason which the best of the ancients exemplified, and, above all, the virtue of religion; he is as well prepared for death as the Bishop of Marseilles, whose selfless courage, during the visitation of the plague in 1720, had made his name a byword. "Marseille's good bishop" is mentioned by Pope in the *Essay on Man,* and we are told that "wherever the poorest lay, there he went confessing, consoling, and exhorting them to patience. To the dying he carried the Sacrament, to the destitute the whole of his money in alms."[55] Swift's ideal of goodness is a man not of detached Stoic virtue but of the charity and compassion necessary in a world of imperfect and interdependent creatures.

So religion is for Swift the only possible way to bring order and certainty into the chaos of human motives without ignoring some part of our nature and heritage. Only revelation, being independent of man, can provide the fixity which Swift in his consciousness of the confusion of human life so strongly desires. So Montaigne had said, after his consideration of the weakness and deceit in which we live, in the *Apologie of Raymond Sebond:*

"But then what is it, that is indeed? That which is eternall, that is to say, that which never had birth, nor ever shall have end; and to which no time can bring change or cause alteration."[56] Reason cannot provide or reach what "is, indeed," because reason in man is at the mercy of self-love, but religion can be reconciled with self-love and so the way can be opened for the turning of man's mixed nature to the services of good. To try to live by reason is to attempt what is contradictory to our nature, but religion can be grounded in our self-concern and yet lead us out of the welter of our own personal preoccupations to share in a good far more complete than that of the moral or rational man. Again by adjustment and compromise among the conflicts of his day Swift contrives to hold, however precariously, to something of the old certainty and the old inclusive conception of the complexity of man. Man is not simply and naturally good; he is complicated, changeable, wrapped up in his own self-love, his reason wavering and his passions strong and ingenious to deceive. Yet on that basis, if we will accept it and not pretend that we can live morally by trusting in ourselves, it is possible to build a degree of goodness. The greatest mistake we can make is to suppose virtue to be natural and easy; it is an effort always, but without the firm support of religious faith it is practically impossible, and so that support must, with whatever difficulty, be maintained.

Always, therefore, Swift is engaged upon that necessary contemporary task which Pope describes, in his account of the "design" of the *Essay on Man* as "steering betwixt the extremes of doctrines seemingly opposite."[57] Pope's way of achieving this in his poem is a complex one, but it is possible to see the antithetical heroic couplet as one result of the effort which faced Augustan poets. Pope in particular uses the couplet to set out a pair of contrasts, extremes whose balance will produce a truth more central than either though that truth itself is not, usually, directly expressed. The lines addressed to Martha Blount, and describing a good woman—Martha herself—are constructed in this way; she has

> Reserve with Frankness, Art with Truth ally'd,
> Courage with Softness, Modesty with Pride.[58]

But the best example, and the one most clearly applicable to the task in which Pope and Swift, despite the efforts of their friend Bolingbroke, were alike engaged, is the passage at the opening of Epistle II of *An Essay on Man,* in which the nature of man is described:

Plac'd on this isthmus of a middle state,
A being darkly wise, and rudely great;
With too much knowledge for the Sceptic side,
With too much weakness for the Stoic's pride,
He hangs between; in doubt to act, or rest,
In doubt to deem himself a God, or Beast:
In doubt his Mind or Body to prefer,
Born but to die, and reas'ning but to err;
Alike in ignorance, his reason such,
Whether he thinks too little, or too much:
Chaos of Thought and Passion, all confus'd;
Still by himself abus'd, or disabus'd;
Created half to rise, and half to fall;
Great lord of all things, yet a prey to all;
Sole judge of Truth, in endless Error hurl'd:
The glory, jest, and riddle of the world![59]

Here is chaos manipulated into order by the skilful handling of the couplet form; in the marshaling of extremes the truth is implied. Swift, with the same aim, evolves in the great satires a more complex version of the same method. Man is himself a paradox in whom all these partial truths exist; he cannot be explained by any one of them alone. Any simplification must be an error, and Pope's description includes many of the opposed errors which faced his generation and Swift's. The view of man's nature here expressed is substantially that of Swift, and it is the basis not only of the two great philosophical satires, *A Tale of a Tub* and *Gulliver's Travels,* but also of his political writing. Swift refuses to simplify; as moral being or as political being man is a complex creature, and only a process of compromise can produce, in any sphere, a state of things which will do justice to his complexity.

That Swift's hold upon this practical solution was precarious is clear enough from his own comments. It involved, as the middle way so often does, an unending effort of adjustment and especially, one may suppose, the continuous suppression of the doubts which so worried him. He thought they might be forgivable if he allowed them no influence on the conduct of his life; he trusted that scruples might be forgiven to the wise man at the Day of Judgment. But these doubts, even if forgivable, he seems always to have believed to be wrong, and even at the cost of a rigid control of his reason he must keep faith in the only answer to man's predicament that seemed to accord with experience and to afford a reconciliation between the sharply separated worlds of chaos and of order. This sense of difficulty, of the forces which were ranged against the ancient stronghold of revealed religion, is behind his comment on his task as a clergyman, in "Thoughts on Religion": "I look upon myself, in the capacity of a clergyman, to be one appointed by providence for defending a post assigned me, and for gaining over as many enemies as I can. Although I think my cause is just, yet one great motion is my submitting to the pleasure of Providence, and to the laws of my country."[60] No doubt the post had to be defended, not only against Catholic and Dissenter, against Shaftesbury and Bolingbroke and Collins, Mandeville, and Hobbes, but also against his own unruly thoughts, always in a ferment and needing constant occupation. Swift's willingness to compromise with self-love may lessen the consistency and systematic quality of his thinking, but it has its own kind of honesty. He holds to what he believes to be important, whatever desperate shifts he has to take to keep his grasp.

Chapter V
THE INDIVIDUAL AND THE STATE

No one, I think, would claim that Swift was at all a profound political thinker, though much may be claimed for his honesty and sincerity of purpose. But his political ideas, particularly those which bear upon the individual and his relation to the state, are interesting because they arise from the same attitude to man's nature as do his ideas on morality. It would not have occurred to him that political convictions could arise from any other source than one's conceptions of what sort of creature man is. Living in an age when political parties were only beginning to divorce themselves from opposed religious and moral positions, and when government was only beginning to need specialized knowledge and techniques, Swift remained in the older world. We know that government always seemed to him a matter not for the expert but for the well-informed and well-disposed man, and that he believed the politicians, by their deliberate secretiveness and knowing airs, made it seem far more difficult and specialized a thing than it really was. Swift's political allegiance turned, really, on the affairs of the church; he saw Whig and Tory in terms of tolerance or orthodoxy, and uppermost in his mind were the threats of Catholicism, Deism, and Dissent. The strength of the Anglican Church was his main concern, and the Church must be strong because man, being what he was, stood in desperate need of it. Among the conflicting ideas and "systems" of the age, in the midst of doubts and dangers, the one thing that stood firm and must continue to stand firm was the Christian truth embodied in the Church of England.

There is, however, a more precise relation between Swift's moral and political ideas than this general one of the weakness of man which makes a strong church essential. Like Mandeville, he is much concerned with the relation between the good man and the state in which he must live, and when he writes on religious subjects he often devotes much thought to goodness as it is seen in a public, a social context. This is a common enough practice in the period, perhaps because the problem which Mandeville stated so

91

bluntly and unpleasantly was very much in people's minds. The modern commercial state was establishing itself, and one of the obvious concerns, for people who cared about moral problems at all, was to try to relate this modern state with its commercial values to traditional standards of behavior. For centuries there had been, at least in theory, no contrast between private virtue and the good of the state. The same moral standards could be applied to both, to man and to the body politic, and whether or not they were actually attained they were there as a firm foundation to private and public life. Now, with more modern methods of trade, with the quick expansion of credit and speculation, "bubbles"·and "projects," with luxury seeming essential to the financial well-being of the country, with the rapid rise of the "moneyed interest," the old values were gravely undermined. To the more old-fashioned, it seemed as though the true good of the country was forgotten, and as though nothing now mattered to the people and their rulers but a frantic pursuit of riches: that virtue was not only not achieved, but not even recognized as an achievement to be desired. Under the Hanoverians, Pope's poetry is full of contrasts between the old standard, virtue, and the new, money:

> 'Tis the first Virtue, Vices to abhor;
> And the first Wisdom, to be Fool no more.
> But to the world no bugbear is so great,
> As want of figure, and a small Estate.
> To either India see the Merchant fly,
> Scar'd at the spectre of pale Poverty! . . .
> Here, Wisdom calls: "Seek Virtue first, be bold!
> As Gold to Silver, Virtue is to Gold."
> There, London's voice: "Get Money, Money still!
> And then let Virtue follow, if she will."
> This, this the saving doctrine, preach'd to all
> From low St. James's up to high St. Paul.[1]

The citizen Balaam, Pope's modern version of Job, is tempted not by affliction but by success, for

> Satan now is wiser than of yore,
> And tempts by making rich, not making poor.

Under the Devil's contrivance,

> Stocks and Subscriptions pour on ev'ry side,
> 'Till all the Daemon makes his full descent,
> In one abundant show'r of Cent per Cent,
> Sinks deep within him, and possesses whole,
> Then dubs Director, and secures his soul.

And this modern kind of temptation is more effective than the old, for unlike Job "sad Sir Balaam curses God and dies." Indeed this third epistle of the *Moral Essays*, "Of the Use of Riches," is a powerful treatment of the evil effects of modern finance and the pursuit of wealth as an end in itself. Gold, though "Trade it may help, Society extend," also "lures the Pyrate, and corrupts the Friend," and hidden corruption is helped by paper-credit:

> Pregnant with thousands flits the Scrap unseen,
> And silent sells a King, or buys a Queen.[2]

Thus helped by modern methods does "secret Gold sap on from knave to knave"; new ways are opened in which age-old vices may more easily operate.

Pope does not only condemn, however; he sees that, corruption and bribery apart, there is a very real problem to be faced. Under modern conditions as interpreted by the eighteenth century, the vice of a particular man may truly contribute to the well-being of many. Riches like Timon's, tastelessly squandered in megalomaniac pride, yet give employment:

> Yet hence the Poor are cloth'd, the Hungry fed;
> Health to himself, and to his Infants bread
> The Lab'rer.bears.[3]

And more, Timon gives direct to the poor, not indeed through charity, but through "charitable vanity." The phrase expresses concisely the way in which a vice can produce the good results of a virtue. But for Pope it is not a matter of simple opposition between private virtue and public good. Private vice may produce public benefit, but so may private virtue, and his example is John Kyrle, the Man of Ross, who on five hundred pounds a year contrived to transform his immediate neighborhood through an active charity.

Swift's solution of this absorbing problem of his day is similar, and arises out of his definition of virtue—or rather out of his refusal to make a clear-cut definition based on reason only, or self-denial only. He is as conscious as Mandeville of the opposition between the purist and the worldly standards of behavior, and probably more troubled by it, for to Mandeville the matter seems to be an interesting intellectual puzzle, stirring him to anger only when people like Shaftesbury blur the fascinating paradox. Swift likes clear thinking too, but moral understanding is more important to him, and indeed thinking, when divorced from moral premises, is to him an irrelevant exercise. There is no moral indignation or distress of the spirit in Mandeville when he contemplates the problem he has formulated so clearly, and one feels that this is true because he does not really take seriously the radical standard of goodness which he sets up against the standards of a modern society, and would not be sorry if it were altogether abandoned. But Swift takes it very seriously indeed. He believes in ultimate perfection, and seen against this, man is utterly evil. "Miserable mortals! Can we contribute to the honour and Glory of God?" And he believes too that man, whatever he might have been capable of in a state of innocence, is not capable now, having forfeited his grand privileges, of approaching that perfection. As Glanvill puts it, "He that looks for perfection, must seek it above the Empyreum; it is reserv'd for Glory."[4] Another standard of behavior, based on the attainable and not on the perfect, is a necessity under such conditions. It is not surprising therefore that Swift so often makes use of a dual standard of judgment in his work. His conception of the doubleness of reason, "reason itself" which is true and just, and the wavering reason of every particular man, has its counterpart in the acceptance of a necessary duality in judging the behavior of man in society. Swift has Mandeville's consciousness of the inconsistency between human theory and human practice, but for him that inconsistency is an inevitable result of man's condition, something that must be made the basis of practical endeavor and not, as for Mandeville, to be contemplated as an absurd and unnecessary contradiction or a mere sop to human hypocrisy. Mandeville, for all his perfunctory denials, would seem to imply that the paradox should be resolved by dropping one-half of it;[5] Swift, that one must accept it, as only one aspect of the greater paradox, man, and make what one can of it.

The obvious example is the *Argument against Abolishing Christianity,* because the subject here treated is so like Mandeville's in *The Fable of the Bees,* and in "A Search into the Nature of Society," where he remarks firmly, "Religion is one thing and Trade is another." In the *Argument* the duality is set out quite clearly by an author impatient of the outmoded restraints of religion and anxious only to rid the country of these without losing those results of Christianity which contribute to its material well-being. The duality is between real or primitive Christianity[6] and "nominal Christianity; the other having been for some Time wholly laid aside by general Consent, as utterly inconsistent with our present Schemes of Wealth and Power."[7] This double standard, and the impatient dismissal by Swift's mouthpiece of primitive Christianity, his scorn even of the "nominal" version, of course makes very good satire; it is a startling way of showing up that difference between profession and practice which is the perpetual concern of the satirist and particularly of Swift. But it is not only a happy choice of satiric method. It is Swift's acknowledgment of the dilemma of the secular state which calls itself Christian, and more than that, of the dilemma of man himself. Primitive Christianity is a real standard by which all our schemes of wealth and power, all our values as political beings in a great modern state, must be condemned of course; yet to try to attain that standard in society as a whole would be worse than useless. It would be, says the author, "a wild Project; it would be to dig up Foundations."[8] The "author" is not Swift, but the whole tendency of the *Argument* is towards this conclusion. Beneath the foundations of the societies we know lie the foundations of human nature; what use can it be to tear away the accumulated building of the past, when it is to these deepest foundations that we must always return? So Jack, in *A Tale of a Tub,* had come to disaster, tearing away not only unnecessary ornament but the very fabric itself of the coat that was his inheritance. "It is possible," says Swift in *Examiner*

No. 29, "that a Man may speculatively prefer the Constitution of another Country, or an Utopia of his own, before that of the Nation where he is born and lives; yet from considering the Dangers of Innovation, the Corruptions of Mankind, and the frequent Impossibility of reducing Idea's to Practice, he may join heartily in preserving the present Order of Things, and be a true Friend to the Government already settled."[9] The remark is typical of him. The standards of Christianity must always be before us as human beings, in all their inexorability, and it is our private responsibility to approach them as nearly as we can, but this is all we can do. The state as such, "the entire Frame and Constitution of Things," is necessarily concerned with other matters.

But the kind of Christianity that can exist in the context of government in a modern state has its uses, nominal though it is. Blasphemy can be punished, restraints can be laid upon human nature, one day at least can be saved, by the action of the state, from trade, business, and pleasure, to allow the individual member of that state to work out his own salvation. The freethinking writer of the *Argument* is being used to put forward, however obliquely, Swift's practical comment on the problem that Mandeville had set out a few years before in "The Grumbling Hive." Swift is always ready to believe that though absolute and disinterested virtue is rare indeed, things in themselves indifferent or even undesirable, considered by absolute standards, may in time help to produce a genuine goodness. The state, imperfect though it must be, may not only discourage and punish irreligion and vice, but give positive encouragement to virtuous conduct and so become an instrument of such partial goodness as may be expected in the world.

The *Project for the Advancement of Religion* is also relevant to the problem of the individual and the state. There is considerable divergence of opinion about the exact purpose of this tract, and whether it is to be regarded as a straightforward plan or as a satire; it has been described as a Tory tract "clothed in the language of morality."[10] No doubt Swift intended to suggest that those public men who respected and supported the Established Church would be best qualified for posts under the scheme, put forward by his "Person of Quality," that the Queen should cause enquiries to be made into the conduct of those in office, and of members of her household, "with respect to their morals and religion, as well as their abilities." That he had the church party in mind seems plain from this passage:

But, it must be confessed, That as Things are now, every Man thinks he hath laid in a sufficient Stock of Merit, and may pretend to any Employment, provided he hath been loud and frequent in declaring himself hearty for the Government. It is true he is a Man of Pleasure, and a Free-Thinker; that is, in other Words, he is profligate in his Morals, and a despiser of Religion; but in Point of Party, he is one to be confided in; he is an Asserter of Liberty and Property; he rattles it out against Popery, and Arbitrary Power, and Priest Craft, and High-Church. It is enough: He is a Person fully qualified for any Employment in the Court, or the Navy, the Law, or the Revenue; where he will be sure to leave no Arts untried of Bribery, Fraud, Injustice, Oppression, that he can practice with any Hope of Impunity.[11]

This freethinker and hater of priestcraft is certainly an embodiment of Whiggish principles as they appeared to a staunch churchman. But as always Swift relates politics to more fundamental questions. The *Project* contains much direct moral comment on the condition of a country in which even nominal Christianity is fast dying out. For instance:

I suppose it will be granted, that hardly One in a Hundred among our People of Quality, or Gentry, appears to act by any Principle of Religion. That great Numbers of them do entirely discard it, and are ready to own their Disbelief of all Revelation in ordinary Discourse. . . . The Consequences of all which, upon the Actions of Men, are equally manifest. They never go about, as in former Times, to hide or palliate their Vices; but expose them freely to View, like any other common Occurrence of Life, without the least Reproach from the World, or themselves.[12]

Even the most nominal Christianity is of use since it prevents wickedness from being taken for granted or even becoming a thing to boast of; it makes men conceal their vices through fear of public condemnation, and so a climate of opinion is produced in which vice is less likely to spread and in which virtue is made easier.

It is altogether consistent with Swift's attitude, as fragmentarily expressed throughout his works, that he should be ready to accept any way to the improvement of public morals. The state, as state, can by its very nature make use only of nominal Christianity, but it should at least do that, by "making it every Man's Interest and Honour to cultivate Religion and Virtue; by rendering Vice a Disgrace, and the certain Ruin to Preferment or Pretensions."[13] The reply given to the expected objection that the project might increase hypocrisy is perfectly realistic; even hypocrisy is preferable to open wickedness, since it lowers the worldly prestige of vicious and irreligious conduct, and so lessens the temptations of the weak—always a prime concern of Swift's; his resentment against freethinkers is due largely to their deliberate dissemination of ideas which may turn unthinking heads. And hypocrisy, acting as if we were good, may sometimes result in real goodness;

But if One in Twenty should be brought over to true Piety by this, or the like Methods, and the other Nineteen be only Hypocrites, the Advantage would still be great. Besides, Hypocrisy is much more eligible than open Infidelity and Vice: It wears the Livery of Religion, it acknowledgeth her Authority, and is cautious of giving Scandal. Nay, a long continued Disguise is too great a Constraint upon human Nature, especially an English Disposition. Men would leave off their Vices out of meer Weariness, rather than undergo the Toil and Hazard, and perhaps Expence of practising them perpetually in private. And, I believe, it is often with Religion as it is with Love; which, by much Dissembling, at last grows real.[14]

From a sober and surely unironic opening this passage turns into wry satiric comment, and of course in the *Project* as in the *Argument,* the very modesty of the author's hope for reform is itself satire upon the state of the country's morals. But the passage is, none the less, based on Swift's real and considered opinions; it can be paralleled in the sermon "On the Testimony of Conscience": "It is very possible for a Man who has the Appearance of Religion, and a great Pretender to Conscience, to be wicked and an Hypocrite; but, it is impossible for a Man who openly declares against Religion, to give any reasonable Security that he will not be false and cruel, and corrupt, whenever a Temptation offers, which he valueth more than he does the Power wherewith he was trusted."[15] From the point of view of the public, a hypocrite whose vices are hidden is preferable to an openly and shamelessly wicked man. The same opinion is expressed in *Examiner* No. 29, where it is suggested that a man who is not truly religious or even regards religion merely as a device for keeping the vulgar in awe, but conceals his opinions, may be in a deplorable condition as to his own future state, "yet Providence, which often works Good out of Evil, can make even such a Man an Instrument for contributing towards the Preservation of the Church."[16]

The acknowledgment, opposed to purists like Shaftesbury and cynics like Mandeville, that even good actions undertaken for bad reasons may result, not merely in benefits to the state, but perhaps in reformation in him who undertakes them; the willingness to be satisfied with one pious man out of twenty; the acceptance of such incomplete good as the state can achieve: all this is typical of Swift's attitude. It is not, for him, simply a matter of keeping up appearances, for there is always the hope that the appearances themselves may in time produce a reality, and by much dissembling religion may at last grow real, when once men have given it a fair trial in their daily lives. There is no more that the state can do; the real task of achieving such virtue as we may is not for states, species, or the "animal called man," but for men, for individuals. "You may force men, by interest or punishment, to say or swear they believe, and to act as if they believed: You can go no further."[17] The government can and should remove difficulties and temptations, can punish and encourage, in terms of the more or less nominal Christianity which alone can be its concern, since real Christianity is a contradiction of the very nature of the modern state.

The state is not, therefore, as for Mandeville, a completely nonmoral entity. Nor is it the result of man's naturally social disposition, an emanation of our true nature, as it is for Shaftesbury, to whom the Hobbist definition of the state of nature as a state of war is "a virulent Maxim."[18] Swift's conception of the state and the individual's relation to it steers, like so many of his conclusions, betwixt extremes seemingly opposite. The state is for him something which has developed over the centuries through a historical process of trial and error, of shifting stresses as mistakes, or perhaps well-meaning actions which give too much opportunity to the wickedness in man, have to be redressed. Swift was after all a practical politician in a sense that Shaftesbury and Mandeville were not. He was in a position to appreciate the confused atmosphere in which political action does, really, take place; how measures taken in good faith and for good motives may produce bad results through the pressure of circumstance or the selfishness of others, how an admirable measure may be put through for the worst of motives or through some haphazard and almost accidental sequence of events into which conscious motive scarcely enters at all. In "A Voyage to Laputa," Gulliver too discovers "the Springs and Motives of great Enterprizes and Revolutions in the World, and of the contemptible Accidents to which they owed their Success. . . . How a Whore can govern the Back-stairs, the Back-stairs a Council, and the Council a Senate."[19] Experience of the political world could only have strengthened Swift's conviction of the chaos in which we live, and his determination not to ignore chaotic circumstance and take refuge in the simplifications either of Mandeville or of Shaftesbury, but to accept and use it. Swift's readiness in political controversy to appeal to the self-interest, or parochialism, or fear, of his readers has frequently been remarked upon, but it is not surprising in view of his opinion of man as a social and political animal. In the absence of absolute standards of right and wrong in the state, a practical man must still make his choice as best he can among the policies available, since, as Swift remarks in *The Sentiments of a Church of England Man,* "it seems every Man's Duty to chuse one of the two Sides, although he cannot entirely approve of either."[20] And having chosen, he must do all that is possible to bring about the success of the policy he believes to approximate most nearly to the right.

To Swift, the theory of politics is a matter of a few basic principles, but to establish these principles in practice one needs much good sense, adaptability, and knowledge of men, as opposed to theories about man. He seems never to have been a passionate party man; here again his faith is in individuals rather than in the professions of either party as a whole. When the Whig leaders failed him in the matter of Queen Anne's Bounty, he gave his loyalties less to the Tory party than to Harley, "the greatest, the wisest, and the most uncorrupt Minister, I ever conversed with," he calls him in "A Letter to the Lord Chancellor Middleton."[21] He respected Harley as a good and honest man, more likely than anyone else to govern well and moderately, and to bring about those conditions, especially in the relations of church and state, which Swift thought most conducive to a decent order in the country. Later, he was ready to approach even Walpole in the hope that something might be done for Ireland. He was certainly no diehard Tory, for what took him and held him to the party was its professed concern for the church and its opposition to the toleration on which the Whigs prided themselves and which Swift attacks in the sermon "On Brotherly Love" and elsewhere. There is no sign in him of the Jacobitism which existed in the Tory ministry itself and in many of the rank and file of the party, and it is generally agreed that he knew nothing of the secret negotiations carried on with France. It is the measure of his honesty that he can expect his readers to believe, as he expected Archbishop King to believe, on his word alone, that he had seen no evidence among the "great men" with whom he had associated in London of a desire to bring in the Pretender;[22] and his word does, indeed, convince us. Swift had little love for the Hanoverians, but he would have had still less for a Papist Stuart.

Certainly Swift was in no way committed to the extreme wing of the party which he had chosen, though no doubt he could not "entirely approve of either." His theory of government is Whiggish enough, and lends color to his frequent claim to be in politics (as opposed to church matters) a Whig of the old persuasion who had made common cause with the Tories because he believes in their leaders and in their church policy. Thus he writes to Steele in 1713, "I think, principles at present are quite out of the case, and that we dispute wholly about persons. In these last, you and I differ; but in the other I think, we agree, for I have in print professed myself in politics, to be what we formerly called a Whig."[23] And again to Lady Betty Germain in 1732-3, "I am of the old Whig principles, without the modern articles and refinements."[24] He dislikes in the modern Whigs such innovations as "septennial Parliaments, directly against the old Whig principles, which always have been mine."[25] He sees the government of England as based on "the Gothic system of limited monarchy,"[26] and his account of it is substantially the same as that of Steele in, for example, No. 28 of the first series of his Whig periodical *The Englishman.* The theories of both writers, the Whig Steele and the Tory Swift, owe much to Sir William Temple, whose views, according to his biographer Abel Boyer, were acceptable to both parties because of their moderation: "He ever was a zealous stickler for the Established Church and Monarchy, and therefore not to be suspected by our modern Tories: He was at the same time a constant Enemy to Popery and a French interest; and therefore not obnoxious to the Whigs."[27]

Swift, who had been introduced to the world of affairs by Temple himself and had a great admiration for him, takes up a consciously similar attitude. He says in *The Sentiments of a Church of England Man,* "I should think that, in order to preserve the Constitution entire in Church and State; whoever hath a true Value for both, would be sure to avoid the Extreams of Whig for the Sake of the former, and the Extreams of Tory on Account of the latter."[28] This, he says, is the best way of choosing a middle between two ill extremes, and an allegorical version of the same idea can be seen in *Gulliver's Travels,* where one of the Laputan projectors has a scheme for sawing off the occiput of each violent party man "in such a Manner that the Brain may be equally divided" and transferring it to the head of an equally violent member of the opposing party, thus producing "Moderation as well as Regularity of Thinking."[29] Swift's advice to his congregation in the sermon preached, according to custom, on the "day of humiliation" designated to commemorate the death of Charles I, runs on similar lines. The sermon, like most of those preached on this day of commemoration, January 30, is of a political turn, and in it Swift gives his version of the events which led up to, and followed upon, the death of the king, and a statement of his political faith as a moderate Tory churchman. He closes by advising his listeners to take a middle course between the extreme opinions which existed concerning the obedience due to a ruler:

102

. . . One great design of my discourse was to give you warning against running into either extreme of two bad opinions, with relation to obedience. As kings are called Gods upon earth, so some would allow them an equal power with God, over all laws and ordinances; and that the liberty, and property, and life, and religion of the subject, depended wholly upon the breath of the prince; which however, I hope, was never meant by those who pleaded for passive obedience. . . .

On the other side, some look upon kings as answerable for every mistake or omission in government, and bound to comply with the most unreasonable demands of an unquiet faction, which was the case of those who persecuted the blessed martyr of this day from his throne to the scaffold.

Between these two extremes, it is easy, from what hath been said, to chuse a middle; to be good and loyal subjects, yet, according to your power, faithful assertors of your religion and liberties.[30]

Like so many Englishmen of his time who abhorred the rebellion of 1641 but accepted the settlement of 1688, Swift found himself somewhere between two extreme and consistent points of view. Faced with the necessity, in a "Martyrdom" sermon, of setting out a coherent theory which will tactfully express his own disapproval of current tendencies, he accepts the moderate position best expressed by that spokesman of the necessary Augustan compromise, John Locke. But he is not deeply concerned to achieve a theoretic consistency; politics is to him an empirical matter, part of the giddy circumstance of man's world in which the same action may be at one time right and at another wrong; at one time a worth-while risk and at another an incalculable danger. The process of avoiding extremes, which he recommends to his congregation, is the process he follows himself, not so much because that is the only way open to him in which a fairly consistent theory can be maintained, but because it is the only way in which sensible government can be carried on. Harley's efforts to achieve a moderate and broad-based administration which could blunt the sharper distinctions between Whig and Tory must have met with strong approval from Swift. In avoiding extremes, his method is to take from each side what seems best and, especially, most practicable. His letter to Pope in January 1721-2, giving an account of his political opinions "in the time of her late glorious majesty" is very much a practical document in which his attitude to the succession depends not only on legal right but on the opinion of the people:

> Neither did I ever regard the right line, except upon two accounts; first, as it was established by law, and secondly, as it has much weight in the opinions of the people. For, necessity may abolish any law, but cannot alter the sentiments of the vulgar, right of inheritance being perhaps the most popular of all topics; and therefore in great changes, when that is broke, there will remain much heart-burning and discontent among the meaner people, which, under a weak prince and corrupt administration, may have the worst consequences upon the peace of any state.[31]

This is one of the many instances in which abstract theory has to be modified by, and checked against, the actual feelings of the people, whose untrained and perhaps unreasonable attitude can break the most admirable schemes and settlements. Nor will Swift be drawn into the current arguments about the right of subjects to rebel under certain circumstances. Right or no right, the fact is that when the people are provoked beyond endurance rebel they will, and to expect otherwise is absurd. "When oppressions grow too great and universal to be borne, nature or necessity may find a remedy."[32] Another practical empiric, Swift's fellow Tory Samuel Johnson, was to express a similar opinion when he uttered that "generous sentiment" which so stirred Boswell: "And then, Sir, there is this consideration, that if the abuse be enormous, Nature will rise up, and claiming her original rights, overturn a corrupt political system."[33]

This being so, rulers, Swift points out, must be careful not to emulate Nero, Caligula, or King John, and so provoke their subjects by continual oppressions. Similarly the people should consider, before they exert their power in such a case, whether their practical advantage will really be served by it, and should take care not to leave themselves worse off, through a revolutionary change, than they were before:

> As to what is called a revolutionary principle, my opinion was this; that whenever those evils which usually attend and follow a violent change of government, were not in probability so pernicious as the grievance we suffer under a present power, then the public good will justify such a revolution. And this I took to have been the case in the Prince of Orange's

expedition, although in the consequences it produced some very bad effects, which are likely to stick long enough by us.[34]

The same opinion of "the Prince of Orange's expedition" is expressed in the sermon "Upon the Martyrdom"; it is judged upon its merits as a risk that had to be taken, and by it the country was delivered from great misery, but it brought misfortunes of its own: "But, as a house thrown down by a storm is seldom rebuilt, without some change in the foundation, so it hath happened, that, since the late Revolution, men have sate much looser in the true fundamentals both of religion and government, and factions have been more violent, treacherous, and malicious than ever, men running naturally from one extreme to another."[35] As one might expect, Swift's attitude towards such a profound upheaval is one of, at most, reluctant acceptance of an accomplished fact. Such drastic action must bring about a change in the very foundations of the country's life, the "true fundamentals" are shaken, and the people oscillate between extremes. For Swift this was an inevitable result of the adoption in any sphere of radical action even in the direction of reform. Balance is achieved by a slow and gradual process, and once lost it is hard to find again.

With theory so constantly related to what is likely actually to happen in a world which consists not of legal right, divine right, or contract, but of the reactions of a number of fallible and indeed muddle-headed people, Swift is far from being a doctrinaire in politics. In the early *Sentiments of a Church of England Man*, which offers criticism to Whigs and Tories alike, he again considers forms of government as a matter of expediency and convenience rather than of legal right or theoretical excellence. "But although a Church-of-England Man thinks every Species of Government equally lawful; he doth not think them equally expedient; or for every Country indifferently. . . . There may be a great deal in the Situation of a Country, and in the present Genius of the People." Successful government is a slow development, "the adjusting Power and Freedom being an Effect and Consequence of maturer Thinking,"[36] but for this country and for this time, a limited monarchy has shown itself, through a process of trial and error, to be the system which best achieves this delicate adjustment through its balance of power between king, people, and nobles, which enables it better to avoid the "several depravations" of the three classical forms of government.[37] It has been attained through centuries of struggle between these three centers of power, and as often nearly lost because of greed or weakness or the mere pressure of events. For example, in "Upon the Martyrdom of King Charles I," Swift traces briefly those events which, he believes, led up to the Great Rebellion. The prodigal distribution of crown lands among favorites, and the greed of Henry VIII, which resulted in the distribution of church lands also, upset the balance of power by weighing it too much on the side of the people as against the crown, whose power was further weakened later as an indirect result of the persecutions under Queen Mary, for when the exiled Protestants returned from Geneva in Elizabeth's reign, they had learned "to quarrel with the kingly government." Finally the ill advice of ministers and the "weakness and infatuation" of Charles himself precipitated the Rebellion. The exile of the royal family to France, where James at least had been "seduced to Popery," was the cause of his misgovernment when he became king and so of his deserved rejection by his people. The second revolution, unlike the previous "execrable rebellion," had been justified; yet it is seen as the result of an earlier loss of balance through the appropriation, by one section of the community, of more than their due share of power. And though William of Orange had fortunately been available to restore order, the earlier fine balance[38] could not be regained, for "a house thrown down by a storm is seldom rebuilt, without some change in the foundation."[39]

None of this, of course, is original political thinking. Swift's conclusions can be paralleled again and again in the political theory of the time, but what is significant is the kind of ideas he chose to accept among the welter of extremes and of attempts at a "middle way" which were available, and the reasons why he accepted them. He is accustomed to distrust generalizations and to try to make his way among warring factions; he is sceptical about the absolute worth or the divine sanction of any particular form of government, since for him so much depends upon the

106

vagaries of a muddled world and on the varying and incalculable passions of men. Being thus sceptical, he has resort to empirical solutions: the best government, one might say, is the government that works best at a particular time and place, and when a country has achieved a government which suits it and which works comparatively well, it should be chary of upsetting it and so of having all its work to do again. But any government has, at best, only a limited sphere of achievement and influence; in the end, the power and worth of a state depend less upon its form of government than upon the people who constitute it. "Few States," Swift tells us in *The Sentiments of a Church of England Man,*

are ruined by any Defect in their Institution, but generally by the Corruption of Manners; against which, the best Institution is no long Security, and without which, a very ill one may subsist and flourish: Whereof there are two pregnant Instances now in Europe. The first is the Aristocracy of Venice; which, founded upon the wisest Maxims, and digested by a great Length of Time, hath, in our Age, admitted so many Abuses, through the Degeneracy of the Nobles, that the Period of its Duration seems to approach. The other is the United Republicks of the States General; where a Vein of Temperance, Industry, Parsimony, and a publick Spirit, running through the whole Body of the People, hath preserved an infant Commonwealth of an untimely Birth and sickly Constitution, for above an Hundred Years, through so many Dangers and Difficulties, as a much more healthy one could never have struggled against, without those Advantages.[40]

The importance of the individual member of the state is very much stressed in those few of Swift's sermons which remain. He is reputed to have said that he preached "pamphlets" and the sermons have frequently a certain political content. The sermon "On the Martyrdom" is a special case, but that "On the Causes of the Wretched Condition of Ireland," and that on "Doing Good," with its references to Wood's Halfpence, are just as obvious examples. But political questions are always linked convincingly, and as far as can be seen sincerely, with problems of conduct. Indeed the sermons read not at all like political propaganda but like examinations of right and wrong behavior seen in relation to the public good and consequently illustrated by events and actions which have a bearing on the political situation. There is no doubt of Swift's conscientiousness as a guide and teacher of his parishioners, and he is here honestly concerned to expound what he believes to be the duty of a good Christian in his dealings with the state. The sermons, whether or not politics enter into them, do read like the "plain honest stuff" that he told Stella he proposed to preach before Queen Anne. The sense of the importance to the state of its individual members, which is present in the political writings, is felt here also, and the subject is naturally treated at more length, since Swift is here speaking as a clergyman properly concerned with the moral welfare of each soul committed to his charge. "Doing Good," the sermon delivered on the occasion of Wood's Project in 1724, no doubt intends Wood himself by its references to "the meanest instrument"[41] who can do mischief to the public upon principles of avarice or malice, but the whole sermon presents a consistent picture of the commonwealth as composed of single men who all, rich or poor, have the power to help or harm it. Swift's purpose is not merely to declaim against the fact that one mean instrument has the power to ruin Ireland; he recognizes the power of every man for good or evil, for he knows that even a state founded upon the wisest maxims, and so theoretically as good as it can be made, may yet be utterly corrupted by a few bad men. But conversely, one virtuous man may save a state: "Solomon tells us of a poor wise man who saved a city by his counsel. It hath often happened that a private soldier, by some unexpected brave attempt, hath been instrumental in obtaining a great victory. How many obscure men have been authors of very useful inventions, whereof the world now reaps the benefit?"

But even the obscure man who has no such particular opportunities for the felicitous exercise of his bravery or his intelligence has his part to play in the country's welfare, for a man who is honest in his dealings with his fellows has an influence which may spread through the whole of society.

The very example of honesty and industry in a poor tradesman, will sometimes spread through a neighbourhood, when others see how successful he is; and thus so many useful members are gained, for which the whole body of the public is the better. Whoever is blessed with a true public spirit, God will certainly put it into his way to make use of that blessing, for the ends it was given him, by some means or other: And therefore it hath been observed in most ages, that the greatest actions, for the benefit of the commonwealth, have been performed by the wisdom or courage, the contrivance or industry, of particular men, and not of numbers.[42]

When the state has done what little it can to minimize evil in society, it is on the efforts of the individual members of that society that its physical and moral welfare must depend. It is John, Peter, and Thomas who are the powerful reality, not an abstraction like man, society, the people: and though the state as a whole may have little to do with morality, the morality of individuals may have a great deal to do with the state.

Swift's answer to those who with Mandeville question the relation of virtue to our modern schemes of wealth and power is in effect to agree that the modern state is not a moral entity, but to assert none the less that individual men can live morally within it, and even contribute to its well-being by their honesty and goodness. He will not, like Shaftesbury, require of men in relation to society that they should be guided entirely by benevolence and not by self-love, nor will he suppose with Mandeville that because the member of a modern trading community cannot live by rigorous definitions of virtue he is not concerned with right and wrong at all. There are degrees of attainable good within the community, and the industrious and fair-dealing tradesman is an honest man even if, as is probable, he considers his own and his family's prosperity rather than the good of his fellow-men. Even his neighbors, who emulate him because they "see how successful he is" yet behave more honestly as a result, and whatever their original motives they and the community are the better for it. After all, "The motives of the best actions will not bear too strict an inquiry." Indeed Swift begins this sermon, "Doing Good," with the firm statement: "Nature directs every one of us, and God permits us, to consult our own private Good before the private Good of any other person whatsoever." In fact "the law of nature, which is the law of God" disposes us not to social benevolence but to love of self. But on this basis Swift builds up an argument for public virtue. For though self-love is the first and natural urge of man, and so is in its way the law of God, we have also a more specific law, a direct command of God, which has to be reconciled with the first.

109

We are commanded to love our neighbors as ourselves, and therefore "if, by a small hurt and loss to myself, I can procure a great good to my neighbour, in that case his interest is to be preferred. For example, if I can be sure of saving his life, without great danger to my own; if I can preserve him from being undone, without ruining myself, or recover his reputation without blasting mine; all this I am obliged to do: And, if I sincerely perform it, I do then obey the command of God, in loving my neighbour as myself." And if we are obliged to follow God's command in loving our neighbor considered as a private person, we are equally obliged to apply it to "our neighbour in his public capacity, as he is a member of that great body, the commonwealth."[43] In exerting ourselves for the public good, we are carrying out both the natural law of self-love and the more particular command of God, since we ourselves as well as our neighbors are contained in that great body. Thus by a compromise that the extremists would have scorned, Swift is able to reconcile virtuous public conduct with man's natural self-love. Care for our neighbors is not the result of natural benevolence but something we are obliged to by the law of God, and if we are ready to believe that the motives of the best of men are necessarily mixed by the law of his nature, we can persuade him to do good to his neighbor and his country by showing him where his religious duty and his own interest lies. At least by this acceptance it is possible to bring about some practical result; Swift would no doubt have felt that both Shaftesbury's attitude and Mandeville's were likely to lead to discouragement in refusing, in their different ways and for their different reasons, to recognize degrees of good.

The particular person in the commonwealth has, then, a positive duty towards it, and that duty is governed, primarily, by divine command. Our present schemes of wealth and power still leave opportunities for the performance of our Christian duty. A wise man should assist with his counsels, "a great Man with his Protection, a rich Man with his Bounty and Charity, and a poor Man with his Labour." The unmoral working of the state, which is concerned primarily with matters of trade and foreign policy, does not mean that individuals should omit their duty of hard work and above all of helpfulness and charity. "Nay, even the poor Beggar hath a just Demand of an Alms from the Rich Man, who is guilty of Fraud, Injustice, and Oppression, if he doth not afford Relief according to his Abilities."[44] Again, in "The Causes of the Wretched Condition of Ireland," the number of beggars is imputed to oppressive government and cruel landlords, but none the less the duty of relieving their distress falls upon the individual. Nor should we consider too closely whether in a particular case a man's poverty is caused entirely by the wretched condition of the country or whether his own faults have been partly responsible. After all, the duty which God has laid upon us is to help our fellow-men, not trying, as imperfect men ourselves, to form too exact a judgment of their deserts: "However, since the best of us have too many Infirmities to answer for, we ought not to be severe upon those of others; and therefore, if our Brother, thro' Grief, or Sickness, or other Incapacity, is not in a Condition to preserve his Being, we ought to support him to the best of our Power, without reflecting over seriously on the Causes that brought him to his Misery."[45]

Thus, in his consideration of man in society Swift holds firmly to his conviction of the importance of the particular man, and is ready to abandon theoretical consistency if by so doing he can present a truer picture of the needs and duties of men. If the state can never function morally, at least it should not become so immersed in schemes of wealth and power as to forget those individual members who compose it. This is what Swift is saying, in a very different tone and with the indirection habitual to him as a satirist, in *A Modest Proposal for Preventing the Children of Ireland from Being a Burden to Their Parents or Country*, where private vices become public benefits in so singular a manner. Swift appears to have accepted the assumption of the mercantilist theory of the day that the natural strength of a nation consists in the number and increase of the inhabitants, and the *Modest Proposal* turns upon this conception.[46] His acceptance of the theory can be seen in his reference, in "A Short View of the State of Ireland," to "encreasing the Number of their People; without which, any Country, however blessed by Nature, must continue poor,"[47] and

111

again in "An Answer to Several Letters Sent Me from Unknown Hands": "If labour and people make the true riches of a nation, what must be the issue where one part of the people are forced away, and the other part have nothing to do?"[48] But in his hands the idea that each person is "an economic unit whose annual value to the nation could be exactly computed"[49] is changed indeed. To him the "people" are not only the riches of a country; they are moral entities towards whom their rulers have the responsibility of ensuring that they can live decently. In *A Modest Proposal* it is the purely economic attitude of their superiors towards the "labour and people" that is attacked. The English government and the Irish landlords regard the people merely as cattle to be exploited, and indeed one of the reasons for the misery of the people of Ireland, and for their wholesale emigration, is the rapacity of the landlords in turning over so much arable land to pasture, "the unhappy practice of stocking such vast quantities of land with sheep and other cattle, which reduceth twenty families to one."[50] Bishop Synge of Ferns and Leighlin similarly blamed, for the emigrations, the rackrenting practices of the landlords and the behavior of the gentry who "chuse to stock their lands with Beasts rather than Men."[51]

A purely monetary evaluation of the inhabitants of a country can only lead to regarding them as the equivalents of cattle, and the desperate project put forward in *A Modest Proposal* starts from the assumption that the wealth of Ireland is now not in men but in beasts, and that the best course for the men is to compete with the conquering beasts in their own field. Breeding children for the table, it is pointed out, can be profitable no less than breeding cattle; the flesh compares favorably, and "will be in Season throughout the Year," and the skin, like that of beasts, can be made use of, for, artificially dressed, it "will make admirable Gloves for Ladies, and Summer Boots for fine Gentlemen." Under existing conditions, this is the only use that can be made of the people of Ireland, the riches of the nation, "for we can neither employ them in Handicraft or Agriculture; we neither build Houses, (I mean in the Country) nor cultivate Land."[52] A less striking form of the same remedy is to be found in "Maxims

Controlled in Ireland," where Swift angrily suggests that if Ireland had "the African custom or privilege, of selling our useless bodies for slaves to foreigners, it would be the most useful branch of our trade, by ridding us of a most unsupportable burthen, and bringing us money in the stead. But, in our present situation, at least five children in six who are born lie a dead weight upon us for the want of employment."[53] In his Irish tracts he is frequently roused to anger by the complacent claim that Ireland is a rich country, when the most superficial observation proves that the boasted wealth lies only in money held by a very few, and that the people, the true "riches," are dying of starvation.

But the real answer to the desolation of Ireland is in the visionary schemes that the businesslike projector of the Modest Proposal regards as hopeless, and it is in effect a moral answer.

Therefore let no man talk to me of other Expedients: Of taxing our Absentees at five shillings a Pound: Of using neither Cloaths, nor Household Furniture except what is of our own Growth and Manufacture: Of utterly rejecting the Materials and Instruments that promote Foreign Luxury: Of curing the Expensiveness of Pride, Vanity, Idleness, and Gaming in our Women: Of Introducing a Vein of Parsimony, Prudence and Temperance: Of learning to love our Country, wherein we differ even from Laplanders, and the Inhabitants of Topinamboo: Of quitting our Animosities, and Factions; nor act any longer like the Jews, who were murdering one another at the very Moment their City was taken: Of being a little cautious not to sell our Country and Consciences for nothing: Of teaching Landlords to have, at least, one Degree of Mercy towards their Tenants.

Governments should not make it difficult for the individual to function morally, should not produce a situation in which the selling of children for slaughter can be ironically recommended because it would "encrease the Care and Tenderness of Mothers towards their Children" and because "Men would become as fond of their Wives, during the time of their Pregnancy, as they are now of their Mares in Foal, their Cows in Calf, or Sows when they are ready to farrow; nor offer to beat or kick them, (as is too frequent a Practice) for fear of a Miscarriage."[54] And the "particular person" in his turn should not forget that he is to be guided, in his public capacity, not only by economic laws but by the laws of God which must govern his relations to the other members of

113

society. Moral and humane behavior may, for Swift, contribute to the true well-being of a state.

It is noticeable that in the Utopian sixth chapter of "A Voyage to Lilliput," in which are described the original institutions of that country "and not the most scandalous Corruptions into which these People are fallen by the degenerate Nature of Man," the laws which are described are chiefly those which aim to encourage honest dealings among the individual members of the state, by the only methods available to a state as such, those of reward and punishment. False informers are severely punished: "All Crimes against the State, are punished here with the utmost Severity; but if the Person accused make his Innocence plainly to appear upon his Tryal, the Accuser is immediately put to an ignominious Death; and out of his Goods or Lands, the innocent Person is quadruply recompensed for the Loss of his Time, for the Danger he underwent, for the Hardship of his Imprisonment, and for all the Charges he hath been at in making his Defence."[55] To Swift, it would seem, the riches of a nation consist not only in people, but in honest people. Honesty is part of the true well-being of a country, and the Lilliputians "look upon Fraud as a greater Crime than Theft, and therefore seldom fail to punish it with Death: for they alledge, that Care and Vigilance, with a very common Understanding, may preserve a Man's Goods from Thieves; but Honesty hath no Fence against Superior Cunning: And since it is necessary that there should be a perpetual Intercourse of buying and selling, and dealing upon Credit; where Fraud is permitted or connived at, or hath no Law to punish it, the honest Dealer is always undone, and the Knave gets the Advantage." "The Lilliputian laws properly apply the tools of government, for as well as punishing the guilty they reward all who can prove they have observed the law for a certain period of time, and Gulliver's comment is, "Although we usually call Reward and Punishment, the two Hinges upon which all Government turns; yet I could never observe this Maxim to be put in Practice by any Nation, except that of Lilliput." Moreover they are able, in a Utopian state, to carry out a more thoroughgoing version of the *Project for the Advancement of Religion,* for "in chusing

Persons for all Employments, they have more Regard to good Morals than to great Abilities."[56]

Thus even in Lilliput, a miniature version of the modern highly developed, commercial state, with its "perpetual Intercourse of buying and selling, and dealing upon Credit," there are certain ways in which the state can encourage good behavior in its citizens. In the less sophisticated country of Brobdingnag, we hear little of government except indirectly, through the king's comments on what Gulliver tells him of Europe, and indeed government in the land of the giants seems to Gulliver of a very simple and primitive kind. That there should be such a conception as that of the "Art of Government" is, to the king, ridiculous; he has no secrets of state and despises "all Mystery, Refinement, and Intrigue, either in a Prince or a Minister." His notions of government are simple, moral, and humane, being confined "to common Sense and Reason, to Justice and Lenity, to the Speedy Determination of Civil and criminal Causes; with some other obvious Topicks which are not worth considering." He sees his task as one of practical usefulness, and believes "that whoever could make two Ears of Corn, or two Blades of Grass to grow upon a Spot of Ground where only one grew before; would deserve better of Mankind, and do more essential Service to his Country, than the whole Race of Politicians put together." His guide is not, primarily, politics but morality; he is simply a good man, and he does not believe, as Gulliver does, that in relation to his country, and to establish his public power, a man may follow different principles from those that prevail in his private life. He would rather lose half his kingdom, he tells Gulliver, than learn the secret of gunpowder, thus letting slip an opportunity "that would have made him absolute Master of the Lives, the Liberties, and the Fortunes of his People." His rule appears to be eminently successful. He is almost adored by his people, and a high standard of conduct exists in his country, for Gulliver tells us that "as to the Decision of Civil Causes, or Proceedings against Criminals, their Precedents are so few, that they have little Reason to boast of any extraordinary Skill in either."[57]

Brobdingnag is, indeed, exceptionally well governed. It is perhaps fortunate in its simple agricultural economy, in its lack of foreign enemies, and above all in its king, who has no wish to make himself absolute master of his people, and who is both good enough to wish for the well-being of his subjects and wise enough to know in what their true well-being lies. The people, for their part, respond as they should to his wise and kindly rule; the country's case depends largely on the disposition of the king and of his subjects. But Brobdingnag is by no means perfect. It has had its difficulties in the past, and those difficulties are the same that England has had to settle. Not all the giant kings had been as wise as the one Gulliver knew, and some had tried to seize absolute power, for the giants were "troubled with the same Disease, to which the whole Race of Mankind is Subject; the Nobility often contending for Power, the People for Liberty, and the King for absolute Dominion."[58] Brobdingnag is an ordinary country with the usual troubles, but it has found a better way of solving them than have the countries of Europe, and it is particularly admirable in its refusal to separate public and private morality. It is the best-governed state in the whole of the *Travels,* for Laputa and Balnibarbi are in a condition of uneasy and resentful truce, avoiding tyranny or rebellion only because any such action would be mutually destructive, while their practical government is chaotic, contrasting sharply with that of Brobdingnag. As for Houyhnhnm-land, the Houyhnhnms, being wholly governed by reason, need no other government than this, and their only public body is the Assembly, "a Representative Council of the whole Nation," which meets every fourth year at the vernal equinox to settle the regulation of families and to "inquire into the State and Condition of the several Districts; whether they abound or be deficient in Hay or Oats, or Cows or Yahoos?" In the rare event of any district showing a lack of these commodities, the remedy is simple, prompt, and unopposed: the want "is immediately supplied by unanimous Consent and Contribution."[59] The Houyhnhnms supposed that "our Institutions of Government and Law were plainly owing to our gross Defects in Reason, and by consequence, in Virtue; because Reason alone is sufficient to govern a

116

Rational Creature."[60] Such is the nature of the Houyhnhnms that their country governs itself, and is as efficient as it is primitive. And while the Houyhnhnms are beyond government in our sense, the Yahoos, as unreasoning beasts of burden, are beneath it. There is little, in this strange land of extremes, that can be of practical use to a muddled, struggling state of human beings, and it is to the Brobdingnagians, "least corrupted" of men, that we must look for guidance in matters of government, as Gulliver gives us to understand: "I shall say nothing of those remote Nations where Yahoos preside; amongst which the least corrupted are the Brobdingnagians, whose wise Maxims in Morality and Government, it would be our Happiness to observe."[61]

Thus in *Gulliver's Travels* as elsewhere, government is closely linked with morality in individual men, for the well-being of a country depends ultimately not on the form of its government but on the moral condition of each one of its people. Tracts like *A Modest Proposal* or *The Drapier's Letters* are concerned as much with moral principles as with political expedients, while on the other hand the sermons, dealing as they do with the duty of actual men under the pressure of a state governed by non-moral motives and the further pressure of a multitude of conflicting theories of behavior, form a comprehensive guide to the proper conduct of the "particular man" in his relation to the community. Like all his opinions, Swift's political views are rooted in his conception of the nature and needs of man, and in his anxiety that the state should, at least, not complicate further the problems of deceived and deluded humanity. In the chaos which man has made for himself the only secure guidance is to be found in "moral and Christian virtues," and the little Swift asks of the state is that it should not deprive us, the animals capable of reason, of our only help. Theoretical consistency in politics has no importance for him; his only concern is to find a balance of forces which will control our evil tendencies and perhaps persuade us, in our own interest, to good. As a moralist, Swift is always consistent, and his political writings like his poetry are not "without a moral view."

Chapter VI
GIDDY CIRCUMSTANCE

It has been the purpose of the preceding chapters to suggest that Swift, both by nature and by reason of the confused and transitional age in which he lived, was disposed to see the conditions of human life as chaotic and difficult. Desiring the order and unity and simplicity of traditional aspiration, he saw little hope of attaining it in man's world of deceit, and the ways of achieving order that were being tried in his lifetime could only succeed by leaving out half the truth about man and his world. Faced by extreme philosophies, extreme moral and political systems, each with its own neat little parody of completeness, Swift assumes a position between them, follows the middle way which will allow him to take advantage of the partial truths on either side and to drop what seems to him valueless. This necessity affects the form and the content of his satires alike. Swift is one of the most difficult writers of the very allusive and complicated satire of the seventeenth and eighteenth centuries because he is trying to perform a particularly difficult task. For the problems which he saw, there could be only a tentative and partial solution: he is concerned to hold the precarious balance of a traditional view of man, his nature, his relation to his fellows, his God, and the world about him, in conditions increasingly hostile to it. To know that truth exists, but to acknowledge the difficulty of attaining it, to weigh the claims of mind and body, of eternal truth and inescapable "circumstance," was to be assailed from all sides. Extreme rationalism and enthusiasm, the determined optimism of Shaftesbury and the cynicism of Mandeville, all these divergent attitudes were in some way upsetting the balance, oversimplifying the complex and difficult reality and so moving further into the dangers of deception, making still harder the lot of man struggling to know himself and such truth as he may grasp. Swift's satire, consequently, is of a very complicated kind, for the extremes which he attacks are aberrations from a norm which is itself a compromise difficult to express in positive terms and existing in avoidance of error, that error of stressing one aspect of the human situation to the detriment of the rest which is perhaps best summed up in Swift's own neat comment upon the Stoics: "The Stoical Scheme of supplying our Wants, by lopping off our Desires; is like cutting off our Feet when we want Shoes."[1]

In most of the problems which he presents to us in his satiric and other writing Swift's solution is, then, necessarily one of compromise. At worst, in the realm of practical politics for instance, this is an uneasy balance of forces; at best, as in *Gulliver's Travels,* a true reconciliation by which essential yet apparently opposed truths can be brought together. Such a reconciliation can only be expressed by a complexity of method which is Swift's equivalent of the seventeenth century literature of paradox and the eighteenth century literature of antithesis. In government there must be a balance of power between king and aristocracy and people, while for the individual the best way is to avoid the harmful extremes of either party, Whig or Tory. As for the morality of the state, again Swift sees the solution in a middle way: the state, concerned with its schemes of wealth and power, cannot be a truly moral entity, but it can help and encourage virtue, even if its motives in doing so are not of the highest, and the "particular person" in his relation to the state can help both it and himself by honesty. But behind all these lesser compromises lies the fundamental compromise of man himself; man the creature of self-love whose passions lead him astray but who yet, if he recognizes and uses these passions, may become more actively and usefully and fully virtuous than the passionless Stoic can ever be; man who is no longer innocent but can become good if he recognizes himself for what he is. At the heart of all Swift's writing is the animal, man; all his problems and solutions are related to his strong sense of the complexity of our nature, "the best and worst that may be had," and of the necessity of somehow reconciling passion and reason, body and mind, to reach the kind of goodness attainable by, and proper to, so mixed and limited a creature. Perhaps in no writer do we feel more strongly the insistent presence of humanity. As moralist, preacher, political theorist, Swift is never abstract. Always the "particular person"—the honest trader, the humble listener in the congregation, the apparent author or the apparent audience—gives vividness and actuality to his words; always we feel ourselves in touch with a human being, always with Swift himself in his humor and affection, his angry compassion, his desire to be of practical use, and intermittently with his narrators, stupid, complacent, well-meaning, or urbane. In each case, we have to deal not with ideas only, but with ideas as they are formulated by a person with all his oddities, vanities, "prejudices," indignations; not with mind only, but with that mixture of mental activity with bodily impulses which makes up the animal capable of reason. Swift's impatience of "Ideas, Entities, Abstractions and Transcendentals" is everywhere obvious; he is not interested in theories or systems except as they affect or are affected by John, Peter, and Thomas. No system can long survive unchanged when it has to take its chance with unpredictable mankind, and most ineffective of all are the systems which try to schematize man himself. Only revealed religion can account for man, and the Christian view is one which allows full value to his complexity.

This preoccupation with man is to be felt in all Swift's work, satiric or not, but in the satires it is overwhelmingly strong. Satire, of course, must be concerned with human beings, but Swift's major satires are concerned with humanity at a deeper level than that of individual oddities or wickedness. He investigates, rather, the nature of man from which behavior arises, and criticizes those philosophies and systems which are based on a misunderstanding of that nature. People of all kinds throng his pages, contributing to his investigation; giants and pygmies, ancients and moderns, Gulliver and Bentley and the author of *A Tale of a Tub,* and whether or not they are presented as consistent characters each one of them is, at each given moment, a most convincing representative of confused humanity. For it is the complexity of man's nature which is Swift's chief point; complexity, inconsistency, fallibility, the variousness of his self-deceit, and the humility and effort which are necessary if he is to grow into the kind of goodness possible to him. By indirection, by ridicule of false extremes and simplifications, the positive is implied, and the positive is the traditional Renaissance view of man as a limited creature in whom mind and body are at odds and must be, as far as possible, reconciled. Swift said of his poetry, light though much of it seems, that he wrote no line "without a moral view,"[2] and this is even more true of the great prose satires. Even *The Battle of the Books,* starting from the literary argument in which Sir William Temple had so unfortunately involved himself, has behind it a firm conception of the nature of man, and from the *Battle* and the *Tale* to *Gulliver's Travels* this conception is essentially unchanged, though experience strengthened and deepened it. *A Tale of a Tub,* the "young man's book," is a brilliant presentation of the predicament of man on his isthmus of a middle state, and of the absurdity of his attempts to better himself, though its very brilliance does in a way obscure the central conception on which the book is based, because we are conscious chiefly of a dazzling intellectual activity on the part of Swift himself as he shifts and maneuvers to display all the varying absurdities he wishes to satirize. It is mind in all its pride and energy that we feel in *A Tale of a Tub;* yet what the book is primarily about is the weakness of mind, so easily governed by bodily desires or diseases, by vanity or self-interest, or by the deceit of the senses. The point is made most clearly in the case of the Aeolists, or the great conquerors, whose mental activity is caused by, and warped by, the merest physical accident. But both for Swift and for his readers, through most of the *Tale,* this truth is as yet a matter of intellectual acceptance and intellectual enjoyment, rather than of experience. What is constantly in Swift's mind is the glorious absurdity of man's pompous claims and of his blindness to his predicament; he is less concerned, in this youthful work, with the predicament itself, though that underlies all the ridiculousness of the Aeolists and of the "modern" author. But in *Gulliver's Travels* the human situation has been deeply felt and painfully experienced, and the technique as well as the attitude has matured. Here body as well as mind is constantly, even oppressively, present; no longer can the intellect range freely in wild parodies of speculation, but is caught in the minuscule bodies of Lilliput or in the clumsy bodies of Brobdingnag, and in each case obviously and inescapably influenced by the body in which it dwells. In *A Tale of a Tub,* the paradox of man is posed and contemplated, a source of laughter and delight: in *Gulliver's Travels*

121

the two sides of man's nature are kept gravely before us, forcing us to experience for ourselves, as never in the *Tale,* the inexorability of the human situation. And when we are sufficiently convinced, sufficiently resigned, a solution—the only solution possible for Swift—is unobtrusively suggested. Sublunary chaos, giddy circumstance, is no longer simply displayed, however delightfully; through Gulliver and the varied creatures he meets on his travels, chaos is grasped and ordered, so far as man can order it.

The Battle of the Books is perhaps the least interesting, as well as the least characteristic, of Swift's longer satires, and for that reason may be first considered, though parts at least of *A Tale of a Tub* were written earlier. It has an air of real detachment—as distinct from the assumed detachment of *A Modest Proposal*—which is unusual in him. He makes the satirist's formal pretense to impartiality: "I, being possessed of all Qualifications requisite in an Historian, and retained by neither Party; have resolved to comply with the urgent Importunity of my Friends, by writing down a full impartial Account thereof."[3] The joke here is that we are supposed to see at once how exceedingly partial the author is, though he is only writing, as so many claimed to be, through the "urgent Importunity" of his friends, and of course it is plain enough from the outset that the *Battle* is a blow on behalf of the ancients and of their supporters, chiefly Boyle and Sir William Temple, who are represented as honorary ancients. But as we read on, the ironic claim begins to seem almost a double bluff, for though Swift has chosen his side and believes he has chosen rightly, he seems not very deeply concerned in the matter. The actual battle, led on one side by the formidable combination of Homer, Pindar, Euclid, Plato, Aristotle, Herodotus, Livy, and Hippocrates, and on the other by a rabble of contenders for the chief command, is a lighthearted affair in which Swift's interest, and ours, lies not so much in the rights and wrongs of the argument as in the fun of the parody of heroic language and incidents and in the ingenuity of the episodes. The exchange of armor and the projected exchange of horses between Virgil and Dryden, or Wotton's abortive attack on Temple, who "neither felt the Weapon touch him, nor heard it fall," and indeed most of the contests, are amusing and neat in their translation of literary differences into physical encounters, but the ingenuity is the thing here, as in Pope's hilarious heroic games in *The Dunciad*. Swift was not by nature disposed to see things in plain black and white; perhaps the issue here, necessarily prejudged for him as a supporter of Temple against the well-armored Bentley, was too simplified to be real, and made too little appeal for him to feel deeply involved, though his admiration for Temple and the life that Temple stood for was real enough. In his later work he does not show himself ready to applaud or condemn either party without reservations, and even here several of the moderns are courteously treated, Cowley, Denham, Milton (whom Swift certainly admired) and, notably, Bacon, among them.

The satiric method, too, seems almost groping, considering the apparent ease and confidence with which the other early work, *A Tale of a Tub,* is written and shaped despite its far more complex theme. The *Battle* is clever but episodic, with allegories, parody, mock-heroic, each one neat in itself but all loosely strung together, and the satire is, for Swift, unusually simple and direct. It is not his normal habit to show his hand so plainly as he does here, with his opening allegory of the twin peaks of Parnassus and the causes of war, which are poverty and want on the part of the aggressor. As for the mock-heroic of the battle in St. James's Library, this was a mode of writing which at the end of the seventeenth century not only gave a clear warning of satiric intention but indicated pretty precisely how the satire would go; it is a far cry from this to the business-like approach of *A Modest Proposal,* or the factual sober air of Gulliver's *Travels. A Modest Proposal* could, at first, be yet another in that spate of impractical suggestions for improving the state of Ireland which so wearied Swift; the *Travels* could, at first, be another adventure story or at most another version of those many voyages to the moon or to the Antipodes which the reading public had been enjoying for so many years. We discover very quickly, it is true, that neither is what it seems, but it takes us a great deal longer to discover what, exactly, it is, and the false start is part of the effect. The recognition of the full satiric intention in these works of Swift's maturity involves reorientation and a necessary concern on the part of the reader; in *The Battle of the Books* we are complacently certain at the outset of the course to be run, and our complacency is never disturbed.

Indeed, we are here in a far more solid and familiar world than the one which Swift usually prepares for our discomfiture. Both the form and the supposed author are what they seem, though in fact the author contributes little to satiric meaning. Perhaps nowhere in Swift's work is the method simpler, except in political tracts where for the moment all that is in question is attack on, or ridicule of, a particular person or policy. Indeed the situation here is similar to that in a political pamphlet; an enclosed area of human experience has to be considered, in which attitudes approximating to right and wrong may be seen and in which it is necessary to "chuse one of the two Sides, although he cannot entirely approve of either." The intention of the satire is limited, and not of a kind to inspire Swift's more characteristic effects, and the method is, consequently, comparatively uncomplicated. The author is, for the most part, a mere eyewitness, reporting what he has seen and heard; he approaches most nearly to the modern author of *A Tale of a Tub* in his portentous opening remarks, and in the series of ingenious analogies which prove so little and please him so much. "NOW," he says proudly, after his argument from the causes of war as seen in the Republick of Dogs, "NOW, whoever will please to take this Scheme, and either reduce or adapt it to an Intellectual State, or Commonwealth of Learning, will soon discover the first Ground of Disagreement between the two great Parties at this Time in Arms."[4] But there is only a hint of the joyous lunacy of *A Tale of a Tub* in these parodies of ingenious, pointless argument; usually the parody is as straightforward as that of the "Tritical Essay," and soon we find ourselves in the Library of St. James's, watching the contest between the books in whose rival merits Swift is not deeply concerned.

But behind the rivalries of Virgil and Dryden, Cowley and Pindar, as behind the whole seventeenth century quarrel of the ancients and the moderns, lies the larger issue of what man is capable of: the difference between those who believe that his powers are strictly limited and those who believe in his power to improve upon existing knowledge and achievement.[5] The real importance of the quarrel in England was not literary but scientific and philosophic; and here it touches questions which were vital to Swift. One of the encounters in the battle is between Aristotle and Bacon; Aristotle shoots, but his arrow "mist the valiant Modern, and went hizzing over his Head; but Des-Cartes it hit; The Steel Point quickly found a Defect in his Head-piece; it pierced the Leather and the Past-board, and went in at his right Eye. The Torture of the Pain, whirled the valiant Bow-man round, till Death, like a Star of superior Influence, drew him into his own Vortex."[6] For Swift, Bacon as experimenter working humbly upon the matter of experience and as an opposer of those who domineer over nature was not unacceptable; it was Descartes, progenitor of the race of modern system-makers, who was representative of all that was presumptuous and dangerous in rationalizing modernism. James Keill, Newton's associate, sums up this attitude. Descartes, he says, has encouraged "this presumptuous pride in the Philosophers, that they think they understand all the works of Nature, and are able to give a good account of them. . . . He was the first world-maker this Century produced, for he supposes that God at the beginning created only a certain quantity of matter, and motion, and from thence he endeavours to shew, how, by the necessary law of Mechanisme, without any extraordinary concurrence of Divine Power, the world and all that therein is might have been produced."[7] This aspect of the quarrel is dealt with in the encounter between the Spider and the Bee, the one passage in the book in which the allegory is rich with compressed meaning. Various aspects of modern presumption are drawn together in this episode by means of allusion; it is an early example of the density which Swift can achieve in his prose, though rarely in the poetry, where one might rather expect to find it. Some of the meaning is expounded, fittingly enough, by Aesop, master of the beast fable; as he points out, the two insects have, by implication, summed up the whole situation. Indeed the uncouth and choleric spider, with his boasts of self-sufficiency, of being "furnisht with a Native Stock within my self," is an excellent symbol of the particular vice of modernism, especially since the buildings

125

on which he prides himself constitute in fact not a "Fortress" or a "large Castle" but a cobweb, ephemeral and flimsy as the cloud embraced, in mistake for Juno, by Bishop Huet's rationalist philosophers. The elaborate structure spun from the spider's own entrails is quickly shattered by the mere presence of the bee, though it makes no deliberate attack upon the fortifications, and the bee's civilized demeanor and polished utterance as quickly shows up the barbarism and ignorance of the spider. The contrast between an urbane traditional culture, always in touch with the world about it, and the unbalanced pride of word-spinning and system-spinning modernism, could scarcely be better displayed.

Several more particular applications can be made of the episode. It is, for instance, an excellent illustration of the difference between the traditional neoclassic literary theory and the new developments which were already opposing it. The bee's description of its activity as being "That, which, by an universal Range, with long Search, much Study, true Judgment, and Distinction of Things, brings home Honey and Wax"[8] suggests the old conception of literature as a reshaping, through the vigorous effort of the individual, of existing materials; the spider follows the easier course of a self-expression uncontrolled by reference to anything beyond himself, and so lacking in that discipline which is forced upon the bee by the effort to interpret the outside world and extract from it honey and wax, or as Aesop puts it "the two Noblest of Things, which are Sweetness and Light."[9] Sir William Temple had used the bee as a symbol of proper creative activity in his "Essay of Poetry," referring to the art and labor, and the difficult task of judging and selecting, involved in the bee's choice of flowers, extraction of honey, and separation of the wax. But the bee and the spider belong also to those philosophical and scientific differences which were undermining the ways of thought from which classical literary theory sprang; they had been used to symbolize the quarrel between those who were content to observe and experience, and those who were overeager to theorize. Francis Bacon had seen scholasticism as a spider, spinning useless cobwebs of learning out of little matter and infinite agitation of wit; in *Novum Organum* he compares the men of experiment with the ant, who only collects and uses, the reasoners with the spiders, "which spin webs out of their own bowels," and the true philosopher with the bee, who takes a middle course, for "she draws her materials from the flowers of the garden and the field, and yet changes and digests them by a power of her own."[10] Bacon's middle way would no doubt appeal to Swift as an assertion of the ordering and shaping power of the mind within the limits he would regard as possible and permissible. Mind has a strenuous part to play, but a limited part; it must take into account the confusion of the world and work upon it, for though we cannot escape from chaos we can by difficult effort compose it into meaning.

The spider and the bee were, therefore, already familiar symbols when Swift wrote, and others before him had related Bacon's spider to rationalists of all kinds, Cartesian as well as scholastic. One of the most notorious of contemporary system-makers was Dr. Thomas Burnet, who a few years before had spun what was perhaps the most intricate and flimsy cobweb of all in his account of the creation and subsequent history of the world, *Telluris Theoria Sacra*. This extraordinary work was seen to be not only an unfounded hypothesis but a dangerous one, tending to the denial of the Biblical story of man's creation and fall, and taking too little account of final causes; and such de-spiritualizing of the universe was detestable to Swift as to many of his contemporaries. In the *Battle* he has a passing hit at these system-makers with their absorption in efficient causes and their failure to relate them to the Final Cause, in the passage describing the visit of Fame to Jupiter. She tells him of the impending battle, and having consulted the Book of Fate he summons a number of menial gods: "These are his ministring Instruments in all Affairs below. They travel in a Caravan, more or less together, and are fastened to each other like a Link of Gally-slaves, by a light Chain, which passes from them to Jupiter's great Toe: And yet in receiving or delivering a Message, they may never approach above the lowest Step of his Throne, where he and they whisper to each other thro' a long hollow Trunk. These Deities are call'd by mortal Men, Accidents, or Events; but the Gods call them, Second Causes."[11] This is a lightly turned comment on the pursuers of second causes; follow the chain of causation as far as they will, there will still be an un-bridgable gap between it and the final cause. They can reach no further than the lowest step of God's throne, and the divine in-tentions cannot be penetrated by such investigations. They will succeed only in cutting themselves off from the true understand-ing which can be reached by accepting the mysterious purposes of God; as Meric Casaubon put it, men who kept their minds fixed on matter and secondary causes might "forget that there be such things in the world as spirits, and at last that there is a God, and that their souls are immortal." The divine decrees become, to mankind, mere "Accidents, or Events." Mysteries must and will remain, for all the explanations given from second causes by the moderns.

It has recently been demonstrated that Swift's spider has par-ticular reference to Burnet, who recounts an eastern legend of a cosmic spider which spun the universe and governs it as it would a web[12]—as do the system-makers themselves—while the bee, on the other hand, is a familiar symbol of the good life, ancient and modern. Marvell's "Garden," for instance, the place of all tra-ditional God-centered wisdom, is the home of the bee, working intelligently upon the glories of the created world, and it is the bee who closes and sums up the poem:

> Where, from above, the milder sun
> Does through a fragrant zodiac run,
> And, as it works, the industrious bee
> Computes its time, as well as we![13]

The contrast of bee and spider bears upon the fundamental moral problems of the age; it is not surprising that in this episode Swift's satire becomes more complex and less direct, drawing many allu-sions and meanings into a small space. It is more characteristic of him than is any other part of *The Battle of the Books,* and not the least typical aspect of the passage is its embodiment of theory in persons—for the insects have recognizably human personalities. One of the implicit arguments against modern theorizing is that it produces a Bentley or a Burnet-spider; one of the arguments for ancient humility is the wise bee, or the courteous and magnan-imous Charles Boyle. As always, attitudes of mind are displayed through, and judged by, the results they produce in conduct. Although they are obscured by the topical jokes of the battle itself, there are important issues hinted at in this otherwise rather impersonal and, for Swift, rather unorganized and simple, book. The real function of man in the world is already his main interest, and the good life with its unambitious achievement of order and meaning within the framework of traditional acceptances, is set against the fantasy world of the reasoners in their strongholds which can be broken at the first touch of reality.

The comparative directness of method in *The Battle of the Books,* arising from the comparative simplicity of the material, is especially noticeable in the handling of the allegory and of the narrator or mouthpiece. The allegory is, for the most part, a matter of simple mock-heroic equivalences and surface meanings; the narrator is managed just as straightforwardly. But in Swift's greatest and most characteristic satire, allegory or mouthpiece, or in *Gulliver's Travels* both, constitute his chief means towards the indirect and ironic presentation of a number of qualifying ideas and attitudes. To accept the allegorical narrative of Book IV of the *Travels* as simply as we do that of the *Battle* would be a fatal mistake—in a sense, the mistake that Gulliver himself makes. It is because he takes the allegorical figures of Houyhnhnm-land at their face value that he errs so gravely and learns, in effect, the wrong lesson. His error is part of the total meaning, for in *Gulliver's Travels* it is not the allegorical narrative simply, but the visible and purposeful manipulation both of the narrative and of its narrator, which gives us Swift's full intention. The ironic treatment of the particular form chosen and of Gulliver, its ostensible author, is, I believe, more effective and more precisely suited to its complex purpose than in any other of the satires, even than in the more immediately striking *Tale of a Tub,* but it is only the best example of a constant practice. In *A Modest Proposal* as in the *Travels,* a literary form—in this case the humble one of a practical economic project—and its author are put before us only to be twisted and manipulated in the way that will express most completely and most sharply the views and emotions of Swift himself. Such terms as "parody" and "mask" suggest some-

thing too consistent and too simple, though it is hard to think of
more adequate ones. Swift's manipulations are too complicated
and too rapidly changing to be easily tabulated, except as part of
the indirection which is essential if he is to express several things
at once, as he is usually trying to do. In the interests of complete
expression the allegory or the parody may be broken, the narrator
inconsistent or vanishing from our notice, the story or the project
spoiled, for all these things are to Swift merely so many tools to be
taken up or dropped, to be made use of as his satiric meanings
require. He takes pains to impress this upon us, for by such means
as satiric treatment of the author, or by making him speak at one
moment with naïve acceptance and at another in a way that quite
openly expresses the opinions of his creator, he makes us aware
that we have to do not with a narration, whether it be a story or a
plan or an account of the state of English letters or religion; not
even with a simple reversal of values with its one reiterated
ironical point; but with a narration which, along with its "author,"
is being used to satiric and moral purpose by the mind which has
created them both.

The amount of use made of the "supposed author" varies considerably, and sometimes where the satire does not require very
complicated ironies he has too little to contribute to be usefully
considered as a separate entity. This is so in *The Battle of the
Books* and in *An Argument against Abolishing Christianity,*
where time and again a passage can technically be attributed, with
perfect appropriateness, to the shadowy, simple-minded "author"
but yet in reading is recognized at once, by its tone, as the direct
comment of the true author; in such passages nothing is really
gained by thinking in terms of the supposed author, and we are
actually aware only of the play between direct and ironic comment:

". . . Would any indifferent Foreigner, who should read the
Trumpery lately written by Asgill, Tindall, Toland, Coward, and
Forty more, imagine the Gospel to be our Rule of Faith, and con-
firmed by Parliaments? . . .

". . . Will not Heydukes and Mamalukes, Mandarins, and
Potshaws, or any other Words formed at Pleasure, serve to dis-

tinguish those who are in the Ministry from others, who would be in it if they could?"[14]

It often happens, of course, that even those "authors" who contribute most to satiric effect merge in this way with their creator; Gulliver's comment on the good king of Brobdingnag—"it would be hard indeed, if so remote a Prince's Notions of Virtue and Vice were to be offered as a Standard for all Mankind"[15]—is felt as ironical comment by Swift, though it can be conveniently regarded as a piece of pompous complacency on the part of Gulliver. Indeed Gulliver, though he seems more solid than the rest of Swift's mouthpieces (partly because he is actor as well as narrator) is conceived in the same way, but in his case as in that of the authors of *A Tale of a Tub* and *A Modest Proposal* it is convenient, even necessary, to speak of the author or narrator or mouthpiece as a person, while recognizing that even as we read we know him to be a satiric fabrication. As with all Swift's mouthpieces, his purpose is purely satiric, and he is given as many characteristics, consistent or not, as his inventor requires for that purpose, or he may from time to time disappear altogether. The brilliance of the handling of Gulliver lies in the precision with which the inconsistency of the satiric mouthpiece is used progressively for a further satiric effect, and contributes to the rich meanings of the work as a whole. In each book Gulliver functions satirically in more ways than one, but his predominant generosity in Lilliput, contrasted with his peevishness in Brobdingnag, is part of a deliberate effect, while the "Voyage to the Houyhnhnms" turns upon Gulliver's capacity for misunderstanding. Similarly, though less elaborately, in *A Modest Proposal,* we are always conscious of Swift's presence, yet the nature of his puppet-author helps, by interrelation with the plan itself, to enforce the satire. The fact that the author is, above all, well-meaning, that he recognizes the misery of his fellow-countrymen but can think of no plan to help them but this very modest proposal, in itself expresses the horror of the situation. It is his desire to help which has produced his ingenious scheme, for help, as he has been forced to see, can only be given within the context of English assumptions. Only a commercial proposition will be given a hearing by the English

131

government or by the Irish landlords, and the most telling irony of all is that the plan really would be a way of "providing for Infants" and of "relieving the Poor," since the children would be saved by death from the greater misery of living, and since they would be assured of treatment as good as that received by such pampered creatures as lambs and calves. The proposal is not only economically sound, it is humane, the only form of practical helpfulness left. In a passage like the following it is Swift's presence that we feel, and Swift's helpless angry pity, but the modest proposer has served his purpose in suggesting the moral confusion into which even well-meaning men can be thrown as they contemplate the horror of Ireland.

I desire those Politicians, who dislike my Overture, and may perhaps be so bold to attempt an Answer, that they will first ask the Parents of these Mortals, Whether they would not, at this Day, think it a great Happiness to have been sold for Food at a Year old, in the Manner I prescribe; and thereby have avoided such a perpetual Scene of Misfortunes, as they have since gone through; by the Oppression of Landlords; the Impossibility of paying Rent, without Money or Trade; the Want of common Sustenance, with neither House nor Cloaths, to cover them from the Inclemencies of Weather; and the most inevitable Prospect of intailing the like, or greater Miseries upon their Breed for ever.[16]

Of all Swift's mouthpieces, the "supposed author" of *A Tale of a Tub* is one of the least tangible. Gulliver, though changeable, is generally, except for particular uses, solid enough at a given moment, and the full extent and the precise nature of the satiric treatment he is to receive is only gradually revealed. But the Author of the *Tale* is from beginning to end a fantastic creature, a mere bundle of unrelated qualities. Though it is useful to speak of him so, it is not really possible to regard him as a person, when he is given such lines as these:

In my Disposure of Employments of the Brain, I have thought fit to make Invention the Master, and give Method and Reason, the Office of its Lacquays. The Cause of this Distribution was, from observing it my peculiar Case, to be often under a Temptation of being Witty, upon Occasion, where I could be neither Wise nor Sound, nor any thing to the Matter in hand. And, I am too much a Servant of the Modern Way, to neglect any such Opportunities, whatever Pains or Improprieties I may be at, to introduce them.[17]

The presentation of nonsense is, indeed, the Author's primary satiric function; fantasy, unreality, is what he is there to express. In a sense he is more simply conceived than Gulliver, being essentially a conglomeration of incompatible attitudes, all equally important, or unimportant, but in detail he works in a particularly elusive and shifting way. Swift's mouthpieces are one of his most flexible methods of indirection, of expressing his complicated meanings, but the Author of the *Tale* is least rigid of them all, for he has the special function of plunging us into chaos, confusion, self-deceit, a world of upheaval and destruction in which our own task, as readers, is to collect the scattered raw materials and rebuild our own attitudes to form a structure more firmly based upon reality.

In *A Tale of a Tub,* therefore, complexity is the rule, not, as in *The Battle of the Books,* an exception. The *Tale* is Swift's plunge into the chaos of mindless experience, "the unreality of the 'uncreating word'—the 'true No-meaning' which 'puzzles more than wit.' "[18] In it our mad world is parodied and heightened to a point where we can no longer believe it to be sane; every fragment of the broken truth is shattered into still smaller, scintillating pieces, and only the barest and most casually indirect hints are given to help us in the task of fitting them together into their proper shape. In all this activity Swift is, of course, far from irresponsible; the process is one of deliberate and purposeful destruction, and the simpler parts of the book, those which constitute the allegory of the three churches in the shape of the brothers Peter, Martin, and Jack, are a kind of key to the method and intention of those dazzling chapters which contain so much of the meaning and which are with wilful wrongheadedness described as "Digressions."

Apart from satiric hits at particular practices of the Roman Catholics and the Dissenters, and a good deal of incidental fun, the main theme of the allegory of the churches is of a gradual departure from given truth, a steady descent into self-deceit. Because they wish to do various things which under the terms of

133

their father's will they are not permitted to do, the three brothers allow themselves to be deceived and become more and more adept at using their reason in the service of their passions until, by great ingenuity, they are able to find in the will permission to add whatever decorations they wish to their simple coats. The plain command "to wear no sort of Silver Fringe upon or about their said Coats" is evaded by a judicious use of mythological and allegorical senses; shoulder-knots are found to be permissible by the fitting together of separate letters in the will, a method invented by Peter: " 'Tis true, said he, there is nothing here in this Will, *totidem verbis,* making mention of Shoulder-knots, but I dare conjecture, we may find them *inclusivé,* or *totidem syllabis."* And having failed here: "Brothers, there is yet Hopes; for tho' we cannot find them *totidem verbis,* nor *totidem syllabis,* I dare engage we shall make them out *tertio modo,* or *totidem literis."*[19] Peter remains in this mad world of fantasy excused by a show of reason, but the other brothers, having been kicked out of doors, begin to reflect seriously upon their misfortune and its causes, and decide to return strictly to the terms of their father's will. Martin pulls off all the lace, fringe, and other decoration that he can, but stops when he finds that some of it is so tightly attached that he cannot remove it without tearing the coat itself, "resolving in no Case whatsoever, that the Substance of the Stuff should suffer Injury; which he thought the best Method for serving the true Intent and Meaning of his Father's Will."[20] Jack, however, tears away decoration, coat, and all, ending in rags and tatters still ornamented by a few of Peter's most elaborate embroideries. In fact there is great danger in tearing away too drastically the deceits of our passions and desires; some of them may be, or may have become, an integral part of our nature. There are, as so often, two satiric standards: the will, by which all the churches, as all humanity, stand condemned, and the compromise standard, the best that can practically be achieved by half-blind humanity, the conduct of the reformed Martin.[21]

The story of the three brothers has, in itself, less than Swift's usual power, and perhaps the lowering of intensity has the same cause here as in *The Battle of the Books,* that all is too plain; the work has been done for us. The compromise solution has been reached and exists before us in Martin. But though it is comparatively low-powered if taken in isolation, the allegory of the churches has an essential part to play in the work as a whole, for the Digressions circle about a very similar theme. The Author of the *Tale* is himself an example of the very process through which Jack, the dissenting brother, passes in the story which he himself recounts to us. He indulges in all the word-spinning which all three brothers use under the guidance of Peter, and with his wild theories and elaborate analogies, with his digression in praise of digressions, he is a perfect instance of the modern spider producing a cobwebby book out of his own entrails, just as the Dissenters initiated, according to Swift's sermon "Upon the Martyrdom," a "sect of religion that grew out of their own bowels."[22] But though he is in fact so totally immersed in deceit that he can utter only nonsense, he considers himself to be a great reasoner, and a formidable enemy of "prejudice." Like Jack, and with as sorry results, he proposes to free himself from all such deceit, but he exists in the incoherent world of giddy circumstance that his whirling style and his proud presentation of nonsense so perfectly symbolize. Recognizing neither the weakness of reason nor the strength of deceit, he struggles, caught in his own cobweb but believing it to be a strong and rational structure; and in so nonsensical an atmosphere the difficulty for the reader is in determining, from the chaotic opinions of the supposed Author, what conclusions the true author intends us to reach.

From the outset we are aware that the Author is the object of satire, since this is established immediately by the use of parody; and from his opening words to Prince Posterity, self-importantly submitting "the Fruits of a very few leisure Hours, stollen from the short Intervals of a World of Business, and of an Employment quite alien from such Amusements as this," to the final promise to pause "till I find, by feeling the World's Pulse, and my own, that it will be of absolute Necessity for us both, to resume my Pen,"[23] he is clearly there to be laughed at. Having seen this, we assume that by reversing his values we will arrive at his creator's meaning; the Author, we feel complacently, may be astray in a

135

fairyland of dreams, but we at least have our wits about us; we can see what is really intended. But this confidence is soon shaken by the intellectual pyrotechnics of Swift himself; we are continually pulled on to what seems to be firm ground, where we feel that we know just what is absurd in the remarks of the Author— and therefore, by implication, what is sensible—only to be pushed briskly off again into chaos. The experience is purely enjoyable; what we feel is a breathless exhilaration at being swept along in this lively mental activity, rather than a sense of loss and alarm. We share the true author's creative liberty, not the supposed Author's captivity in chaos. This, perhaps, is why the *Tale* has less power to disturb than *Gulliver's Travels;* in the later work we are faced by a frightening emptiness which forces us to the task of reconstruction, but here we can be content to enjoy, with Swift, the vigorous power of mind. And if there is less incentive, and less urgency, in working out meanings—as in Swift's satire we are always required to do—there is also more difficulty; because of the utter incoherence of the Author it is harder than usual to recognize where Swift is leading us.

In *Gulliver's Travels* and the shorter satiric pieces we have firm guidance from Swift; when once we are accustomed to his tone of voice we can gauge with some accuracy what we should take seriously and what not. We are familiar with the apology for some suggestion which everyone will think foolish, as in the paradox timidly put forward by the author of *An Argument against Abolishing Christianity* that he does not yet see the absolute necessity of extirpating the Christian religion; with the scorn for a point of view, as in Gulliver's sneer at Brobdingnagian "Prejudices, and Narrowness of thinking"; with the grudging approval—"the least corrupted are the Brobdingnagians." We recognize Swift's guidance in Gulliver's enthusiasm first for Britain and later for Houyhnhnm-land, in his exaggerated complaints in his letter to his cousin Sympson, and in the exaggerated calm with which the writer of the *Modest Proposal* puts forward his desperate remedy. But in *A Tale of a Tub* all the opinions expressed appear equally ridiculous and are expressed in the same fantastic style; the Author is himself a style rather than a person, and his function is to display the madness of deceit and the greater madness of supposing that we are ever free of it, this being the greatest deceit of all. Various philosophies and particular philosophers are put forward as examples of the modern Author's madness, again and again self-deceit masquerades as reason, and in this atmosphere all value is negated. If we concentrate too exclusively on the fantastic Author as the object of the satire, exact meanings are difficult to catch, for he can misunderstand, misrepresent, contradict his own findings, with the utmost complacency, and he has no firm, even momentarily firm, opinion which with Swift's guidance we can learn to disregard. The *Tale* consists, so far as the Digressions are concerned, entirely of aberrations from a norm which is barely suggested; in none of Swift's satires is positive value more indirectly expressed. This, presumably, is why it has been called negative and destructive intellectual activity designed to no end. Yet there are values in the *Tale,* though we must shake off the supposed Author in order to see them, for he is not, like Gulliver, a man of mistaken and changing values, which we can allow for, but a man of no values at all, intended not so much to express meaning as to nullify it.

It has been demonstrated in recent years that in several passages of *A Tale of a Tub* Swift is specifically attacking certain modern positions,[24] particularly those which are frankly materialist, like "Epicureanism" and Hobbism, or those which so cencentrate on systematizing the physical world that the spiritual basis of that world is forgotten. To Swift, of course, either materialism or a blind pursuit of second causes is wrong, morally as well as intellectually, since for him the world can only be properly interpreted in a context of moral truth enforced by divine authority. This firm positive standard is present throughout the allegorical part of the *Tale,* and in reading we do in fact carry over into the Digressions the standard we have absorbed from the story of the three brothers, comparing not only Peter and Jack but the Author and all the philosophies he jumbles together, with the sound and sensible Martin, and, behind him, with the supreme authority of *"Christiana Religio absoluta et simplex"* which he does his human best to embody. The flimsy uncertain world of the Digressions is seen against the certainty, solidity, and centrality of the Will and the three coats made of cloth "so neatly sown, you would swear they were all of a Piece." The two parts of the book are deliberately linked at several points; for instance, the satire on materialism in Section II, the description of the tailor idol and of his worshippers' belief in the micro-coat and macro-coat, takes the story of the three coats into the world of the Digressions, as the clear factual narrative style slips into the fantastic analogies and proudly produced false conclusions, so dear to the heart of the Author:

What is that which some call Land, but a fine Coat faced with Green? or the Sea, but a Wastcoat of Water-Tabby? Proceed to the particular Works of the Creation, you will find how curious Journey-man Nature hath been, to trim up the vegetable Beaux. . . .

That the Soul was the outward, and the Body the inward Cloathing; that the latter was *ex traduce;* but the former of daily Creation and Circumfusion. This last they proved by Scripture, because in Them we Live, and Move, and have our Being: As likewise by Philosophy, because they are All in All, and All in every Part. Besides, said they, separate these two, and you will find the Body to be only a senseless unsavory Carcass. By all which it is manifest, that the outward Dress must needs be the Soul.[25]

But the *Tale* is not primarily an attack on modern materialism as such. In his account of the doctrine "That the Soul was the outward, and the Body the inward Cloathing" Swift parodies not Hobbist but Scholastic terminology, for all such intricate reasonings move steadily away from reality; even when soul is not denied it is reasoned out of any useful existence, and with it morality, until religion is a cloak, honesty a pair of shoes worn out in the dirt, and a man can cry, "That Fellow has no Soul; where is his Shoulder-Knot?" Modern and ancient philosophies are attacked not so much in and for themselves but as illustrations of the spider-like reasoning which, because it disregards the firm outlines laid down by morality, tradition, and experience, moves into fantasy and leaves the mind spinning in a dead world, devoid of the true meaning which only "unrefined reason," the reasonable acceptance of revealed truth and morality, can find and which Martin approximately represents. Without the madness of uncontrolled reasoning and systematizing all mankind would be reduced to the "same Belief in Things Invisible."[26] The world of fantasy presented in the Digressions is dead because it lacks the meaning which can be given to it only by a mind content to keep close to the known, to experience, and humbly depending upon the divine mind which alone can interpret its own creation. As so often in Swift, much is expressed by an accumulation of imagery, and the language of the *Tale* is full of images of lightness, shallowness, superficiality, and all that can suggest the meaningless. The Author is obsessed by surfaces and rinds and shells, by the footless Bird of Paradise which must fly up until it crashes to the ground, by "Edifices in the Air," by all that is "light enough to swim upon the surface for all Eternity," all that is "lofty and light" and soars above the earth. The pulpit of dissent is a symbol of the writings of the modern saints, "as they have spiritualized and refined them from the Dross and Grossness of Sense and Human Reason,"[27] because it is made of rotten wood, full of wormholes and shining in the dark, giving out the ghostly "Inward Light" of phosphorescence. Dead wood, rotten and treacherous and shining with an unreal light—the image sums up the whole world of madness, as does the Aeolist substitution of wind for spirit. The primary error of the Aeolists is that in their anxiety to escape from a world of sense into pure spirituality they have only sunk deeper into the power of the body, the passions, and the deceiving senses: and this happens to all who try to escape, whether by way of the spirit or by way of the reason. They end in a place of no-meaning, where revelation gives way to the Delphic oracle, where Saints and conquerors and philosophers are indiscriminately engendered and where a man may be a comparatively harmless Aeolist or an Alexander or a Descartes, doing infinite damage. For in this state, no moral standards exist.

The power of the human body and the impossibility of escaping its influence is here most forcefully brought home to us in the figure of the purple-faced, belching Aeolist priest who believes himself to be rapt into the spirit. Since in his major satires it is the nature of man as an animal, though one capable of reason, which is his main theme, Swift writes much in terms of physical humanity; it is people of all kinds who best make his satiric points.

The Author's whirling and disconnected comparisons often come jolting home to their real end in an image of the human body. His long disquisitions on appearance and reality end with Pythagoras, Aesop, and Socrates, with a "senseless unsavory Carcass," "the Carcass of a Beau," a woman flayed, or a neatly symmetrical skeleton. For it is the Author's misfortune that whatever he exercises his mind upon he succeeds in killing, rendering meaningless. He complains of the superficiality of the readers of the present age, which has forced the Grubaean sages to shut up their great truths within a dazzling exterior, but the wisdom he offers to lay bare, by the typically destructive methods of unwinding or incision, is after all only a worm or a maggot, and the dazzling exterior itself is discountenanced by the comparison with Socrates and Aesop, famous for their ugliness. Socrates's appearance was unimportant because of his inner qualities of wisdom and goodness, but Grub Street ugliness, or "outward Lustre," covers only a maggot. In the Author's world neither exterior nor interior is of the slightest consequence. The meaning he claims to find in Grub Street literature—the "compleat Body of Civil Knowledge"[28] in *Reynard the Fox,* the Pythagorean doctrine of *Tom Thumb*—is as unreal as is the reasoning of Eugenius Philalethes or of Descartes in another sphere. The state of chaotic deceit in which all these people exist is most fully displayed in the famous passage in the Author's Digression on Madness. We are subject to delusion from within ourselves as from without, and indeed human happiness depends on our understanding and our senses being deceived; the pleasures we most value are those which "Dupe and play the Wag with the Senses." We see what is present no more clearly than what is past or future, and things that have place in our imagination may as properly be said to exist as those that are seated in the memory.[29] As for the senses, they are beset by a muddle of secondary qualities and phantasms, the films and images that fly off upon our senses "from the Superficies of Things,"[30] looking no further than "the Colour, the Shape, the Size, and whatever other Qualities dwell, or are drawn by Art upon the Outward of Bodies."[31] In fact we are never able, through the senses, to reach the real truth of things, and it is as well, thinks the Author, that we do not, for "How fading and insipid do all Objects accost us that are not convey'd in the Vehicle of Delusion? How shrunk is every Thing, as it appears in the Glass of Nature? So, that if it were not for the Assistance of Artificial Mediums, false Lights, refracted Angles, Varnish, and Tinsel; there would be a mighty level in the Felicity and Enjoyments of Mortal Men."[32] Reason only serves to make us miserable by destroying our happy delusion, "cutting, and opening, and mangling, and piercing, offering to demonstrate, that they are not of the same consistency quite thro'." This, says the Author, is unnatural; it is to pervert nature, "one of whose Eternal Laws it is, to put her best Furniture forward."

The Author has thus contrived, as usual, to reduce everything to equal meaninglessness. To live in enjoyment of what flies off upon our senses, accepting impressions without shaping them into significance, is to be deluded, a fool; to go beneath the surface is to be wretched and unnatural, a knave. Swift has maintained, through his manipulation of the Author's language—varnish, tinsel, mangling—a delicate balance between two unacceptable extremes, using each extreme as a temporary satiric standard by which to discredit the other. The Author tilts the balance slightly towards reason by his decision to prefer an Epicurean dependence on the evidence of the senses, "that Wisdom, which converses about the surface, to that pretended Philosophy which enters into the Depth of Things, and then comes gravely back with Informations and Discoveries, that in the inside they are good for nothing," but the startlingly vivid image of the human body provides a counterweight and at the same time suggests a solution. "Last Week I saw a Woman flay'd, and you will hardly believe, how much it altered her Person for the worse."[33]

There is no better evocation in all Swift's work of the precarious activities of the mind in its wild sublunary dance. Swift is well aware how much we are at the mercy of "false mediums," and may perhaps share his Author's regret for the "Vehicle of Delusion," but he believes that we must, while always remembering that some delusion is inescapable, try to find such truth and meaning as we may. The true answer to the Author's quandary

141

lies, of course, in what he has left out in his exhaustive survey of
the situation, in the compromise solution of unrefined reason, the
"common Forms," human centrality, and good sense. Nature, the
approximation to absolute truth, which is all we can hope to attain, cannot be known only by the "false Lights, refracted Angles,
Varnish, and Tinsel" that make up the happiness of the senses,
but by the mind that orders and interprets the material which the
senses present. "Who judgeth by apparences," says Montaigne,
"judgeth by a thing different from the subject."[34] But if nature
disapproves of wilful self-delusion, she also disapproves of "an-
atomising," the systematizing reason which is only delusion in
another form. Reason must act, but it must keep within its proper
bounds, and not lay bare what nature herself has hidden, since
that too is only to distort. To pry beneath the skin is to kill reality,
so that either of the Author's extremes ends in nothingness, in
tinsel or in death, the flayed corpse; in the "Crowd of Atoms
justling in a heap" or the mindless body, cold and dead, of the
"Ode to the Athenian Society."

This passage with its two opposing kinds of unreality is properly part of the Digression on Madness, for the madness of Bedlam is only an accentuated form of the Author's irresponsibility,
and that in its turn is only an accentuated form of the delusion
which is our normal state. Bedlam is mad, but so are conquerors
and philosophers, courtiers and city-men, poets and beaux; all
of us are deceived, and one of our greatest dangers is that in our
efforts to escape we will go to the other extreme and tear down
not only delusion but the reality which is inextricable from it.
The Author, used as he is to present so many wrong attitudes, is
himself an example of this error, for though he disapproves of
mangling reason he is a great lover of systems and abstracts and
of anatomizing. He has seen a woman flayed and ordered the
carcass of a beau to be stripped; one of the treatises he tells us he
has written is entitled "Lectures upon a Dissection of Human Nature," another project is "An Universal Rule of Reason, or Every
Man his own Carver," and he presents his book to Posterity as "a
faithful Abstract drawn from the Universal Body of all Arts and
Sciences." He describes himself as the Secretary of the Universe, a

title applied to Descartes by his admirers and to the Rosicrucian John Heydon by himself,[35] and in his guise as Secretary of Nature he makes his most ambitious and fatal attempt: "To this End, I have some Time since, with a World of Pains and Art, dissected the Carcass of Humane Nature, and read many useful Lectures upon the several Parts, both Containing and Contained; till at last it smelt so strong, I could preserve it no longer. Upon which, I have been at a great Expence to fit up all the Bones with exact Contexture, and in due Symmetry; so that I am ready to shew a very compleat Anatomy thereof to all curious Gentlemen and others."[36]

Here he has succeeded in producing not merely a corpse but a skeleton; he has so anatomized human nature that everything has been stripped away and his attempt to reach truth has ended in the substitution of dead bones for the complete body, the flesh and blood of reality. What he has found is neat and systematic but irrelevant to human life; not only bodily "prejudices," tinsel, clothes, but life and reality, have been stripped away. Jack's attitude to the relation of appearance and reality is similar. He sees correctly that the senses are unreliable, but his solution of ignoring them leads only to complete blindness and confusion. Bouncing his head against a post as he walks through the streets with his eyes closed, he remarks:

Now, had my Eyes been open, it is very likely, the Business might have been a great deal worse; For, how many a confounded Slip is daily got by Man, with all his Foresight about him? Besides, the Eyes of the Understanding see best, when those of the Senses are out of the way; and therefore, blind Men are observed to tread their Steps with much more Caution, and Conduct, and Judgment, than those who rely with too much Confidence, upon the Virtue of the visual Nerve, which every little Accident shakes out of Order, and a Drop, or a Film, can wholly disconcert; like a Lanthorn among a Pack of roaring Bullies, when they scower the Streets; exposing its Owner, and it self, to outward Kicks and Buffets, which both might have escaped, if the Vanity of Appearing would have suffered them to walk in the Dark. . . . For, O ye Eyes, Ye blind Guides; miserable Guardians are Ye of our frail Noses; Ye, I say, who fasten upon the first Precipice in view, and then tow our wretched willing Bodies after You, to the very Brink of Destruction.[37]

The practitioners of the art of Mechanical Operation make the same error, "Because the Senses in Men are so many Avenues to the Fort of Reason, which in this Operation is wholly block'd up."[38]

Jack and his Aeolists, the Author and his philosophers, the Laputans of *Gulliver's Travels* and the system-makers of *The Battle of the Books,* all who move away from realistic common forms and common understanding, whether they believe themselves to be reasoners or men of the spirit, end in a world of fantasy. "The World of God, no doubt, is an other thing, than the World of Sense is," but such truth as we can find for ourselves is available only through the world of sense, and if we try to escape from its delusions by ignoring it, it will only capture us more completely. For

However Spiritual Intrigues begin, they generally conclude like all others; they may branch upwards towards Heaven, but the Root is in the Earth. Too intense a Contemplation is not the Business of Flesh and Blood; it must by the necessary Course of Things, in a little Time, let go its Hold, and fall into Matter. Lovers, for the sake of Celestial Converse, are but another sort of Platonicks, who pretend to see Stars and Heaven in Ladies Eyes, and to look or think no lower; but the same Pit is provided for both; and they seem a perfect Moral to the Story of the Philosopher, who, while his Thoughts and Eyes were fixed upon the Constellations, found himself seduced by his lower Parts into a Ditch.[39]

It is when we believe ourselves to be reasoning most ingeniously, feeling most spiritually, that our greatest danger comes and we fall more deeply into the power of flesh and blood and matter, and then our reason for all its energetic activity is really in the power of delusion, moving at the dictates of fancy; "when a Man's Fancy gets astride of his Reason, when Imagination is at Cuffs with the Senses, and common Understanding, as well as common Sense, is Kickt out of Doors."[40] Then the lover and the enthusiast fall into matter, the philosopher is caught in second causes and mathematical systems, the occultist achieves his "methodical muddle of spirit and matter,"[41] and reality is closed to them all, from one extreme they fall into a worse. Yet these are the great reformers of the world; "Pray what is Man," says

Swift in the character of the moralizing Mr. Boyle, "but a topsy turvy Creature? his Animal Faculties perpetually mounted on his Rational; his Head where his Heels should be, groveling on the Earth. And yet, with all his Faults, he sets up to be a universal Reformer and Correcter of Abuses; a Remover of Grievances; rakes into every Slut's Corner of Nature, bringing hidden Corruptions to the Light, and raiseth a mighty Dust where there was none before; sharing deeply all the while in the very same Pollutions he pretends to sweep away."[42] The supposed Author, though he professes to leave nature to put her best face forward, wrote *A Tale of a Tub* "for the Universal Improvement of Mankind."

The power of "Flesh and Blood" is an important part of Swift's theme in *A Tale of a Tub* and the *Discourse concerning the Mechanical Operation of the Spirit*. The *Discourse,* harsher in tone and more openly serious, gives a stronger impression of the overwhelming power of all that comes to us *"par le corps, ou à l'occasion du corps,"* and its intention is firmly summed up in the closing passage on those who, gazing on the constellations, find themselves seduced by their lower parts into a ditch. But in *A Tale of a Tub* also, though the far more indirect method and the sense we have of Swift's own confident intellectual activity makes it less plain, flesh and blood is always being brought to our notice. Jack and his Aeolists, who profess to scorn it, are more fleshly, more physically vivid to us, than any of the characters, but the dead bodies of the Author, his carcasses and skeletons, present more obliquely the necessity for reckoning with the physical urges of humanity and not anatomizing them to death, if we are to remain human beings. Whether we are mastered by flesh and blood, or whether we ignore it, we will live in a meaningless world. Swift here uses his imagery of the human body with the greatest conciseness and economy. By means of it, he can sum up his theme of the intermingling of man's intellectual powers and spiritual aspirations with his senses and passions, and can suggest that though reason must be pre-eminent the search for truth must not involve too radical a weeding-out of the other parts of man's nature, and must not exercise itself in isolation from the ordinary world which both gives it its materials and lays down its necessary

145

limitations. In this way Swift's two important and interlinked themes, the nature of deceit and the nature of man, can be brought together and a vital compromise can be suggested. Because Swift's intention in the *Tale* is to attack the extremes current in his age, because he is concerned not so much to establish a standard as to undermine false standards, his whole method in the Digressions is elusive and paradoxical; one thing is set up against another to be shown as inadequate, and the second standard is then demolished by reference to the first; we are to attain the positive by piecing together hints and implications and indirections, reconstructing the small but firm area of human certainty that remains when what is false has been thrown aside. To some degree this is always true of Swift, but here the process is particularly marked, for in the *Tale* he is leading us deeper into our world of dream and showing us that though in that world the ordering mind has its essential task it must operate with caution, flexibility, humility, and awareness of all the complex issues of our state. We cannot cut through chaos to simplicity, but must order experience by fitting together the shattered fragments of the single truth. Swift's implied standard is limitation and compromise, this being the proper exercise of reason in a creature like man, and it is a standard best hinted at in the figure of man himself. For man with his dual nature is the supreme paradox who sums up all the lesser paradoxes of his world, and who can only properly live by a process of continual and careful compromise. Behind the mad philosophers and enthusiasts, behind the Author and his flayed and dissected corpses, stands Martin, the one sane man of the *Tale,* who has attained his limited completeness through compromise and acceptance of the traditional values of Christian morality. The sanity and balance of Martin, like the sanity of that other representative of the good life, the wise bee of *The Battle of the Books,* is set firmly against all the flimsy spinning of the modern spiders.

The poems too make much use of human characters and of imagery drawn from the human body, and many of them deal with the world of chaos and deceit. Even in the early odes, where the old-fashioned form and the "sublime" style imply a more ambitious attempt to organize experience in the shape of eternal truth than is to be found elsewhere, Swift's real theme is the impossibility of succeeding in such an attempt. His muse is "deluding," poetry an "incurable Disease," an "equivocal Birth," and the whole undertaking a painful effort:

> In vain I strive to cross this spacious Main,
> In vain I tug and pull the Oar.

The "Ode to Sir William Temple" treats Temple, whom Swift no doubt admired sincerely as an example of wise and balanced living, as a second Adam who is to repair the Fall, and uses Marvell's image of the garden to make the point:

> You strove to cultivate a barren Court in vain,
> Your Garden's better worth your noble Pain,
> Hence Mankind fell, and here must rise again.[43]

But the poem as a whole does not show Temple's garden of retirement as a Paradise, an ordered epitome of existence like Nunappleton; the effect is not of diversity in unity but of diversity, with Temple as a hopeful exception to that general confusion which makes up most of the theme. Virtue, like truth, is fallen shattered into small states, never "seated in one single Breast," and never will be unless Temple can contrive it. All the stress is on our deceit and confusion, on "Juggler's Tricks" and "Dregs of Knowledge." In the "Ode to Sancroft" the bishop's "secret regular sphere" is misunderstood and appears of irregular motion to the "strong and num'rous" fools, and its effect in the poem is secondary to that made by such phrases as "our weak knowledge," "Opinion, dark, and blind," "contradiction's vortex," "crazy composition," and the recurring "giddy" and "giddily." In this poem Swift makes overt use of religious comparisons, and his sense of man's intellectual, moral, and spiritual confusion is most vividly expressed. In "To Mr. Congreve," again, the scattered sunbeams, the sun obscured by froth or by swarming insects, the lives of fools which are delusion and "a sort of dreams," are the strongest impressions left upon our minds. The strained attempt to write in terms of the single and simple truth was soon given up as itself delusion, and in the verses written in 1693 on the occasion of Temple's illness Swift abandons once for all the muse who is

> Kindled while reason sleeps, but quickly flies,
> Like antic shapes in dreams, from waking eyes.

With a relief which his readers must share, he ends the poem briskly:

> There thy enchantment broke, and from this hour
> I here renounce thy visionary pow'r:
> And since thy essence on my breath depends,
> Thus with a puff the whole delusion ends.[44]

The contrast between the tugging of the oar in the early poems and the easy movement of the less ambitious ones which follow can leave little doubt that he was right.

The later poems revert, for the most part, to a satiric presentation of disorder. The images of confusion and deceit which fill the Odes now find their proper place, as in "The Bubble," a description of that period of the South Sea project when man's normal susceptibility to delusion was so oddly heightened. Here we meet again the cheating jugglers, the appearance of a shilling in a vessel of water, when "The Liquid Medium cheats your Sight," the ambitious and deluded Icarus, the delirious mariner. On its smaller scale, it accurately evokes the world of *A Tale of a Tub,* and there are many poems in which our disorderly world is presented in something nearer its usual state, sometimes charmingly as in "The Furniture of a Woman's Mind" or "A Description of the Morning," sometimes with the deliberate unpleasantness of "The Progress of Beauty" or "The Lady's Dressing Room." Often the intention is plainly anti-romantic, and here Swift's claim to moral purpose in his verses is most obviously justified. He will have no short cuts, no false pretense of order or goodness or beauty where none exists; better to face the muddle and imperfection of human life as it really is. Romance, with its blindness to what human beings are like, its simplification of motives, is as much a distortion of reality as Stoicism or Aeolism, and in its way as dangerous. Phillis, the unfortunate heroine of "The Progress of Love," runs away with John the Butler because

> It was her Fate; must be forgiven;
> For Marriages are made in Heaven,

and leaves a letter for her parents:

> 'Tis always done, Romances tell us,
> When Daughters run away with Fellows.

But Phillis's rarefied notions soon vanish when she has to face reality, and having no more adequate ideas to support her she quickly "falls into Matter" until at the end of the poem she and John can thus be described:

> They keep at Stains the old blue Boar,
> Are Cat and Dog, and Rogue and Whore.[45]

Again and again Swift deliberately presents disorderly reality and rejects spurious romantic or poetic interpretations, which impose upon reality a false order achieved only by omission. "The Progress of Poetry" throws the poetic cant of Pegasus and Hippo-crene into the existing background of Grub Street poetry, but more usual in Swift is the kind of theme he treats in "The Progress of Love," where the cult of unreality is more clearly re-lated to immorality. "The Progress of Beauty" is perhaps the best example, because it blends Swift's frequent attack on literary ro-manticism with more overtly serious purpose, and shows the "moral view" that lies behind his parodies of poetic diction. On one level, the poem is a literary *jeu d'esprit,* an extended conceit of the "diminishing" kind, in which the conventional comparison of the chaste lady with the pure Diana is reversed and as many parallels as possible are found between the unchaste Celia and the consequently unchaste moon, for

> 'Twixt earthly Femals and the Moon
> All Parallells exactly run.[46]

It is to be compared with such contemporary works as Gay's *The Shepherd's Week,* though Swift's precise reversal of a con-ventional compliment has the sharper wit; in each case, the charming unreality of a poetic convention is being neatly broken. But the moral theme of the poem is clear enough: Celia, when once her face is repaired, is "the Wonder of her Sex"; "rotting

Celia" is mistaken for a "lovely Nymph," and takes her place among the beauties of love poetry. Corinna, of "A Beautiful Young Nymph Going to Bed," named like Celia after the exquisite creatures of pastoral, is similarly treated. If poets could see the truth about Celia and Corinna they would be silenced, for in them the physical corruption which is a mark of their moral corruption has been covered by paint and poetic convention:

> The bashful Muse will never bear
> In such a Scene to interfere.[47]

Perhaps the best comment on the "moral view" of such poems as these is a passage from Montaigne, part of his attempt to "trample this humane pride" by showing man's uniqueness in evil:

. . . Let us moreover observe, that man is the onely creature, whose wants offends his owne fellowes, and he alone that in naturall actions must withdraw and sequester himselfe from those of his owne kinde. Verely it is an effect worthie consideration, that the skilfullest masters of amorous dalliances appoint for a remedie of venerian passions, a free and full survay of the bodie, which one longeth and seeks-after: and that to coole the longing and aswage the heat of friendship, one need but perfectly view and throughly consider what he loveth.

. . . It is not bashfulnesse so much, as art and foresight makes our Ladies so circumspect and unwilling to let us come into their closets before they are fully readie, and throughly painted, to come abroad, and show themselves.

Whereas in other creatures, there is nothing but we love, and pleaseth our senses: so that even from their excrements and ordure, we draw not only dainties to eat, but our richest ornaments and perfumes.[48]

Of these moral and anti-romantic poems, "The Lady's Dressing-Room," "Cassinus and Peter," and "Strephon and Chloe" are usually regarded as the most offensive; but they are also, if taken together, the most openly moral, even didactic, in intention. "Cassinus and Peter," subtitled "A Tragical Elegy," is less developed than "Strephon and Chloe," but the subject in both is essentially the same: a highly romantic young man, accustomed to think of his lady in terms of pastoral love poetry, as a goddess or a nymph, suddenly discovers that like himself she is "meer mortal Flesh," and is flung from one extreme of unreality to another. Cassinus and the hero of "The Lady's Dressing-Room"

150

end in obsession, their imaginations so sickened by the realization that their nymphs are after all as subject as they are themselves to physical needs and limitations that they can no longer look on any woman without horror. Their unbalanced behavior, their inability to come to terms with reality, is more clearly and powerfully represented in the similar predicament of Lemuel Gulliver, who is unable, after his last voyage, to bear the smell of humanity. Strephon, of "Strephon and Chloe," is another idealizing lover who feels himself too gross to approach "so high a Nymph."

> For, as he view'd his Person round,
> Meer mortal Flesh was all he found. . . .
> Can such a Deity endure
> A mortal human Touch impure?

His wedding is described in terms of the conventional epithalamium, with Venus and her Cupids and sparrows:

> Imprimis, at the Temple Porch
> Stood Hymen with a flaming Torch.
> The smiling Cyprian Goddess brings
> Her infant Loves with purple Wings.

But this is the end of romantic beauty; at Chloe's gross behavior, which her husband quickly copies, goddesses, shepherds, and "romantick Flights" are over, and

> The little Cupids hov'ring round
> (As Pictures prove) with Garlands crown'd,
> Abasht at what they saw and heard,
> Flew off, nor evermore appear'd.

The conclusion here is fully brought out; it is that

> fine Ideas vanish fast,
> While all the gross and filthy last,[49]

and that therefore marriage should be built on a firm foundation. Both parties are wrong, Strephon for romantically ignoring flesh and blood, Chloe for considering nothing else. Strephon should have married for more solid reasons, for sense and wit and decency, and Chloe should "after Marriage, practise more Decorum than she did before." Indeed both should face the facts of human nature, neither forgetting nor wallowing in the physical. There is no answer to the troubles of mankind but in a compromise with reality. The true positive of all these poems lies outside them, in Vanessa's "Decency of Mind," in the "happy Composition" Biddy Floyd, in the merit of Stella, contrasted in "To Stella" with "Chloe, Sylvia, Phillis, Iris," in the charming picture of Mrs. Cope, "Equal to all in Care and Love,"

> Soft'ning with Songs to Son or Daughter,
> The persecution of cold Water.[50]

In his "Letter to a Young Lady" Swift tells her that hers was "a match of Prudence and common Good-liking, without any mixture of that ridiculous Passion which has no Being but in Play-Books and Romances," but he knew too that society required "a little grain of the Romance."[51]

But the anti-romantic poems have a wider application than that of a proper attitude towards marriage and towards relations between the sexes. In them a particular and well-defined situation is examined as an illustration of a general truth about mankind. The physical impact is strong, and much physical detail is given, because that is part of the theme; the human situation is strikingly embodied in particular persons. Elsewhere in the poems the human body is used not illustratively but in the course of personification; this use is found in the odes, before Swift's resolution to enter the world of flesh and blood, of Corinna and Vanbrugh and Baucis and Philemon. In the "Ode to the Athenian Society," Philosophy is pictured as a woman made ridiculous by ages of fools and madmen, overdressed in farthingale and commode, top-knot and ruff, and now to be restored to her true simple beauty. In the "Ode to Sancroft," Religion is similarly personified, but here with a further turn to the thought: the "wild reformers" have contrived

> To tear Religion's lovely face;
> Strip her of ev'ry ornament and grace,
> In striving to wash off th' imaginary paint:
> Religion now doth on her death-bed lie.[52]

Here we approach the theme of *A Tale of a Tub;* it is true that mankind always tends to obscure and confuse the simple truth, as though with paint and elaborate clothes, but in striving to eradicate such prejudices we are still in their power, for the paint we think we see may be imaginary and we may end in the destruction of meaning and life, as the Author of *A Tale of a Tub* so often and so proudly does. Some beauty is real; not all red and white is produced by the paint of Corinna and Celia. The struggle against deception is one that must be conducted with the greatest care, for some of our aberrations from truth and reason are part of our very nature and condition, and we must not strip away too much in our search, must neither kill nor succumb to the body and its deceits. There are matters in which our passions inevitably control our reason, and even self-love, love of fame, and such irrational affections can be an incitement to virtue. Swift well knew "to what dangerous Heights some Men have proceeded" under the notion of prejudices, and in his hands the metaphor of the human body was developed into an image of considerable subtlety and complexity of suggestion, indicating at one and the same time the necessity and the hazard of the search for truth. The canceled passage from "On Poetry: A Rapsody," which describes man as "A mingled Mass of Good and Bad," sums up the view of humanity which is implicit in all Swift's moral writings. Arbuthnot, in his poem "Know Yourself," based on Pascal's *Entretien avec Saci,* presents a similar picture of man, but goes on, like Pascal, to resolve the contrasts and confusions, "Those jarring Truths which Human Art beguile," in the light of revelation which alone can explain the marks of man's birth. Swift too, though less explicitly, presents the same solution in *A Tale of a Tub* and *Gulliver's Travels,* but it is typical of him that his answer is given not in abstract terms but in the figure of a man, in Martin or in the good human beings, the least corrupted Yahoos, encountered by Gulliver. Whether in the form of single images or illustrations, or in the extended symbols of the Brobdingnagians or the Yahoos, it is in terms of the human body that Swift communicates most powerfully with his readers, because these are the terms in which his ideas can be most fully explored and conveyed.

153

Chapter VII
ANIMAL RATIONIS CAPAX

Gulliver's Travels is Swift's most complete and most masterly summing-up of the nature of man and of his proper behavior in a difficult world. As in so much of his writing, he works partly through parody, parody of travel literature and its authors, parody of the conclusions of the philosophic voyagers; but here as in *A Tale of a Tub*, the anti-romantic poems, or the *Modest Proposal*, parody is only a means to a moral end, serving, especially in the fourth voyage, to make Swift's point in the most economical way by a sharp reversal of the findings common in travels to Utopia. The "Voyage to the Houyhnhnms" is so much the most striking and effective that it has often been considered in isolation, but in fact it is the climax towards which the whole work moves. Swift claimed, in his humorous but wholly serious letter to Pope, that the *Travels* in its entirety was built upon the same "great foundation of misanthropy, though not in Timon's manner," and it is true that a consistent purpose is visible throughout. Even the "Voyage to Laputa," once scorned as untidy, superficial, boring, a book of left-overs, can now be seen in its proper eighteenth century context as highly relevant to Swift's general purpose.[1] The whole of *Gulliver's Travels*, though it is timeless in its vision of the unchanging condition of man, is at the same time contemporary, presenting humanity in the particular situation of Swift's scientific, system-making, Deistic, and rationalistic age. Compared with *A Tale of a Tub*, the *Travels* is a model of clarity and order, but it is more inclusive than the earlier work, for Swift's perfect choice of vehicle enables him to deal without confusion, often in the same incident or character, with science, philosophy, politics, morals. The third voyage is conceived in terms of contemporary science, but it has also political connotations and relevance to Swift's primary theme of the proper activity of man; the voyages to Lilliput and Brobdingnag are moral and political, but Swift's chosen allegory of the giants and pygmies, the enormous and the microscopic, has great significance for the new scientific age. Book IV is less concerned with science or with politics, for here we have reached the primary theme itself, and Swift treats openly of the different attitudes to man which underlie differences on the political or scientific level; but the moral lesson, with its basis in Christian tradition, is related to the ideas of Hobbes and Locke, Shaftesbury and Bolingbroke and Descartes, and the progressive and Deistic perfectionism of the philosophic voyagers. Satiric method can never, in Swift, be considered apart from his theme, but here form and content are even more beautifully integrated than in his other work. The "Voyage to Laputa," it is true, is a partial exception, but even here commentators have in the past exaggerated its untidiness and its episodic quality. Miss Nicolson and Miss Mohler have demonstrated the unity of theme which had been lost to the readers of the nineteenth and twentieth centuries, and it is not, I think, special pleading to suggest that here as in *A Tale of a Tub* an air of confusion and wrongheadedness is part of the theme, for the Laputans have plunged into unreality as delightedly as the author of the *Tale*. Structurally it is perhaps a fault to revert to another and earlier method in the midst of an ostensibly factual and sober work, but the psychological effect of this book, placed as it is before the "Voyage to the Houyhnhnms," is well calculated.

The satiric basis of the voyages to Lilliput and Brobdingnag is the conception known as relative size, and regarded purely as a satiric device this is apt and successful: man is seen more clearly and with more detachment when seen from a far lower or far higher physical position. But Swift's methods never can be regarded purely as satiric devices, and in these first voyages he is setting his readers into the context of eighteenth century insecurity. For this is the age of the telescope and the microscope, displaying so excitingly and yet so alarmingly the huge spaces around man, planets perhaps with other living beings, and the world of insects beneath him, tiny yet, to its inhabitants, as infinite as man's world is to himself. The literature of the early eighteenth century is full of awed references to the revelations of these two machines: to the disconcerting animal world of the sceptical Raleigh or Montaigne, incomprehensible to man, are added these other planes of being, the life of the insects and the

155

life of the possibly inhabited worlds. "Relative size" is an aspect of the atmosphere of relativity in which man found himself, no longer the center of the universe but, perhaps, as unimportant and absurd as the insects, who no doubt believe themselves to be valuable creatures. "I dare engage," says the giant king, speaking of Gulliver's race, "these Creatures have their Titles and Distinctions of Honour; they contrive little Nests and Burrows, that they call Houses and Cities; they make a Figure in Dress and Equipage; they love, they fight, they dispute, they cheat, they betray."[2] Similarly Voltaire, later in the century, brought to earth from Saturn the giant Micromégas, who strides unaware across the world until he chances to look through a diamond and sees the tiny animalcules who are men and women, as the scientists had seen through the first microscopes the teeming life of leaf and puddle. Many men of the period were disconcerted by these new discoveries; many wrote of the wonders newly displayed and thought uneasily of the relation of these things to the position of man. Glanvill felt that the new knowledge gave more grounds for his "fear, that we scarce yet see anything as it is," since it is now even more plain that "our Senses extremely deceive us in their reports, and informations." But only Swift saw how relativity could be used, not merely to exhilarate or to shock, but to express in contemporary terms a moral view of man; only Swift turned the idea of man the insect into the clear-sighted condemnation of the King of Brobdingnag: "I cannot but conclude the Bulk of your Natives, to be the most pernicious Race of little odious Vermin that Nature ever suffered to crawl upon the Surface of the Earth."[3] In Swift's hands, what the microscope reveals is related to the ancient Christian and Judaic vision of proud and insignificant man, to Job and Ecclesiastes and Corinthians, to the grasshoppers of Isaiah and to the serpents and snails of the Psalms. The pride shaken by relativity is essentially the same as the pride of the "wicked" of the Old Testament; it is vanity and delusion.

But the denunciation of man by the giant King can only be accepted as the climax of Swift's insect imagery because it has been prepared for with such care and skill. Throughout the first

156

two books there is a steady accumulation of hints and pressures, slight in themselves but preparing us gradually for the King's response to Gulliver's eager praise of European man. The insect and animal suggestions at first are harmless, even charming; in Book I Gulliver feels a small creature, "something alive moving on my left Leg," which turns out to be "a human Creature not six Inches high," one of the Lilliputians whom he calls, at first, "the Creatures." Actual insect reference is hardly necessary in Book I, for we take up our position with Gulliver and naturally regard these tiny human beings much as we would particularly accomplished mice. Much of the effect of relativity is gained through the description of the Lilliputians' own animals, their tiny sheep and geese, "and so the several Gradations downwards, till you come to the smallest, which, to my Sight, were almost invisible."[4] But in Book II the comparison must be more firmly made, for here we must be gradually detached from Gulliver, and must look at him, as representative of mankind, from the point of view of the Brobdingnagians, seeing him as before we had seen the Lilliputians. Accordingly Gulliver is to the giants a "small dangerous Animal" like a weasel, as alarming as a toad or a spider: he fears that the children may torment him as ours do "Sparrows, Rabbits, young Kittens, and Puppy-Dogs." He is carried about by an affectionate monkey, who "took me for a young one of his own Species,"[5] and petted by the giant ladies as if he were something quite inhuman. At best he is a pet, at worst one of a "Race of little odious Vermin," and he is so insignificant that the giants find it difficult to recognize him as a rational creature, though in Book I Gulliver himself had quickly seen that the Lilliputians, small as they were, were human. The charm of insect-like man gives way to the frightened malignancy of the small beast, weasel, toad, or vermin, and as the animal world steadily closes us in we see ourselves, in Gulliver, as the animal man.

Relativity provides Swift, too, with a means of stressing the effect on the mind and character of such physical accidents as size, so that we gain the impression that man's intellectual and moral achievement is to a considerable extent dependent on his physical nature and situation. All the characters in Books I and

157

II are subject to the influence of bodily circumstance on mental qualities. The Lilliputian mind is precise, but petty and limited, just as their vision is; Gulliver tells us with the accuracy of a scientific observer reporting on the fly's "microscopic eye": "Nature hath adapted the Eyes of the Lilliputians to all Objects proper for their View: They see with great Exactness, but at no great Distance."[6] They are neat, efficient, and in their narrow, insect-like way well adapted to their environment, but the arrival of the giant Gulliver brings out their most cruel and treacherous qualities in their efforts to assert themselves, and, with the necessary exception of the lord who warns Gulliver of his danger, they show neither generosity nor gratitude.[7] Despite all that Gulliver has done for them, the Emperor and his Empress—the grandiloquent titles are typical—harbor a malicious resentment for the offenses given to their petty dignity, and Gulliver is finally sentenced to be blinded, though this is represented as an act of great clemency on the Emperor's part. All this is, of course, partly a comment on the immorality of man as a political animal, for one aspect of the insect-like, organized efficiency of Lilliput is political, and this comment is carried further in Book II, in the giant King's opinion of European behavior and also in the sharp contrast between him and the Emperor. The Emperor has no regard for the ordinary human obligations where his schemes of wealth and power are concerned, whereas the King sees cruelty as no more justified in public matters than it is in dealing with private persons. Gulliver, for his part, is at his most attractive, and at his most consistent, in Book I, behaving towards his small captors with great humanity and kindness, and his own gratitude and constancy throw into relief the small-minded selfishness of the Emperor:

Once I was strongly bent upon Resistance: For while I had Liberty, the whole Strength of that Empire could hardly subdue me, and I might easily with Stones pelt the Metropolis to Pieces: But I soon rejected that Project with Horror, by remembering the Oath I had made to the Emperor, the Favours I received from him, and the high Title of Nardac he conferred upon me. Neither had I so soon learned the Gratitude of Courtiers, to persuade myself that his Majesty's present Severities acquitted me of all past Obligations.[8]

158

Yet this same Gulliver in Book II becomes very like a Lilliputian himself, for in his new situation magnanimity is impossible and he feels a constant need to insist on "the Dignity of human Kind" by behavior which he later recognizes as absurd. After being ignominiously carried off by the pet monkey, he tells the King:

And as for that monstrous Animal with whom I was so lately engaged, (it was indeed as large as an Elephant) if my Fears had suffered me to think so far as to make Use of my Hanger (looking fiercely, and clapping my Hand upon the Hilt as I spoke) when he poked his Paw into my Chamber, perhaps I should have given him such a Wound, as would have made him glad to withdraw it with more Haste than he put it in. This I delivered in a firm Tone, like a Person who was jealous lest his Courage should be called in Question. However, my Speech produced nothing else besides a loud Laughter.[9]

This conceited posturing little creature is a different person from the kindly, humble Gulliver of Book I, so much has his character changed with his physical situation. In Brobdingnag he is constantly subjected to great danger both to life and to character from causes in themselves trifling, and the resulting sense of the precariousness of human life and virtue is reinforced by his account of an old Brobdingnagian treatise which he found in the possession of Glumdalclitch's governess, "a grave elderly Gentlewoman, who dealt in Writings of Morality and Devotion." Gulliver's condescending attitude towards this "little old Treatise" warns us that we are to take the passage seriously. The book treats, he says, "of the Weakness of Human kind; and is in little Esteem except among Women and the Vulgar." Certainly the ideas put forward are not new or progressive, being familiar to us as to Swift from countless of the more old-fashioned moral works of the seventeenth century. But though the ideas are trite, and naïvely expressed, the writer's intention, to bring down man's pride by showing him as, "in his own Nature," a weak and helpless animal, is a serious matter. Montaigne is an obvious source, and Godfrey Goodman's *The Fall of Man, or the Corruption of Nature* (1616), a work which presents in the form of a straightforward treatise the view of mankind which Swift found it necessary to express in the poems and *Gulliver's Travels* through at-

159

tack and indirection, makes much of man's natural weakness. Such notions are likely to be dismissed by Gulliver, who is at this point inclined to be complacent about human achievement and is a great lover of mankind. For the writer "went through all the usual Topicks of European Moralists; shewing how diminutive, contemptible, and helpless an Animal was Man in his own Nature; how unable to defend himself from Inclemencies of the Air, or the Fury of wild Beasts: How much he was excelled by one Creature in Strength, by another in Speed, by a third in Foresight, by a fourth in Industry."[10] The author is also convinced of the physical degeneracy of giant man, and believes that at one time he was "not so liable to Destruction from every little Accident of a Tile falling from a House, or a Stone cast from the Hand of a Boy, or of being drowned in a little Brook." From all this were drawn "several moral Applications useful in the Conduct of Life," but Gulliver thinks it needless to repeat them, and shows how ill he has learned the lesson of relativity when he assumes that the large size of the giants, and of their stones and their brooks, invalidates the author's arguments and so, by implication, the view of European moralists that fallen man is insecure, weak, a stranger on the earth. For the author of the treatise is really underlining the theme of the first two voyages, the lesson which the King, with his firm sane moral standards, is so quick to draw from his contemplation of diminutive man: "he observed, how contemptible a Thing was human Grandeur, which could be mimicked by such diminutive Insects as I."[11]

The giants themselves are the third element in the complicated relationships of Lilliput and Brobdingnag, and it is in them that the physical or animal aspects of humanity are most forcibly thrust upon our attention. Their enormous bodies are insisted upon; there are descriptions of their skin and beards and gestures and of the horrors of disease and dirt in the beggars, infested by vermin whose limbs Gulliver could see "much better than those of an European Louse through a Microscope; and their Snouts with which they rooted like Swine."[12] The nastiness of these creatures brings additional force to the King's condemnation of the little odious vermin, man, and the reference to a microscope

160

relates the Brobdingnagians to ourselves, as does the magnifying glass which, Gulliver supposes, would make the fine skin of English ladies look as coarse as that of the giants. The behavior of the Queen's maids of honor brings us close to the anti-romantic poems with their plea for a decent reticence; in both the human body is being used deliberately, not as an outlet for physical disgust in Swift himself but to present a moral truth. The Brobdingnagians are akin to the Yahoos in that they embody the physical and its senses and passions, but they differ from the Yahoos in the same way that Gulliver does; they are not a part of man, but man. In their case the physical is deliberately stressed because through his handling of relativity Swift intends to impress upon us man's weakness and limitations and above all the power of flesh and blood which must always be reckoned with. But the Brobdingnagians are not simple creatures like the Yahoos, or even like the Lilliputians. In Lilliput, everyone is much the same: one can generalize easily enough about the Lilliputian character. In Brobdingnag, there is considerable variation among the people, and as individuals they are more complex than any of the creatures of the *Travels* except the Europeans of Book IV. The giants can be cruel through selfishness and avarice, like Gulliver's first owner the farmer, who wears him out by constant showing and then makes haste to sell him before he dies; they can be jealous like Gulliver's enemy the dwarf, or playfully lascivious like the maids of honor, or stupid through vanity like the scholars. They are, in fact, very like ourselves, easily swayed by self-love and the desires and passions common to humanity. But it is not only our tendency to brutishness and selfishness that is displayed in them; they also possess human warmth, sympathy, and affection; the animal side of man is shown in its capacity for good as well as for evil, and the huge size of the giants can impress upon us not only animality but expansive good humour, magnanimity, and a breadth of moral understanding. The motherliness of the farmer's wife, the graciousness of the Queen, the loyal, protective affection of Gulliver's young "nurse," are attractive examples of human goodness, and Glumdalclitch in particular, so enormous and yet so delicately understanding of the feelings of her difficult charge,

161

is as admirable an illustration of the value of well-regulated affections in human relationships as is the delightful Mrs. Robert Cope of "The First of April." The people of Brobdingnag have the same bearing on human behavior as the government of Brobdingnag has upon human states: there is nothing utopian or ideal about them, but they are the best that man can attain. They have come to terms with reality, and in them mind and body have established a fruitful relationship. They are not interested in abstract reasoning—"as to Ideas, Entities, Abstractions and Transcendentals, I could never drive the least Conception into their Heads"[13]—they are well aware of man's limitations and attempt only what they are capable of. Their reasoning powers are used for practical and benevolent purposes, to ameliorate human conditions, to "make two Ears of Corn, or Two Blades of Grass to grow upon a Spot of Ground where only one grew before."[14]

The wisest and best of the Brobdingnagians is the King, who, as Gulliver admits, is "a Prince of excellent Understanding," but whose intelligence exercises itself strictly within the limits of a firmly moral conception of life. It is because of this that Gulliver regards him as narrow-minded; his contempt for what he has heard of Europe is the result of moral condemnation. No amount of achievement or ingenuity can impress the King if it leads to evil results, to cruelty and inhumanity, and Gulliver is accordingly moved to tell him that this attitude of contempt and disgust "did not seem answerable to those excellent Qualities of Mind, that he was Master of."[15] His own government is essentially moral, based on his human and kingly duties to the governed and concerned with their welfare, and his comments on Europe are expressed in terms of practical morality. He is quick to see what Gulliver will not admit, that humanity on the whole is always ready to distort what seems, in the abstract, a good political scheme, through bribery and self-interest, and it is because he is aware of the need to prevent this that he is such a good ruler. "It doth not appear," he says at last, "from all you have said, how any one Perfection is required towards the Procurement of any one Station among you; much less that Men are ennobled on account of their Virtue, that Priests are advanced for their Piety or Learning, Soldiers for their Conduct or Valour, Judges for their Integrity, Senators for the Love of their Country, or Counsellors for their Wisdom."[16] And it is a mark of his tolerance and charity that he delivers his judgment on the little vermin while gently stroking their representative, the "little friend Grildrig" to whom he shows such affectionate forbearance. The King has, indeed, attained that unillusioned view of man which Swift advocated and tried himself to achieve; his sober clear sight into the motives of mankind is to him a reason not for hatred but for pity and charity and practical help. The clearest instance of his moral thinking and his unfailing humanity is his response to Gulliver's offer to give him the secret of gunpowder: "although few Things delighted him so much as new Discoveries in Art or in Nature; yet he would rather lose Half his Kingdom than be privy to such a Secret." This time even the realistic and tolerant King is horrified at Gulliver's revelation of human depravity, and "amazed how so impotent and groveling an Insect as I (these were his Expressions) could entertain such inhuman Ideas, and in so familiar a Manner as to appear wholly unmoved at all the Scenes of Blood and Desolation, which I had painted as the common Effects of those destructive Machines."[17] Gulliver's comment is "A Strange Effect of narrow Principles and short Views!" But after all, he considers, the remoteness of Brobdingnag necessarily produces "many Prejudices, and a certain Narrowness of Thinking; from which we and the politer Countries of Europe are wholly exempted. And it would be hard indeed, if so remote a Prince's Notions of Virtue and Vice were to be offered as a Standard for all Mankind."[18] Through the disapproval of Gulliver we are made aware that the compassionate King of Brobdingnag is Swift's positive standard for man, and this hint is repeated by Gulliver in the twelfth and final chapter of the "Voyage to the Houyhnhnms," where Gulliver, now obsessed by the pure reason of the alien Houyhnhnm race, and loathing all men, whom he erroneously equates with Yahoos, grudgingly admits that "the least corrupted are the Brobdingnagians, whose wise Maxims in Morality and Government, it would be our Happiness to observe."[19] One can put it that this indirect commendation is all that

Swift's ironic method itself will allow him to make, but it is truer to say that the ironic method itself is the result of Swift's reluctance to put forward an unambiguous standard. For always he is saying not simply, "This is what man should aim at" but rather "This is all that man can aim at." Limitation, compromise, humility, must be inherent in his positives, and so they must be presented indirectly, almost grudgingly, as the best that can be had. Gulliver's words, while they express the supreme irony that in aiming too high he has fallen too low, and is blind to achievable goodness, are also accurate: the Brobdingnagians are not perfect; they are, precisely, the least corrupted of fallen humanity. But this limitation by no means implies despair. The King and the Queen and Glumdalclitch show that the best that corrupt mankind can attain to is high indeed, but that it can only be reached by a humble realism and a recognition that the passions, senses, instinctive affections, if guided by reason working within a moral context, can issue in true human goodness. Swift's ability to embody ideas in the persons of men and women stands him here in good stead, for the warmth and reality, the charm and the human responsibility, of the best of the Brobdingnagians can hardly fail not only to convey his conception of the goodness proper to man but to convince us that it is both admirable and true.

But of course we can only see the Brobdingnagian virtue, and its meaning in the whole structure, when we have read to the end of the *Travels*. The immediate effect of the first two books is of growing unease, not of acceptance of a standard, for the compromise standard has to be worked out when all the creatures are assembled and when what at first seems to be an absolute good— the life of the Houyhnhnms—has been shown to be a false simplification. The world of Brobdingnag is solid and sane, but we are not yet allowed to rest at ease in it. Our amusement and annoyance with the Lilliputians and their antlike organization, and our approval of the decency of unpolitical man as displayed in Gulliver, are turned to uncertainty as we find ourselves in the shifting world of relativity and discover that Gulliver is far from being a norm of behavior and that according to circumstances he can be as mean-minded and vain as a Lilliputian, and even more inhuman. Moreover, Gulliver, we begin to see, is apt to draw very wrong conclusions from his experiences. Even in Lilliput, where he is seen to best advantage, he too readily accepts Lilliputian standards, and talks quite seriously of the great nobles, and of the honors he has received in this ridiculous little state. For instance: "I should not have dwelt so long upon this Particular, if it had not been a Point wherein the Reputation of a great Lady is so nearly concerned; to say nothing of my own; although I had the Honour to be a Nardac, which the Treasurer himself is not; for all the World knows he is only a Clumglum, a Title inferior by one Degree, as that of a Marquess is to a Duke in England; yet I allow he preceded me in right of his Post."[20] In Brobdingnag, his reactions to the King's opinions are quite clearly wrong, and he learns nothing from his visit except to be ill at ease at home, fancying his friends and relatives undersized, and looking at them "as if they had been Pigmies, and I a Giant." In a little time, he came to an understanding with his family and friends, but his wife protested he should never go to sea any more. She was in the right, for Gulliver's malleable character and his aptitude for enthusiastic misunderstanding were to lead to worse and more permanent difficulty after his last voyage, when the furthest accommodation he reports is that "I began last Week to permit my Wife to sit at Dinner with me, at the farthest End of a long Table; and to answer (but with the utmost Brevity) the few Questions I asked her."[21] Thus the qualities necessary to a satiric mouthpiece—the inconsistency, the palpable wrongheadedness and absurdity, that lack, indeed, of a positive character, so essential if ironic comment is to be made on any but the simplest scale—are turned with the greatest precision and economy to further purpose.

The insecurity and uncertainty of direction we feel at the end of the "Voyage to Brobdingnag" is heightened in Book III. The success of this book is not at all easy for a modern reader to gauge. Its sharp contrast in method, with the grotesque figures of the Laputans and the excursions into magic and immortality, certainly breaks the atmosphere of moral realism which pervades the voyages to Lilliput, Brobdingnag, and Houyhnhnm-land; even the rational horses belong to a world of morality, not of fantasy. This third book, the latest written, would be, by us, the least missed. But on the other hand the fantasy world of Laputa, in its madness and delusion, still further shakes our wits and our confidence before the final resolution of Book IV, and the Laputan lunacies have, after all, a moral connotation as we can see if we remember *A Tale of a Tub*. But for us, to whom the scientific outlook is a commonplace, it is not so easy to see the "Voyage to Laputa" in terms of modern vice and traditional virtue, and we find it less striking than the other voyages, where moral problems are more overtly considered though their presentation is influenced by contemporary thinking. Only the episode of the Struldbrugs of Luggnagg, unencumbered as it is by topical satire, strikes us with the immediate force and the moral emphasis of the second and fourth books, for to a modern reader scientific experiment is a less acceptable example of irrelevant thinking than are the speculations of Burnet or of Thomas Vaughan. Swift's opinion of the scientific achievement of his day is, in itself, inadequate, and considered as an attack on science the third book must seem wrongheaded and unfair. But considered as what it really is, an allegorical presentation of the evils of a frivolous attitude to life, it is consistent and effective, however unjust we may consider Swift's chosen allegory to be.

For the visit to Laputa itself, and to the subject land of Balnibarbi, has a more serious intention than the topical one of ridiculing the Royal Society. The flying island, though it has a precise relationship—even as to size—with William Gilbert's dipping-needle,[22] and though it uses Gilbert's idea "of the Earth's whole Body being but one great Magnet; and, lesser Magnets being so many Terrella's sympathising with the Whole," presents through this contemporary scientific interest a political philosophy and a comment on man's relation to nature which go beyond the merely topical: beyond particular scientific discoveries or the relation of the kingdoms of England and Ireland. The flying island, "the King's Demesn," in its devious and sensitive oblique movements, suggests the relationship of king and country. Laputa is ultimately dependent upon Balnibarbi, its motions only allowed by the magnetic quality of the "King's Dominions." It is this quality which has allowed the Laputan king to establish his power over the fixed land, but there is a reciprocal dependence, for if either side pressed its power too far the result would be general ruin. The King's last resource, in case of defiance from the populace of Balnibarbi, is to let the flying island drop upon their heads, but this, though it would certainly destroy both houses and men, would at the same time damage the adamant of Laputa itself.

Of all this the People are well apprized, and understand how far to carry their Obstinacy, where their Liberty or Property is concerned. And the King, when he is highest provoked, and most determined to press a City to Rubbish, orders the Island to descend with great Gentleness, out of a Pretence of Tenderness to his People, but indeed for fear of breaking the Adamantine Bottom; in which Case it is the Opinion of all their Philosophers, that the Load-Stone could no longer hold it up, and the whole Mass would fall to the Ground.[23]

As for the nobles and ministers, they are in part committed to the welfare of both lands, for while they attend at the Laputan court their estates lie on the continent below, so that they will never dare advise the King to make himself "the most absolute Prince in the Universe" by so ruthless and desperate a course. The balance of power, and the delicate relationships which subsist between a monarch and those whom he governs, could scarcely be better represented than by conditions in Laputa and Balnibarbi, and it is typical of Swift that these relationships, though given a color of respect for human life and liberties, are seen to be really dependent upon the exact adjustment of practical necessities; the self-love of each party is carried as far as it can go without that open conflict with the self-love of others which would bring it to destruction.

Further, the relation of the greater and lesser magnets, Laputa and Balnibarbi, suggests the limited usefulness of that understanding of the laws of the universe upon which the Newtonian era so prided itself, and which is one of the main objects of Swift's satiric comment in this book. The Laputan king, for all his knowledge of cosmic circumstance, for all the ingenuity of his flying island, is yet dependent upon the firm earth beneath him for

167

every movement Laputa can make; for all his theoretic achievement man is, in practice, dependent upon and circumscribed by other men and by laws of nature, of which he can take a certain limited advantage but which he can neither alter nor, finally, explain. The astronomers of Laputa, although they have written "large Systems concerning the Stone" whose movements control the course of the flying island, can give no better reason for the inability of Laputa to rise above four miles, or to move beyond the extent of the King's continental dominions, than the self-evident one "That the Magnetick Virtue does not extend beyond the Distance of four Miles, and that the Mineral which acts upon the Stone in the Bowels of the Earth, and in the Sea about Six Leagues distant from the Shoar, is not diffused through the whole Globe, but terminated with the Limits of the King's Dominions."[24] Their pursuit of second causes ends in inscrutable mystery, which their confident exposition can only conceal, not clarify. The allegory of Laputa and of Balnibarbi, "controlled by that which it alone controls," is indeed an epitome of the situation more fully explored in the detailed descriptions of the inhabitants of the flying island and of conditions on the mainland below; the neat, generalized relationships help us to find our way in the confusion of the Academy of Projectors and the alien clarities of the Laputan court.

The Laputans, though they are in human shape, are more obviously allegorical creatures than any in *Gulliver's Travels*. Their physical characteristics express their nature as do those of the Brobdingnagians or the Yahoos, but in a different way. Their effect is made, not through exaggeration or isolation, but through distortion, of the physical, and though by this means much of the force of Swift's greatest figures is lost, this is in itself part of the meaning, since the Laputans have indeed lost their human quality in their abnormal absorption in things remote from the concerns of men. They make little physical effect upon us, for their outer aspect is as unnatural, as purely emblematic, as that of a personification like Spenser's Occasion: "One of their Eyes turned inward, and the other directly up to the Zenith"[25] because they are completely absorbed in their own speculations and in the

168

study of the stars. Their interests are entirely abstract, and they see nothing of the everyday practical world, ignoring the knowledge of the senses as totally as Jack or the philosopher of *A Tale of a Tub*. The Laputan is "always so wrapped up in Cogitation, that he is in manifest Danger of falling down every Precipice, and bouncing his Head against every Post; and in the Streets, of jostling others, or being jostled himself into the Kennel."[26] Because they scorn the evidence of the senses, the Laputans are necessarily "very bad Reasoners,"[27] though very positive and dogmatic ones, for the senses are "so many Avenues to the Fort of Reason," which in them as in the mechanical operators of the spirit is wholly blocked up. These strange figures are akin not only to the mechanical operators but more closely to the spider-like world-makers. Like the author of *A Tale of a Tub,* they are less consistent than inclusive, summing up various departures from the middle way. One eye looks outward, but only to a remote world of abstractions where, in the regular motions of the heavens, mathematics and music join. One eye looks inward, to the mind where systems are spun out of a "Native Stock," not built up from that basis of observed fact which, however faulty our senses, is yet the only material upon which our reason can work constructively and practically. Laputan thinking produces results as flimsy and useless as a cobweb—Gulliver's ill-fitting suit, the devastated countryside of Balnibarbi.

The King and his court are devoted entirely to two subjects, music and mathematics, the most abstract of sciences. There is a topical reference, in that an interest in these "two eternal and immutable verities" and in the analogies between them serves to identify the Laputans as members of the Royal Society, but for centuries an interest in the relationship of mathematics and music had existed, so that it was by no means an exclusively contemporary concern. In the Middle Ages music, regarded as a mathematical science, had been one of the purest embodiments of unchanging law, and the Laputans with their absorption in music, mathematics, and astronomy, represent specifically the members of the Royal Society but more generally all those who believe that, by turning away from the impressions of the senses and the ordinary concerns of human nature they can ignore sublunary confusion and reach eternal truth. Swift's reference to the music of the spheres emphasizes this more general meaning; the Laputans spend hours at their instruments, preparing themselves to join in the music of the spheres, which they claim to be able to hear. Since mankind is traditionally deaf to this music because of the grossness of the senses through sin, the claim implies that the Laputans believe themselves to have escaped from such tyranny. To their impracticality is added the presumption of ignoring the inherited wisdom which sees man as a fallen creature separated, through his own fault, from the order, truth, and justice figured in the celestial harmony of the nine enfolded spheres.

The narrowness, even to inhumanity, of the Laputans is indeed stressed throughout. They have cut themselves off completely from all that is humanly creative and constructive. Even their food approaches as nearly as possible to the rarefied atmosphere in which they live, for their meat is carved into geometrical shapes and their poultry trussed up "into the Form of Fiddles."[28] Nor have they any conception of physical or sensuous beauty, since they see beauty only in mathematical abstractions, and judge not by sense impressions but by an arbitrary relation of animal forms to abstract shapes existing in their minds: "If they would, for Example, praise the Beauty of a Woman, or any other Animal, they describe it by Rhombs, Circles, Parallelograms, Ellipses, and other Geometrical Terms; or else by Words of Art drawn from Musick . . . the whole Compass of their Thoughts and Mind, being shut up within the two forementioned Sciences."[29] But the world of human beings cannot be adequately dealt with in mathematical terms, and their wives, as a consequence, have fallen into matter, escaping whenever possible into a life altogether physical and degraded, as exaggeratedly animal as that of their husbands is exaggeratedly intellectual. The King has no interest in "the Laws, Government, History, Religion, or Manners of the Countries"[30] Gulliver has visited, and his realm of Balnibarbi is chaotic. Gulliver "could not discover one Ear of Corn, or Blade of Grass"[31] except in a few places, during his journeys, and our minds revert to the kingdom of Brobdingnag, the land which has been called a "simple Utopia of abundance," where government is conducted with practical good will and a due regard for traditional wisdom, and where the King regards his task as one of promoting increase and life, making "two Ears of Corn, or two Blades of Grass, to grow where only one grew before." The Laputans, on the other hand, produce a world of death, and the results of their efforts are purely destructive because their aims are impossibly high and are unrelated to real conditions. Some day, they say, "a Palace may be built in a Week, of Materials so durable as to last for ever without repairing. All the Fruits of the Earth shall come to Maturity at whatever Season we think fit to chuse, and increase an Hundred Fold more than they do at present; with innumerable other happy Proposals."[32] In the meantime, houses are ruined, land uncultivated, and people starving, and the only result of Laputan enterprise on the prosperous estate of the old-fashioned Lord Munodi has been to destroy the mill which had long provided his family and tenants, in order to make way for one which should, on scientific principles, be better, but which somehow fails to work. Samuel Johnson sums up in similar terms the humanist sense of the Royal Society's irrelevance to true and living values:

When the philosophers of the last age were first congregated into the Royal Society, great expectations were raised of the sudden progress of useful arts; the time was supposed to be near, when engines should turn by a perpetual motion, and health be secured by the universal medicine; when learning should be facilitated by a real character, and commerce extended by ships which could reach their ports in defiance of the tempest.

But improvement is naturally slow. The Society met and parted without any visible diminution of the miseries of life. The gout and stone were still painful, the ground that was not ploughed brought no harvest, and neither oranges nor grapes would grow upon the hawthorn.[33]

That Munodi, the one successful landowner in Balnibarbi, should be a traditionalist is only to be expected; "being not of an enterprizing Spirit, he was content to go on in the old Forms; to live in the Houses his Ancestors had built, and act as they did in every Part of Life without Innovation."[34]

The activities of the members of the Academy of Projectors, though they involve experiment, are yet related to the abstract

171

thinking of the King. For the most part, they are based on some wrongheaded abstract conception, and are really examples of what Pope calls reasoning downward, taking "the High Priori Road"; they are aspects, therefore, of the great modern heresy of ignoring "the old Forms" and relying on a spider-like spinning of thought. By blending experiment and High Priori reasoning in the Academy at Lagado, Swift is able to show scientific "projects" as yet another example of that whole development of thinking which leads away from the ways of a Christian and humanist tradition, and Pope's lines would refer as well to the mathematicians of Laputa and the scientists of Lagado as they do to Hobbes, Descartes, Spinoza, and Samuel Clarke:

> Let others creep by timid steps, and slow,
> On plain Experience lay foundations low,
> By common sense to common knowledge bred,
> And last, to Nature's Cause through Nature led.[35]

Indeed one of the projects is an exact allegorical equivalent of the process of reasoning downward to, instead of upward from, the foundations of plain experience: "There was a most ingenious Architect who had contrived a new Method for building Houses, by beginning at the Roof, and working downwards to the Foundation; which he justified to me by the like Practice of those two prudent Insects the Bee and the Spider."[36] We are not told the results of this method, but in other cases the ideas of the projectors do not well stand up to experiment; for instance, the notion of "plowing the Ground with Hogs to save the Charges of Plows, Cattle, and Labour" results, "upon Experiment," in no crop and a great deal of trouble and expense.

The experiments and their results allow Swift to collect together various images which, as so often, express his meaning through producing a certain atmosphere which must affect our response to Laputa and Balnibarbi. These projects leave an impression of uselessness, dirt, ephemerality, or death; the Academicians present for our inspection a spider web, a hog rooting up acorns, a muddle of painters' colors, a dead dog. Their efforts are summed up in an illustrious member who has been given the title of "the Universal Artist," and who has been for thirty years

172

directing his followers in various ways of converting things into their opposites, thus turning the useful into the unusable and the vital into the atrophied. Air is made tangible and marble soft, land is sown with chaff and naked sheep are bred; and perhaps most exact of all as an epitome of the achievements of the Academy, the hooves of a living horse are being petrified. The projects of Lagado are, in fact, conducted in an atmosphere similar to that of *A Tale of a Tub,* an atmosphere of aimless activity, distorted values, and a perversion of things from their proper purpose even to the point of removing all life and meaning from them. The results produced are woolless sheep, dead dogs, horses whose living hooves are turned to stone. The mechanism of the *Tale* exists in Lagado too, in the machine which is to replace the thinking and creating mind of man and will, by pure chance, eventually produce "Books in Philosophy, Poetry, Politicks, Law, Mathematicks and Theology."[37] While the prevailing effect of the images we associate with Lilliput and, especially, Brobdingnag is of man and other animals as vigorous physical presences, the effect of Laputa and its subject kingdom is of a wilful abandoning of the physical and of the vital for the abstract, the mechanical, and the unproductive. The prevailing images here are not of real people and animals, even "little odious vermin," but of ruins, mechanical constructions, men who look like allegorical figures and women who are thought of as rhomboids or parallelograms. Animals are only negatively present, as in the pathetic horses and sheep of the Academy. Even Laputa itself is a mechanical device, and the flying island expresses not only the Laputans' desertion of the common earth of reality but their conversion of the universe to a mechanism and of living to a mechanical process.

From Lagado Gulliver makes his way to Glubbdubdrib, where again he is in a world of no-meaning, of delusion and death, darker and more shadowy than Laputa. In the palace of the sorcerer who is governor of the island he has a series of singularly uninformative interviews with the ghosts of the famous dead, and Alexander and Hannibal, who as conquerors and destroyers had little to recommend them to Swift, make particularly trivial replies. We are given a gloomy enough picture of both the ancient and the modern world, and upon this ghostly history follows the most somber episode of all, that of the Struldbrugs of Luggnagg, in which the lesson of Laputa with its naïve hopes, its misplaced ambition, and its eventual sterility is repeated with more open seriousness. A right sense of values, a proper attitude to living, is here suggested not through the handling of contemporary aims and habits of thought but through the figure of man, immortal yet still painfully recognizable, and perhaps owing some of its power and poignancy to Swift's own fear of death and, still more, of decay, of a lingering old age giving way at last to helpless lunacy. Gulliver, hearing of the immortals, cries out "as in a Rapture," exclaiming upon the wisdom and happiness which they must have achieved. They must, he says, "being born exempt from that universal Calamity of human Nature, have their Minds free and disingaged, without the Weight and Depression of Spirits caused by the continual Apprehension of Death,"[38] and he is only too willing to tell his hearers how he would plan his life, if he were a Struldbrug, to bring the greatest possible benefit to himself and his country. In fact, of course, the immortal and aged creatures, though free from the fear of death, are yet as full of fears and wretchedness as any other men: being what we are, we will always find occasion to display those vices which as human beings we will always have, however long we may live. The Struldbrugs certainly do not keep their minds free and disengaged, and for them the prospect of endless life does not conjure up visions of endless improvement in wisdom and virtue. They regard their immortality as a "dreadful Prospect" even as other men regard their death, and indeed they long to die as did the wretched Sibyl in Petronius's *Satyricon,* regarding with great jealousy those of their acquaintance who go "to an Harbour of Rest, to which they themselves never can hope to arrive."[39] Immortal man is still man, limited in his capacity for growth, sinful, fearful, dissatisfied; the somber simplicity of the passage, and indeed of the whole of the visit to Glubbdubdrib, is reminiscent of Johnson's methods rather than of Swift's, and the message is essentially similar. Gulliver, who has dreamed of being a king, a general, or a great lord, and now dreams of being a Struldbrug,

174

has to learn the same lesson as the Prince of Abyssinia: that life is a serious, difficult, and above all a moral undertaking, that whatever excuses we may find for ourselves, however we may dream of the greatness we could have achieved under other conditions, we will realize at last that humanity is always the same, and that there is no escape from our vices and our trivialities. Gulliver says that he grew "heartily ashamed of the pleasing Visions I had formed; and thought no Tyrant could invent a Death into which I would not run with Pleasure from such a Life,"[40] and that he would have been willing, if it had not been forbidden by the laws of Luggnagg, to send a couple of Struldbrugs to England to arm the people against that fear of death which is natural to mankind.

So the "Voyage to Laputa," which opens among a people essentially frivolous in its refusal to face the facts of human existence, ends face to face with inescapable reality. Laputa, where the search for the clarity of abstractions involves such confusion in the living world, seems at first merely hilarious and absurd, but as confusion turns to mechanism and destruction this remoteness and unreality becomes not only ludicrous but evil, and the countries about Laputa and Balnibarbi are seen to be places of superstition, sorcery, and tyranny, of ghosts and the corpselike immortals of Luggnagg. The voyage to illusion, the escape from facts, ends in a darker reality than any Gulliver has yet encountered. Gulliver himself, in this book, becomes a part of the world of illusion and distorted values. Already in the earlier voyages the shifting, inconsistent quality which Gulliver shares with all Swift's satiric mouthpieces has been made to contribute to effects of relativity, and to suggest the hold of physical circumstances over mankind. That he is, generally, a different man in Brobdingnag and in Lilliput is made into part of Swift's presentation of human nature. In the "Voyage to Laputa," any still surviving notion that Gulliver is a safe guide through these strange countries is ended. He ceases to have any character and, in effect, vanishes, so that for the most part the satire speaks directly to us; the "mouthpiece" performs no real function. The transparent account of "Tribnia, by the Natives called Langden," where "the Bulk of

175

the People consisted wholly of Discoverers, Witnesses, Informers, Accusers, Prosecutors, Evidences, Swearers,"[41] owes nothing to Gulliver, and would be quite inconceivable from what we have known of him before; in the second voyage he had "wished for the Tongue of Demosthenes or Cicero, that might have enabled me to celebrate the Praise of my own dear native Country in a Style equal to its Merits and Felicity."[42] Here he is being frankly used for ironic comment, as his exaggerated enthusiasm shows; in the description of Tribnia, he is not being used at all. From time to time he is given a momentary reality, but of the most perfunctory kind; there is no attempt to endow him even with the one or two dominant characteristics that he is given elsewhere. His approval of projects, or his tendency to dream about impossible situations instead of getting on with the business of living, his dismissal of obviously desirable political reforms as "wild impossible Chimaeras," are, quite openly, mentioned for satiric purposes of a very simple kind. The handling of Gulliver is in fact far less interesting, and his contribution is far slighter, than in any other book, probably because his function had been worked to its limits in the voyages already written, which included the "Voyage to the Houyhnhnms." But whether or not Swift planned it so, Gulliver's virtual lack of function, indeed of existence, in the "Voyage to Laputa" has a certain effectiveness in contributing to the atmosphere of meaningless activity and self-deceit, leading to a shadowy despair. The gradual undermining of the comparatively solid worlds of Lilliput and Brobdingnag was achieved partly through a shift in Gulliver's position; here he merges completely into his surroundings, and serves merely to describe what he sees, so that we cannot take him seriously as an interpreter. When he reappears in Book IV, we are well prepared to find that his function will not be a simple one either of sensible comment on the vagaries of a strange country, or of admiration for a Utopia, for we have accepted him as one of the many figures in the *Travels,* expressing meaning by his relationship to them, and no more exempt than they from satiric treatment. As a completion of the processes begun in Lilliput and Brobdingnag, and as a preparation for the resolution in Houyhnhnm-land, the Laputan voyage performs its task adequately, though without the formal elegance and neatness of the other books.

Of all the voyages, the fourth is perhaps the most satisfying, both in its fullness of content and in the completeness of its expression. It is also the voyage about which there has been most divergency of view, and though there is no longer any question of its being regarded, as it once was, as the splenetic outburst of a man consumed by hatred of "the Human Name, and Face," critical opinion is still divided on the question of Swift's precise meaning. It was formerly assumed that the Houyhnhnms were intended as perfected human beings whom man should try to copy, or alternatively as faultless rational creatures whose nobility serves to show up the evil of mankind. But if the Houyhnhnms are Swift's positive ideal, attainable by man or not, many difficulties arise; for this interpretation must mean that his satiric method is much more simple and direct than elsewhere, and that the attitude of mind is quite different from that which his other work has led us to expect. In recent years there has been increasing support for the view that Swift did not intend his Houyhnhnms as a simple positive standard, and various possible alternatives have been put forward.[43] Opinion varies, also, as to the success of this book; it is sometimes said that it fails to make its meaning effective and clear, and that Swift has mishandled his allegorical narrative and the creatures within it. But in fact it is, I believe, the most perfectly managed of all Swift's satires. Of course it is partly dependent on the earlier books for its success, but Swift takes full advantage of the meanings established, and the psychological effect made, in them, and in the "Voyage to the Houyhnhnms" he sums up, with the utmost economy of means, the suggestions made in Laputa, Lilliput, and Brobdingnag. In a way, it is a summing up of all his work, for it is his most complete and effective presentation of that central conviction from which his moral, political, and social views arise, a conviction about the nature of man. Implicit in all his work, this preoccupation here becomes explicit in the creatures of Houyhnhnm-land, in the Houyhnhnms themselves, the Yahoos, Gulliver, the Portuguese sea-captain Don Pedro, and, by association, the Brobdingnagians.

177

But though Swift's concern with the moral nature of man here becomes explicit, and is no longer seen through particular human activities such as science, politics, literature, it is still indirectly expressed. The components of meaning are given plainly enough, but the conclusion, though present, is present by implication as the middle way, the acceptable and vital compromise between two sterile extremes. The meticulous balance of figures expresses meaning, and gives shape and point to the more discursive methods of the earlier voyages, while the figures themselves are the most perfectly conceived of all Swift's symbols.

Clear and precise though it is in its main outlines, the fourth voyage carries a great weight of meaning, and though it is less obviously tight-packed with learning than *A Tale of a Tub,* much of Swift's reading, as well as of his thinking and his conversation, lies behind it. Part of its force is due, indeed, to the fact that in it the experience of a lifetime, whether personal or public, the experience of political and social life or of solitary reading and thinking, is ordered into complete expression, so that it relates at many points to his other writings. By reference, imagery, parody, the clear issues of Houyhnhnm-land are linked with the actual life of civilized man. The literary connections of this voyage are particularly obvious and, of course, vital to its understanding. The voyages to Lilliput and Brobdingnag owe little of importance to travel literature; the matter-of-fact tone and the detailed exactness of description may have been borrowed from it, but these were effects Swift had always been able to produce for satiric purpose, and the possible debts to Cyrano or to Francis Godwin are hardly significant. The "Voyage to Laputa," the least original of all, is in the tradition of the fantastic and satiric voyages, but its relation to them is simple and derivative; the complications of Laputa depend on the handling of topical interests, not on the handling of an existing literary form. But in the "Voyage to the Houyhnhnms," we have to deal with an ancient, formidable, and ambiguous tradition, that of the rational Utopia; and on our interpretation of the relationship between Houyhnhnm-land and that tradition depends our interpretation of meaning. In considering this, we must remember what had been made of the

Utopia tradition in Swift's own time, for in all his writing he is a man of his age, concerned as an Augustan writer was always concerned with the attitudes of his own contemporaries. He deals with the fundamental concerns of humanity, but his way of dealing with them is conditioned by what other men are making of them, and this is as true of the "Voyage to the Houyhnhnms" as of the visit to Laputa, or of *A Tale of a Tub*.

In the later seventeenth century the Utopian voyage, in the general sense of an account of a visit to a land of perfect or near perfect beings who are then used as a standard to condemn societies of men, was often used, especially by the *libertins* of France, as a convenient and comparatively safe method of attacking Christianity. The primitivism which had resulted from tales of the noble savages discovered by explorers lent color to such accounts; and though these voyages are necessarily ambiguous and sprinkled with pious comments the conclusion really meant to be drawn from contemplation of the virtuous pagans is, often, not that since they have reached such goodness without the aid of revelation Christian societies should be able to achieve far more, but that their goodness shows the moral failure and the falsity of revealed religion. For the freethinkers their purpose is, in fact, the same as that of the philosophers of the ancient world as set out by Swift in his sermon "Upon the Excellency of Christianity"; from their superior wisdom and virtue reached "purely upon the strength of their own reason and liberty of thinking," we are intended to draw the conclusion that "either all Revelation is false, or what is worse, that it hath depraved the nature of man, and left him worse than it found him."[44] These Utopian races were generally guided by reason, like the *"Hommes raisonnables"* of Claude Gilbert,[45] who are truly happy, their happiness being *"conforme à la nature et à la raison, qui ont établi les règles qui doivent l'assurer."*[46] Denis Veiras's *Histoire des Sevarambes,* which after appearing in England and France in the late 1670's was printed as part of a spurious third volume of *Gulliver's Travels* in 1727, attacks religion through its presentation of the virtuous Australian Sevarambes, akin to men but living in a society based on reason and natural law. One of the most extreme

179

of these voyages is that of Gabriel de Foigny, free liver as well as free thinker, who as an unfrocked monk later expelled from Geneva doubtless conceived a particular spite against revealed religion. Foigny's *La Terre Australe Connue* was published in 1676, recast in 1692, and translated into English in 1693. There is no indication that Swift had read this, or any of the voyages I have mentioned, but it is at least possible that he had, since we know that he read travel literature and since *Gulliver's Travels* itself displays a thorough familiarity with "voyages" of various kinds. The fourth voyage above all, with its easy handling of the conventions and ideas of the philosophic or Utopian voyage, could scarcely have been written in ignorance of the tradition as it had continued through the seventeenth century, whether or not these particular examples of it were known to Swift. Certainly there are likenesses between this voyage and *La Terre Australe Connue* as far as its materials are concerned, likenesses both in particular instances and in the general arrangement of figures; but Foigny's book is only a typical example of such voyages, though in the sharp contrast between the rational inhabitants of Australia on the one hand and man, regarded by the Australians as near-bestial, on the other, the point of this kind of travel literature is made with a peculiar sharpness. The striking difference between Swift's version of the seventeenth century Utopian voyage and that of Foigny is that the gulf is bridged: Yahoo and Houyhnhnm are as far apart as Fondin and Australian, but between them stands a third figure, that of man as he can be, animal indeed, but not bestial for all his irrationality. For the destructiveness of Foigny and Veiras is substituted a positive approach. Swift supplies what they have left out, and so by his manipulation of an existing form finds an economic means of expression. The fourth book is therefore in one of its aspects a comment on the opinions implied in a well-known form, the philosophic voyage of the seventeenth century, with its rationalist, Deist, or anti-Christian pictures of mankind perfected in goodness through the exercise of reason in an untrammeled state of nature; and one way—among several converging ways—towards an understanding of the book is to see it as a significant variation on a familiar theme, and so to set it against its appropriate background. Foigny's account of la Terre Australe, so like and yet in its total effect so different from the account of Houyhnhnm-land, may serve as an example of the genre which is here used to present Swift's summing-up of mankind.

The race which Foigny's traveler Sadeur meets in Australia, and which he regards with such reverence, is a race of tall, six-fingered hermaphrodites, their physical peculiarity being a sign of their completeness and perfection, of their lack of passion, and of the love and unity which exist among them. They regard themselves as *"hommes entiers," "vrays hommes,"* an opinion in which Sadeur soon concurs, for these people are the perfection of human nature. They look upon other races as *"demi-hommes,"* and though they at first suppose that Sadeur, who happens also to be a hermaphrodite, is one of themselves they soon realize from his behavior that he too is a half-man, having *"de petites étincelles de raison"*[47] but ruled for the most part by passion and so sharing the nature of the beasts; and he narrowly escapes being put to death. According to the old man through whose conversation Sadeur learns most about the Australians, "L'homme véritablement homme étoit toujours homme, c'est-à-dire humain, raisonnable, débonnaire, sans passion, par ce que c'est en ce point que consiste la nature de l'homme."[48] Man cannot be truly man if he does not differ completely from the beasts, full as they are of passions and of those faults, arising from the passions, from which man must be wholly free. Sadeur is most impressed by this uncompromising view, which has been reached entirely by the light of nature and reason, and which is certainly startlingly different from the traditional acceptances of the Christianity he professes to embrace. The virtuous Australians are of course total strangers to revelation, though nature and reason have led them, as they led the European Deists of the seventeenth and eighteenth centuries, to belief in a Supreme Being, or First Cause, regarded as something remote and ultimately incomprehensible, never to be discussed because reason can form no clear idea of it beyond the fact of its existence. The conception of a more personal relationship between God and man they regard as absurd, and the

181

old Australian dismisses revelation on those rational grounds which Swift ridicules in his parody of the Deist Anthony Collins, that it cannot reasonably be supposed that a benevolent God would declare the truth only to a few. Sadeur soon decides that he would be wise to say no more about Christianity, since the old man's reasonable mind is sure to make it seem ridiculous.

As might be expected, the Australians live simply. They eat no flesh, for this might contaminate them with the animal nature they regard with such horror. They have all things in common and, since they are all completely reasonable and therefore think rightly and uniformly on all subjects, they live in unbroken amity and so in freedom and equality, no government being necessary. With this rational uniformity and equality in virtue there is no cause for them to prefer one to another, and so they have an equal benevolence towards all of their kind. "Ils s'aiment tous d'un amour cordial, et l'amour est égal pour tous."[49] Not being ruled by self-love, they have no sense of personal ownership, and their rational benevolence is not disturbed by any instinctive preference for their own kin. They have, of course, no wars among themselves, since no possible cause of war exists among them, but they carry out extensive massacres among the other inhabitants of the country, a race of ordinary though uncivilized human beings of the same nature as Sadeur. These people are regarded as bestial creatures whose numbers it is only reasonable to keep down, and Sadeur finds himself in trouble through his sense of kinship with them and consequent reluctance to kill them. From the nature of the "true men" it is not to be wondered at that they wear no clothes, which they regard as contrary to nature. Their nakedness, like their bisexuality, is a sign of their lack of passion, their purely reasonable nature, the absence in them of any sense of sin or, consequently, of shame. Sadeur points out the symbolic nature of this characteristic: "Il n'est que le péché qui nous ait donné de l'horreur de nous-même et qui, ayant sali notre âme devant Dieu, nous ait rendus insupportables."[50] Whether the real intention is to accept the existence of original sin or, as seems far more likely from the context, to jibe at religion for having inculcated a sense of sin, clothes are here being used as a symbol for man's conviction that he is sinful, a conviction wholly lacking in the Australians. The signification was an old one among Christian moralists, who inferred from Genesis that the urge to clothe ourselves is an urge to cover our nakedness both of body and of mind, and a direct consequence of the Fall.[51]

It is clear enough that the adventures of Sadeur have something in common with those of Gulliver, and that the inhabitants of the two countries which these travelers visit have certain similarities. In each there is a virtuous race guided by nature and reason, an inferior race regarded by the other as subhuman, and a human visitor. The materials of Swift's fourth book are those of a rationalist philosophic voyage, but it is hardly to be expected that his handling of these materials should be straightforward. Voyages of this kind present a view of man and an attitude towards religion which Swift constantly opposed; in the terms of his day reason and nature were the catchwords of the Deist, not of the Christian moralist. It is his frequent habit, moreover, to adopt an established form to satiric purpose, as he does in *A Modest Proposal* and in *An Argument against Abolishing Christianity,* through parody involving a sharp twist of meaning. Swift's habit of mind, and the satiric methods which result from it, do not predispose us to expect a simple Utopian voyage in which the actual depravity of humanity is contrasted with the virtue of "true man," nor do Gulliver's earlier voyages raise such an expectation. And in fact the characters, and their relation to one another, are so handled as to suggest that the philosophic voyagers have rather misunderstood the situation, and have contrived to find the wrong answer to the problem set them in the land they visit. Swift uses their materials as an economical and typically indirect way of giving the right answer, which is less simple than theirs.

The Houyhnhnms, though physically quite different from the people of Foigny's Australia, are of similar nature. The fact that they are in the shape of horses, instead of in that of more complete human beings like the Australians, is in itself significant, and not a matter of satiric distance alone. Foigny's rationally virtuous creatures are improved men, men whose physical completeness is

183

a sign of their wholeness and self-sufficiency. Swift's are beings whose physical difference from man is thrust upon our notice to suggest that they are of quite a different order, and that their rational virtue is alien to mankind; the efforts of Deists, rationalists, haters of Christianity, or believers in the innate nobility of man are all irrelevant to the true situation. As symbols they are curiously effective, both suggesting and contradicting certain traditional associations; they are both familiar and disconcerting. The horse is one of the noblest of animals, one of the most perfect creations of the natural world; it is also a symbol of passion and power, to be held in check by reason as, in poetic theory, the winged Pegasus must be checked and guided by judgment. That the creature which we expect to represent passion and force is here in no need of domestication and control strikes us with a certain oddity and even disappointment: the Houyhnhnms lack the life and force that their shape would lead us to expect, and it is with a sense of loss that we see them sitting quietly at their mangers, drawn in their sledges, threading needles and drinking milk. These are symbols which have a negative as well as a positive connotation.

Like Foigny's Australians, the Houyhnhnms are creatures of nature and reason, but Swift takes some pains to impress upon us what their shape suggests, that they are not simply more virtuous and rational, more fully in control of their passions than we; they are not human beings at all. The contrast between the Houyhnhnms and the other characters is very marked and firmly sustained. The Houyhnhnms are by nature virtuous: "As these noble Houyhnhnms are endowed by Nature with a general Disposition to all Virtues, and have no Conceptions or Ideas of what is evil in a rational Creature; so their grand Maxim is, to cultivate Reason, and to be wholly governed by it."[52] The point of the description lies in "as" and "so." The Houyhnhnms can live by reason because their nature is different from ours; they have no shame, no temptations, no conception of sin. They are totally unable to comprehend the purpose of lying, for they define the ends of speech in purely rational terms and argue that "if any one said the Thing which was not, those Ends were defeated." That speech

184

could be used to further other than rational ends—to satisfy self-love, for instance—is inconceivable to them. It is the same with the other common temptations of man, and Gulliver takes days to explain to his master the ravages, among human beings, of the passions, "of the Desire of Power and Riches; of the terrible Effects of Lust, Intemperance, Malice, and Envy."[53] Nature and reason, in the Houyhnhnms, are one and the same, and no passions exist in them to complicate the business of living. They have no "natural affections" in our sense; nature, they say, has taught them to be equally benevolent to everyone, and to make distinction of persons only on the rational grounds of "a superior Degree of Virtue." "They have no Fondness for their Colts or Foles: but the Care they take in educating them proceedeth entirely from the Dictates of Reason. And, I observed my Master to shew the same Affection to his Neighbour's Issue that he had for his own. They will have it that Nature teaches them to love the whole Species, and it is Reason only that maketh a Distinction of Persons, where there is a superior Degree of Virtue." Marriage is undertaken simply as "one of the necessary Actions in a reasonable Being," and their mates are chosen by their parents and friends with due regard to color, strength, and comeliness. They select such colors as will not produce a disagreeable mixture in the breed, and further "Strength is chiefly valued in the Male, and Comeliness in the Female; not upon the Account of Love, but to preserve the Race from degenerating."[54] These considerations are entirely for the good of "the whole Species," so that matches are made on the purely rational principles according to which, among human beings, animals are bred. And perhaps most striking of all, they have no fear of death, that passion which Swift believed to be implanted, together with the passion of love, in all men, perhaps through the deliberate action of Providence so that mankind might be the less likely to die out. In this as in so much else, the Houyhnhnms are like Foigny's hermaphrodites, who regard death as a good because the agitations of life will then give way to repose, and who take Sadeur's unreasonable fear of death as an additional proof that he is not truly human. The Houyhnhnms carry Stoic indifference even further, and look forward to death

185

no more than they fear it. Rather they accept it as casually as a journey, and call it retiring to their "first Mother." This term, with its pagan air, suggests the complete naturalness of death, as of life, to the Houyhnhnm mind; they are buried as obscurely as possible, and their relations express "neither Joy nor Grief at their Departure; nor does the dying Person discover the least Regret that he is leaving the World, any more than if he were upon re-turning home from a Visit to one of his Neighbours."[55] They die only of old age, or occasionally from some accident, and are never ill: indeed their bodies seem only an extension of their minds, as though the physical in them were not merely under the control of the reason, but not differentiated from the reason. Since they have no bodily passions, none of the tensions native to man, in whom reason and passion struggle for mastery, are visible in them. They live as easily and naturally in their state of reason as do the beasts in their state of instinct, for reason is, in them, in-stinctive, inborn and all-embracing, reason "true and perfect," as it is "in itself." Whereas for us the exercise of reason leads to con-troversy and dispute, Houyhnhnm reason leads to unanimity, as with the people of la Terre Australe who will consider only those things of which they have clear and distinct ideas. Gulliver tells us:

Neither is Reason among them a Point problematical as with us, where Men can argue with Plausibility on both sides of a Question; but strikes you with immediate Conviction; as it must needs do where it is not mingled, obscured, or discoloured by Passion and Interest. I remember it was with extreme Difficulty that I could bring my Master to understand the Meaning of the Word Opinion, or how a Point could be disputable; because Reason taught us to affirm or deny only where we are certain; and beyond our Knowledge we cannot do either.[56]

Indeed the Houyhnhnms are what Gulliver says their name implies, the "Perfection of Nature," and it is nature or reason (in them identical) which alone "teaches" and "guides" them. This is constantly insisted on; they assert that "Reason alone is suffi-cient to govern a Rational Creature" and again that "Nature and Reason were sufficient Guides for a reasonable Animal."[57] For Foigny's Australian likewise "sa raison c'est la loy, c'est la règle, c'est son unique guide."[58] Being sinless they are, like the Australians, naked, and when Gulliver, who is desperately concerned to keep on his clothes as a distinguishing mark from the Yahoos, begs that he may not be compelled to "expose those Parts that Nature taught us to conceal," his master replies that "he could not understand why Nature should teach us to conceal what Nature had given."[59] To him, of course, the covering of human nakedness as a consequence of sin would be incomprehensible, and the contrast between his use of the term "nature" and Gulliver's sharply points the difference between human nature, only to be explained by the "Scripture-system of man's creation," and that of the Houyhnhnms. The Yahoos too are naked and in a way sinless, for they as much as the Houyhnhnms act according to their nature, and are no more to be blamed for their odiousness than a beast. The sin and shame which are anciently symbolized by the covering of our bodies are the distinguishing marks of humanity: nature indeed cannot teach us to conceal what she herself has given, but man, whether for good or ill, is not a child of nature in the same sense as Houyhnhnm and Yahoo.

The Houyhnhnms, then, are of the same order as the reasonable beings of the Utopian voyagers, but more clearly and consistently drawn than they, and more sharply differentiated from man. They are conceived entirely in terms of nature and reason, and their actions are a logical consequence from this, while the total result is carefully shown as different not in degree simply, but in kind, from anything possible to man. They are precisely *"animalia rationalia,"* natural creatures which are reasonable, and therefore they are given animal shape; Swift's choice of one of the noblest of the animal creation as a symbol of self-sufficient reason is based upon a traditional view of the uniqueness of man. The Houyhnhnms are the dream of the Deist and the rationalist, and so are, like other of Swift's creations, composite beings embodying different aspects of that belief which underlies the conclusions of Plato or Shaftesbury, Zeno or Bolingbroke, the "scheme of virtue without religion," the assumption that man is self-sufficient and able to achieve virtue under the sole guidance of reason and of "Nature, who worketh all things to Perfection."[60] Thus their life, with its poems of friendship and benevolence and praise of athletic achievement, its diet of milk and oats, its lack of iron, has the simplicity of the Golden Age, the dream of the virtuous pagans; their scorn of systems of natural philosophy reminds Gulliver of the sentiments of Socrates as delivered to us by Plato; they are rational creatures as defined by Marcus Aurelius: "To the rational creature the same act is at once according to nature and according to reason." But all such daydreams merge in the various forms of Deistic thinking current in Swift's own day, and it is in these that the significant parallels may be found.

The insistence on reason as a sufficient guide is of course the chief characteristic of Deism, but many of the polemical Deists or freethinkers were content to use it merely as an argument against Christianity, showing revealed religion as an affront to human reason and also as unnecessary, since reason is a sufficient and even a more successful guide for a rational being. But to find a more detailed account of the effects of living by nature and reason Swift had only to turn to the writings of Shaftesbury and to the letters and conversation of his own friend Bolingbroke. Shaftesbury, with his denial of the power of self-love, and his certainty that man has an inborn moral sense which will lead him to benevolence if it is left free to do so, certainly has his place here. Mandeville, in common with many of Shaftesbury's contemporaries, may have underestimated the amount of self-discipline which he thought necessary to the achievement of virtue, but none the less he is essentially right in his criticism of Shaftesbury as requiring and expecting "Goodness in his Species, as we do a sweet Taste in Grapes and China Oranges, of which, if any of them are sour, we boldly pronounce that they are not come to that Perfection their Nature is capable of."[61] For him man is a natural creature, at home in the universe and finding his true happiness in living in harmony with the whole, loving not individual men but the species; this is to live "according to Nature," and this is what the Houyhnhnms do. Shaftesbury's good men, like Theocles, are very much rational creatures, but he makes less use of the word itself than do many of his contemporaries, substituting for it the term "moral sense" and so freeing himself from the difficulties which surrounded the definition of reason. But the more thoroughgoing Bolingbroke, finding this phrase too enthusiastic, prefers to ground his philosophy on reason, which shows man the "essential differences of things" and that "virtue is the perfection of his nature." Reason, he believes, is the faculty which can lead us to universal benevolence.

[God] has made us happy, and he has put it into our power to make ourselves happier by a due use of our reason, which leads us to the practice of moral virtue and of all the duties of society. We are designed to be social, not solitary, creatures. Mutual wants unite us: and natural benevolence and political order, on which our happiness depends, are founded in them. This is the law of our nature; and tho every man is not able for different reasons to discern it, or discerning it to apply it, yet so many are able to do this, that they serve as guides to the rest.[62]

Bolingbroke's philosophical writings are full of such phrases as "nature and reason," "sound, unprejudiced reason," the guides of the great ancients who are his ideals of virtue. In the letter to Swift, in September 1724, in which he rather angrily and sarcastically defines the term "freethinker," he writes thus of reason: "If indeed by *esprit fort,* or free-thinker, you only mean a man who makes a free use of his reason, who searches after truth without passion or prejudice, and adheres inviolably to it, you mean a wise and honest man, and such a one as I labour to be. The faculty of distinguishing between right and wrong, true and false, which we call reason or common sense, which is given to every man by our bountiful Creator, and which most men lose by neglect, is the light of the mind, and ought to guide all the operations of it."[63] This, put in typical Deist phraseology, is very like the infallible reason of the Houyhnhnms, which "strikes you with immediate Conviction" and which is sufficient to guide them aright in all questions of morality; it is also, despite the difference in terminology, very like Shaftesbury's moral sense in its almost intuitive immediacy; and there is a similarity between Houyhnhnm reason and the Cartesian "rational intuition" of clear and distinct ideas,[64] by which Foigny's Australians appear to be ruled. All these conceptions would seem to Swift equally remote from reality, but in view of the standing argument which was conducted in the letters of Swift and Bolingbroke during the period when *Gulliver's Travels* was being written it seems likely that Bolingbroke's views were much in Swift's mind at this time. Bolingbroke, after all, affected a Stoic serenity during his retirement, and in another letter, in March 1731, he sounds absurdly like a Houyhnhnm in his claim that indifference to death can be achieved simply by following nature: "But we may, nay, if we will follow nature, and do not work up imagination against her plainest dictates, we shall of course grow every year more indifferent to life."[65] No doubt such attitudes had been affected by Bolingbroke before the 1730's, and it is surely to him as much as to Pope that Swift's systematic rebuttal of rational benevolence, the love of the species, is made in 1725: "I hate and detest that animal called man, although I heartily love John, Peter, Thomas and so forth." The Houyhnhnms are "humanity living that law of nature which Bolingbroke describes,"[66] supposing that such a thing were possible, but Swift was certain that it was not. "Passion and prejudice" cannot be so easily dismissed, and nature, in Swift's opinion, does not teach man detachment, serenity, benevolence, nor does his reason teach him the difference between right and wrong. Nature teaches man fear and anger and selfishness, and our nature is not to be fulfilled but controlled and guided by the help of religion. Reason and "moral sense" are alike fallible in man; "there is no solid, firm Foundation of Virtue, but in a Conscience directed by the Principles of Religion."

Since this is what the Houyhnhnms stand for, it is not surprising that, for all their monolithic impressiveness and for all the nostalgic charm of the simple untroubled life they lead, readers of the fourth voyage have found them remote, unsympathetic, and in the end profoundly unsatisfying. They are made so because the philosophy they represent is so, and Swift ensures that we will find them unsatisfying not by telling us that they are, but by the narrative methods proper to the form he is using. He puts them into situations in which they must seem unsympathetic or sometimes faintly absurd; situations which could easily have been avoided and whose tendency Swift, with his sensitivity and humor and his skill in managing his characters, could not have failed to see. The Houyhnhnms are as much subject to ironic treatment as any other of his creations, and there is no need, I think, to suppress a feeling of amusement as we read of their placid, awkward domesticity, or of irritation at their solemn assumption of superiority over all other creatures. Still less should we complain that Swift has blundered; it is we who blunder in expecting, against all the evidence of this and his other works, that he should set us, simply and unequivocally, a standard to follow and admire, especially a standard like that which the Houyhnhnms represent. He deliberately emphasizes their least attractive characteristic, their coldness: a natural result of their purely reasonable nature but one that he would have done well, if he meant to gain our admiration for them, not to thrust upon our notice for the sake of emphasizing their poor opinion of Gulliver. For example, the master Houyhnhnm, Gulliver tells us, "brought me into all Company, and made them treat me with Civility, because, as he told them privately, this would put me into good Humour, and make me more diverting."[67] Again this characteristic coldness and lack of sympathy are displayed in the dispassionate debate of the assembly about the nature and the future fate of Gulliver and the Yahoos, issuing in the calm resolve, on irreproachably rational grounds, to send Gulliver to an almost certain death. Rational benevolence, which teaches them to regard the good of their own species, can find no place for the representative of man. Gulliver finds it impossible to refute their conclusions, but even he, adoring as he is, uneasily feels that his idols lack something of the humane, and that reason might be tempered by pity. Within the framework which Swift has adopted, the limitations of a virtue founded upon reason could scarcely be more forcibly put than in Gulliver's comment: "In my weak and corrupt Judgment, I thought it might consist with Reason to have been less rigorous. . . . I knew too well upon what solid Reasons all the Determinations of the wise Houyhnhnms were founded, not to be shaken by Arguments of mine, a miserable Yahoo."[68]

191

For all the corruption of his reason, Gulliver is considerably more humane than the wise Houyhnhnms, whose purely reasonable nature has none of the qualities from which humanity can arise. Of course the Houyhnhnms are in many ways admirable enough; to follow reason must produce much that is good, and as far as reason can take them these creatures have gone. Swift uses them not only as a satiric norm against which to show up the lamentable activities of mankind as reported to his master by Gulliver, but to embody the reasonable virtues, such as truthfulness and honesty, which we would do well to follow so far as we may. Their customs and institutions—their disapproval of "systems," their education of females—are often those which Swift would approve. But in their blamelessness there is something lacking, the positive goodness of love, pity, gratitude, kindness, which makes life bearable in man's fallen world. Elsewhere in the *Travels* Swift treats with sympathy that deliberate intervention of one man in the life of another which is so different from the Houyhnhnms' equal benevolence, detachment, and rational respect for virtue, but among them the nearest approach to human warmth is the touching devotion of the humble sorrel nag, one of the servant breeds who were "not born with equal Talents of Mind." The nag, with his incompletely rational mind, is the only creature in Houyhnhnm-land to show any affection, and Gulliver's last link with the country as he sails away is the voice of the "Sorrel Nag (who always loved me) crying out—Take Care of thy self, gentle Yahoo."[69]

While the Houyhnhnms lack human warmth because they lack passions and affections, all that the rationalists summed up as the misleading effects of our unfortunate possession of bodies, the Yahoos are at the opposite extreme, inhuman because they have nothing but bodily senses and passions, and are altogether lacking in reason; in them there is nothing to control passion or to shape it into human affection. In them as in the Houyhnhnms one aspect of man's complex nature is isolated. Of all Swift's allegorical figures these are perhaps the most perfectly adapted to their purpose: the physical representation exactly embodies the moral meaning because the Yahoos are that part of human nature which arises from the physical. They embody in visible shape the animal passions of man, in the degenerate form that these passions would assume if isolated from reason, and it is because of this unity of expression and meaning that they achieve such haunting conviction. The sense of man's limitation by his animal nature, which has grown stronger throughout the whole work, here becomes overwhelming, and the more vivid and repulsive these apelike creatures are made, the more physically present they are to us, the more fully Swift's meaning is conveyed. There is no doubt that we are meant to share Gulliver's disgust with the Yahoos, for though Gulliver's own reactions (or those of any of Swift's characters) are not necessarily to be trusted, we are shown enough to judge for ourselves, and are moreover given a further pointer in the carefully chosen associations of uncleanness which surround them. The Yahoos feed upon things which under the Levitical code are forbidden as polluting or unclean—asses' flesh, meat from dead carcasses, rodents, dogs—and they are treated in those terms in which Christian moralists had for so long written of the flesh, the unregenerate man.[70] In a state of nature and with reason totally absent, the animal part of man is entirely given over to sin, or what would be sin in a creature gifted with reason and responsibility, though in a Yahoo it can hardly be called so. The extreme contrast between the hideously physical Yahoos, with their brutish parodies of human behavior, and the Houyhnhnms in whom the body is merely a vehicle for the expression of reason, is an important part of Swift's meaning. To those who consider "Reason alone" as sufficient guide for humanity he is displaying, isolated and therefore exaggerated, those things in us with which reason has to contend. The Yahoos show why man could never be a Houyhnhnm, why the Stoic or the Deist solution to the human problem must always be a failure. But the suggestion of inhumanity in the Houyhnhnms, and the connotations of sin in the Yahoos, indicate also, however lightly, that though the Deist answer will not do there is another answer which can take into account the whole nature of man, resolving the absolute contrast of Houyhnhnm and Yahoo. The Biblical images of uncleanness relate to another dimension in which all the strange beings of *Gulliver's Travels* can be placed in proper relationship. As T. O. Wedel long ago pointed out,[71] the Yahoos live in a "state of nature" nearer to that envisaged by Hobbes than to that of Locke's *Two Treatises of Government,* and infinitely far from that perfection of nature which the Deists believed the churches had done so much to prevent. Their state of nature is a state of war, of unbridled self-love: this is the natural condition of man according to such observers as Hobbes, La Rochefoucauld, Mandeville, and, as the Deists saw, this view was less remote from the traditions of the church than was their own, though it could support only a part of Christian teaching. Swift's handling of the Yahoos is in the tradition of Christian homiletic literature; they are not only examples of the Hobbist state of nature which is a state of war; they are "the body of this death," though their traditional message is adapted to the age of rationalism and dualism, and the new problems that it brought. By the terms in which they are described they imply a context in which brutish self-love is not the whole truth about man, and in which he can be more fully comprehended than by Houyhnhnm reason, which so signally fails to find, in its world of neat and simplified extremes, a place for mankind. These hints are followed up through the relationship of Gulliver to the creatures of Houyhnhnm-land, a relationship which is crucial to Swift's meaning, since it is through his handling of it that his carefully established contrast is finally to be resolved.

The most humiliating experience which Gulliver, that stout upholder of the dignity of human kind, has to endure in all his adventures is the recognition that he is akin to the Yahoos. Only with the greatest reluctance and shame is he brought to admit this kinship even to himself, for he is, like so many of us, deliberately blind to the treasure of baseness in man. Yet the physical likeness is strong and continually stressed, and it is apparent to us while Gulliver is still refusing to recognize it. Being expressed in physical terms, it makes much more impression on us than does the likeness between Gulliver and the Houyhnhnms, which consists in his possession of a tincture of that reason which constitutes the whole of their nature. This of course is what Swift intends, since he wishes to convey the faintness of reason in us, and the strength of our passions, but he is also at pains to show us that Gulliver is different from the Yahoos. For Gulliver can reason, and though he and his fellows share all the selfish instincts of the Yahoos, and though the master Houyhnhnm, like the Brobdingnagian king, recognizes that men too often use their reason to conceal their passions or to gratify them more subtly, the difference is still very great. The Houyhnhnm sums up the situation from his own point of view when he tells the Assembly, according to Gulliver, "That, he observed in me all the Qualities of a Yahoo, only a little more civilised by some Tincture of Reason; which however was in a Degree as far inferior to the Houyhnhnm Race, as the Yahoos of their Country were to me."[72] The Houyhnhnms judge by their own standard of reason, but the inadequacy of their comments on Gulliver and on Gulliver's account of human behavior suggests that this standard is not altogether an appropriate one to apply to mankind. For instance, Gulliver's master, having heard of the distorted ingenuity with which the science of law is conducted in England, remarks that creatures "endowed with such prodigious Abilities of mind"[73] as these lawyers must be, ought to instruct others in wisdom and knowledge: a specific satiric point is made about the state of the law in England, but the Houyhnhnm standard of judgment—"Abilities of mind"—is incidentally shown to be faulty. Indeed the very fact that the Houyhnhnms are used, like any of Swift's characters, to make satiric points even if this involves inadequacy or obtuseness on their part, is an indication that we are not to accept them uncritically, and that they are no more to be regarded as perfect than Gulliver, or the King of Brobdingnag. Again the ineptitude of Houyhnhnm standards of nature and reason when applied to man and used as anything more than a temporary position of satiric vantage, is seen in the passage where Gulliver tries to explain the relative positions of Yahoo and Houyhnhnm (really of man and horse, quite a different matter) in his native country. The Houyhnhnm must, of course, admit that "if it were possible there could be any Country where Yahoos alone were endued with Reason, they certainly must be the governing Animal, because Reason will in Time always prevail against Brutal Strength."[74] But he has to consider man as a natural creature, a being fulfilling its nature in a world in which it is at home, and he goes on to point out that Gulliver is physically ill equipped to employ that reason in the common offices of life. A horse, he implies, is in bodily shape much more fit than a man to live the life of nature and reason, and as far as it goes this criticism is just enough. For man is not, like a horse or a Houyhnhnm, a creature of nature; as such he is more imperfect even than a Yahoo "in point of real Advantage,"[75] as the Houyhnhnm points out almost in the same words on two separate occasions. Man indeed is a most imperfect animal, but then he must be judged by quite different standards, and the effect of the Houyhnhnm's painstakingly logical remarks is to show us that, understandably enough, he has no conception of what man really is. *Gulliver's Travels* is, in part, an examination of the definition of man as a reasoning animal, an examination which the conditions of the time made peculiarly necessary. Swift is concerned to explore not only in what sense man can be called rational, but also, through the continuing play of animal imagery, in what sense he can be defined as an animal. The Houyhnhnms, like the Deists, misinterpret the definition in both its parts, and so in the whole which those parts compose. All that constitutes humanity in its curious mixture of reason and passion, all the complexity of a fallen being ill at ease in a world in which his fellow creatures are at home and yet capable of great good and great achievement: all this lies outside Houyhnhnm standards of judgment. But Gulliver understands none of this; he blindly accepts his master's condemnation, and so adds a further twist to the meaning, for it is in this book that Gulliver makes his greatest contribution, not as a simple mouthpiece but as an example of the disaster to which man can be led through a misunderstanding of his own nature. Gulliver's progress throughout the *Travels* has been in the direction of an increasing fluidity and untrustworthiness; contributing to relativity in the first two books, in the third he is so tenuous a character that we scarcely feel his presence, and by the time Book IV is reached we are well aware that Gulliver, as much as anyone else, is being manipulated in the service of his creator's moral and satiric intention. This is further impressed upon us in the detail of the fourth book itself; for instance, the lengthy condemnation, in Chapters V and VI, of Swift's hated sciences of war, medicine, and law reads like direct satiric attack upon familiar subjects, the stock subjects of satire, and we have no sense that it is being put forward through Gulliver. Rather we feel ourselves to be directly addressed, with the exaggeration usual in a simple attack of this kind, and with an open irony hardly to be expected of Gulliver. The following passage is difficult to relate to any notion we may earlier have formed of Gulliver's character, and not particularly consistent in itself save as the rather heavily and conventionally ironic comment of a satirist. Gulliver has, for the moment, vanished into the brain which conceived him:

> I had formerly upon Occasion discoursed with my Master upon the Nature of Government in general, and particularly of our own excellent Constitution, deservedly the Wonder and Envy of the whole World. But having here accidentally mentioned a Minister of State; he commanded me some Time after to inform him, what Species of Yahoo I particularly meant by that Appellation.
>
> I told him, that a First or Chief Minister of State, whom I intended to describe, was a Creature wholly exempt from Joy and Grief, Love and Hatred, Pity and Anger; at least makes use of no other Passions but a violent Desire of Wealth, Power, and Titles. . . .

And so the passage, with its curious comments on the passions, so ill adapted to Houyhnhnm understanding or Houyhnhnm standards, proceeds to open invective against the political and moral character of Robert Walpole. After this, Gulliver's later claim that he has done all he can to set his countrymen in the best possible light can only add to our feeling that he is now frankly an instrument in his creator's hands; having first told us that the virtues of the Houyhnhnms have opened his eyes to the vices of men, and also taught him "an utter Detestation of all Falsehood or Disguise," he goes on somewhat inconsistently: "However, it is now some Comfort to reflect that in what I said of my Country-men, I extenuated their Faults as much as I durst before so strict an Examiner; and upon every Article, gave as favourable a Turn

197

as the Matter would bear. For, indeed, who is there alive that will not be swayed by his Byass and Partiality to the Place of his Birth?"[76] Thus Gulliver is shown, in Book IV as earlier, to be himself part of the satire; meaning is expressed not through any one character but through the relationship of them all and through Gulliver's misunderstanding of that relationship when he identifies mankind with the Yahoos and at the same time tries to live like a Houyhnhnm, rejecting completely the bodily instincts and passions which the Yahoos represent. Gulliver is always too prone to take on the color of his surroundings, and here he accepts uncritically the rational standards of the Houyhnhnms, with the result that he, like his predecessor the Author of *A Tale of a Tub,* loses himself in a world of extremes, seeing nothing of the larger, more inclusive truth to be gained by moving between them. And as always the truth is only suggested, though more clearly and with more conviction than in the *Tale;* there is now less delight in absurdity, through experience of the disaster to which absurdity can lead, and correspondingly a stronger certainty of the importance of the one answer to the dangers and confusions of life.

Gulliver's first refusal to recognize what man has in common with the Yahoos is of a piece with his earlier concern for the dignity of humankind in Book II, and it is in these two closely connected books that human pride, in the shape of Gulliver himself, is most insisted upon. The same pride, when he is at last forced to recognize the likeness between mankind and the Yahoos, causes him to identify himself, as far as he may, with the Houyhnhnms, accepting their views on himself and his fellows and striving to be like them. The opening of Chapter VII shows how completely he has misunderstood the situation. It is true that he has lost his former pride in humanity, sees human vices more plainly, and thinks less of the honor of his own kind; he has lost his illusions and the pride they nurtured, and he is right to condemn certain human institutions against the standard of Houyhnhnm truthfulness and honesty. As so often with Swift, an extreme standard, a merciless stripping away of illusions, can be temporarily useful for satiric purposes. But Gulliver makes the extreme standard a permanent one, and removes, along with the illusions and the prejudices, those things which are not truly prejudices at all. He judges by pure reason, according to which no good can come of the passions which also exist in man; and because man is not a Houyhnhnm he supposes, as does his master, that he must be a Yahoo:

The Reader may be disposed to wonder how I could prevail on myself to give so free a Representation of my own Species, among a Race of Mortals who were already too apt to conceive the vilest Opinion of Human Kind, from that entire Congruity betwixt me and their Yahoos. But I must freely confess, that the many Virtues of those excellent Quadrupeds placed in opposite View to human Corruptions, had so far opened mine Eyes, and enlarged my Understanding, that I began to view the Actions and Passions of Man in a very different Light; and to think the Honour of my own Kind not worth managing.[77]

The tone of this—and it is by his sensitive modulation of tone that Swift produces some of his subtlest satiric effects—shows us where Gulliver is heading. He has accepted the simple dualism of Houyhnhnm-land not as a satiric device but as a permanent truth, placing Houyhnhnm reason "in opposite View to human Corruptions," and as a result he is disgusted with mankind, whom he falsely identifies with the Yahoos. But his disgust does not really extend to himself, though he calls himself a Yahoo. He has already learned to hate all falsehood and hopes to live with the Houyhnhnms forever; a certain condescension and self-approval, a certain pompous absurdity even—"the many Virtues of those excellent Quadrupeds"—indicates that for one illusion, one source of pride, is being substituted another. Gulliver now sees himself as a potential Houyhnhnm, a correct choice certainly as between Houyhnhnm and Yahoo, but hopelessly unrealistic because, for mankind, the choice does not exist. And when Gulliver tries to live the life of "Reason alone" the results are disastrous, since what is harmless and unavoidable self-satisfaction in a Houyhnhnm becomes in him a fanatical pride, an illusion more dangerous than any he has had before. The demands of the life of reason do not, in fact, allow in man even the blameless and negative virtue of the Houyhnhnms, for like Stoic indifference it can only be sustained through pride. The effort to support his

199

chosen role forces Gulliver into isolation from his fellows, and the charming fondness for his own family which he had earlier shown is replaced not by the equal benevolence of reason but by hatred and contempt. "During the first Year I could not endure my Wife or Children in my Presence, the very Smell of them was intolerable; much less could I suffer them to eat in the same Room. To this Hour they dare not presume to touch my Bread, or drink out of the same Cup."[78] Gulliver has in fact become, through choosing to judge mankind by an alien standard, a ludicrous yet terrible misanthrope, one of *"vous autres"* of Swift's letter to Bolingbroke and Pope, who can only end by hating mankind for its failure to live by inapplicable rules. This, one might say, is what the Utopian voyagers, what Bolingbroke, must come to. The only way to avoid such savage disillusion is to have no illusions in the first place, to recognize the Yahoo in man and to expect of him no more "than such an animal is capable of." Gulliver's course leads him into a self-deceit more complete and disastrous than that of any of Swift's representative figures, even than Peter or Jack, the Author of the *Tale* or the heroes of the anti-romantic poems: he is immersed in chaos, the maddest of them all. In his last inhuman state, he is used to make valid satiric points; we are, no doubt, to accept as justified his strictures on the ridiculous vice of pride in such a creature as man, since that is one of the chief themes of the *Travels,* but it is a further irony that it is Gulliver who makes them in these last proud words: "and therefore I here intreat those who have any Tincture of this absurd Vice, that they will not presume to appear in my Sight."[79]

To make even more clear the unreliability of Gulliver's views, his infinite capacity for getting things wrong by oversimplifying the issues, we are shown him in converse with his horses, who understand him tolerably well, and whom he regards as degenerate Houyhnhnms, and with his groom, because he smells of the stable; while his wife, who from what we hear of her is a very good sort of woman, is detested. This is plain foolishness, and indeed the whole of Gulliver's behavior after he leaves Houyhnhnm-land is so obviously ridiculous that it is impossible he

200

should be taken seriously. The tendency he has always shown to accept the point of view of his hosts is here very marked: he trots like a horse, speaks in a neighing tone, and finds it unnatural that the sailors should talk, "as monstrous as if a Dog or a Cow should speak in England, or a Yahoo in Houyhnhnm-Land." He still thinks of himself as different in kind from his fellows, telling us of Don Pedro that he "spoke so very movingly, that at last I descended to treat him like an Animal which had some little Portion of Reason." Even so, he will wear none of the captain's clothes, except "two clean Shirts, which having been washed since he wore them, I believed would not so much defile me."[80] As though to impress even more forcibly upon the reader that Gulliver's conclusions are themselves the objects of satire, Swift prefaced to his work, in Faulkner's edition in 1735, "A Letter from Capt. Gulliver to his Cousin Sympson," in which Gulliver writes with extreme harshness, arrogance, and self-esteem, still differentiating himself from the Yahoos, "your Species," and preferring to the praise of the whole human race "the neighing of those two degenerate Houyhnhnms I keep in my Stable." His criticisms of party and faction, bad writing, faulty education, and the rest are valid, for he still has his topically satiric function to perform, but that he should suppose that all these things could be reformed within seven months of the publication of his *Travels,* because such reformations "were plainly deducible from the Precepts delivered in my Book," and that "seven Months were a sufficient Time to correct every Vice and Folly to which Yahoos are subject," so that their failure proves them incapable of "the least Disposition to Virtue or Wisdom": all this extremism, with its unrealistic view of what man can achieve followed by utter pessimism when he does not achieve it, shows clearly where Gulliver's error lies. Throughout the "Letter," Gulliver is handled with a markedly heavy irony; perhaps Swift had already found that his meaning had to be underlined.[81]

Yet Gulliver's mistake was avoidable, for he had met on his previous voyages, especially during his stay in Brobdingnag, several examples of that kind of goodness to which it is possible for man to attain. His blindness is part of the satire, but we have no excuse for joining him in it, since there is plentiful evidence throughout *Gulliver's Travels* that man and Yahoo have not an "entire Congruity," and that some members of the human race are far more satisfactory models for Gulliver than are the Houyhnhnms. The King of Brobdingnag, Glumdalclitch, Lord Munodi, even Gulliver's wife or Gulliver himself as we see him in the first voyage, have qualities of kindness or friendliness or generosity, qualities which arise from the passions and affections of man, however controlled or purified, and which cannot exist in the rational Houyhnhnms. Moreover, in the fourth voyage itself Swift takes particular care to set against the inhuman Gulliver human figures of great goodness and tenderness, the Portuguese sailors. In earlier books, the sailors with whom Gulliver comes into contact have been an ordinarily mixed collection of men; Mr. John Biddel, captain of the vessel which picked him up after his departure from Blefuscu, was "a very civil Man," and Mr. Thomas Wilcocks, of the Brobdingnagian rescue, was honest and kindly. In the "Voyage to Laputa" there is a courteous Japanese pirate and an abominable Dutch one—here Swift's private prejudices are coming into play—and in the final voyage Gulliver is abandoned in Houyhnhnm-land by his mutinous crew. All these people are mere narrative devices for getting Gulliver to and from the countries where the satire is carried on, except in the case of the Japanese and the Dutch, whose characteristics are a little more developed to make a particular satiric point. But the captain and crew of the Portuguese ship, which puts in for water on the island where Gulliver is hiding from his kind after his banishment from Houyhnhnm-land, are more fully developed, and we hear much of Gulliver's reactions to their admirable qualities. He behaves very churlishly, displaying only an extreme anxiety to get away from them, but they treat him none the less, as he has to admit, with great humanity, and force him to be saved in spite of himself. Their captain, Don Pedro de Mendez, is particularly humane, compassionate, and forbearing, and Swift emphasizes in him those very qualities which the Houyhnhnms neither possess nor would understand, and which the obsessed Gulliver no longer values, though it is satirically necessary that he should perceive them. Of Don Pedro's goodness Gulliver remarks merely, with the cold and scornful surprise now to be expected of him, that "he was a very courteous and generous Person; he entreated me to give some Account of my self, and desired to know what I would eat or drink; said, I should be used as well as himself, and spoke so many obliging Things, that I wondered to find such Civilities from a Yahoo. However, I remained silent and sullen; I was ready to faint at the very Smell of him and his Men."[82] That it is a physical disgust which Gulliver feels for these sailors and even for his own family, whose smell similarly distresses him, emphasizes the nature of his delusion.

The behavior of the seamen toward Gulliver is quite different from the curiosity of the Houyhnhnms. They regard themselves as responsible for him in spite of the rebuffs they receive; they forcibly prevent him from leaping overboard in an attempt to escape to his former solitude; and Don Pedro persuades him to abandon his design of living as a recluse, following so far as he can the life of rational self-sufficient virtue which the Houyhnhnms have taught him to admire, and instead to commit himself once more to the human relationships proper to mankind. Gulliver's duty as Don Pedro sees it is to return to a life of tolerance and affection among his own kind, and he tries to persuade him on grounds of "Honour and Conscience." As we know from the sermons, conscience for Swift was not a natural sense of right and wrong but a faculty which must itself be guided, by divine law only to be known from a source outside ourselves, from revelation; only a conscience guided by the principles of religion can give us a firm foundation for virtue. And indeed the Portuguese sailors, with their kindness and compassion, their deliberate and responsible intervention in the lives of the unfortunate, form a strong and attractive contrast to the Houyhnhnms' rational benevolence, as well as to the misanthropy of Gulliver. The long-suffering, charitable Don Pedro is perhaps the closest of all Swift's characters to his account, in the sermon "Upon the Excellency of Christianity," of the ideal Christian, who is "affable and courteous, gentle and kind, without any morose leaven of pride or

203

vanity, which entered into the composition of most Heathen schemes."[83] The "scheme" which Gulliver has learned from the Houyhnhnms has certainly an element of that self-sufficient pride which Swift and other churchmen saw both in Stoicism and in the modern schemes of the Deists. Don Pedro, placed in so prominent a position, must make a strong impression on our minds, and the tone of Gulliver's references to him would seem further to suggest that here, among the various figures of the fourth voyage, is to be found the embodiment of the course man should follow. Gulliver speaks of his benefactor with a grudging approval, tinged with contempt for an unenlightened Yahoo, and never accepts the standards by which Don Pedro lives and by which he tries to persuade Gulliver to live. For Gulliver only agrees to go back to England because he can do nothing else: "I complied at last, finding I could not do better." And his comment on Don Pedro, that he had "very good *human* Understanding," is typical of Swift's methods of ironic commendation, made by means of an uncomprehending mouthpiece. Again, through Gulliver, he commends to us the Brobdingnagians, as the poor best that humanity, as contrasted with those truly rational animals the Houyhnhnms, can achieve, and again the grudging, the almost negative, tone is a familiar element of Swift's ironic method: "I shall say nothing of those remote Nations where Yahoos preside; amongst which the least corrupted are the Brobdingnagians, whose wise Maxims in Morality and Government, it would be our Happiness to observe. But I forbear descanting further, and rather leave the judicious Reader to his own Remarks and Applications."[84]

In Don Pedro and the Brobdingnagians we have, then, our positive standard, put forward, as always, ironically and indirectly according to Swift's habit. It is not an ideal standard—that Swift would ever have written a simple Utopia is almost inconceivable—and the indirection itself, the reluctance with which Gulliver recognizes the good qualities of the people he regards as a very poor second best, helps to pin down the meaning precisely. Swift is telling us, as always, not to expect too much and not to simplify what is essentially a difficult matter. The proper life for man is not that of Yahoo or of Houyhnhnm, for he has in him something of both, and in the blending of passion and reason, body and mind, something different from these simple, natural creatures is engendered. The Brobdingnagians and Don Pedro are, in a way, a compromise between extremes, and therefore they are indirectly presented, because we are to understand that we should not aim too high, as Gulliver does when, in trying to ignore part of his human nature, he becomes less than a human being. The best that man can achieve is considerable, but he can achieve it only through acceptance of the truth about himself as a fallen and degenerate creature who if he is to be good must base his endeavors on the whole of his complex nature. Though we cannot be Houyhnhnms we can be something better, and far more suited to the condition of fallen human beings who, as Bishop Butler said, "naturally, and from the condition we are placed in, necessarily depend upon each other." We need not, nor can we, escape that side of our nature which includes passions and affections; carefully guided by conscience and religion, to which reason must be subject, these qualities in man can issue in virtuous action, especially that compassionate assistance to our fellow-men, whether or not our reason judges them worthy of it, which Swift valued so highly and which "the Gentile philosophy" fails to produce. "If our Brother . . . is not in a Condition to preserve his Being, we ought to support him to the best of our Power, without reflecting over seriously on the Causes that brought him to his Misery."[85]

In Gulliver's last voyage utter chaos is thrust sharply against absolute order, and it is this clashing contrast which, in the shape of the Yahoos and the Houyhnhnms, makes the first and strongest impression upon us. But this is not Swift's last word upon the predicament of man. If we cannot escape from confusion to a world of clarity and simplicity, yet we need not, either, be overwhelmed in the meaningless. We must accept and work upon it, each of us making our own order as best we can. Swift sets the extremes firmly before us, but the right course can, by its very nature, be only indirectly shown. For the right course is to avoid extremes and the distortions to which they give rise; and it is also the difficult course, involving a scrupulous balancing of values, a weighing of experience, a determination to include in one's solutions the elements of rightness which exist in the drastic and clamorous claims of Hobbes and Mandeville, Shaftesbury and Bolingbroke. To give too plain an answer would be to defeat Swift's very purpose, which is, in part, to deny that any simple and ready-made answer exists. Don Pedro and the giant king cannot be simply summed up; theirs is the goodness of humility and· adaptiveness, tolerance and human warmth, an imaginative response to the needs of others. In the terms of the satire this positive standard can only be hinted at, but the terms of the satire are themselves chosen as those which express Swift's meaning most exactly, and part of that meaning is that the standard for man is not easy to find or to follow. In *Gulliver's Travels,* as in life itself, we must work out our solution, not denying but wrestling with the chaos we are born to, and refusing any of the tempting simplifications which prove, as in Gulliver's own case, so dangerous. As in *A Tale of a Tub,* the truth lies in what the ostensible author leaves out, in the compromise which includes all partial truths; and though here the true answer is reached, while in the *Tale* we must deduce it from our own examination of the Author's negatives, it can still not be put too plainly before us. In an age of false simplicities it is the chaos of man's life and the paradox of his nature which must be stressed. When that is accepted, we can work upon the whole of our nature for good, with the guidance of conscience and of Swift's one certainty, the Church.

The guidance of religion is not, of course, overtly mentioned in *Gulliver's Travels.* But in relation to the controversies of the day, it is seen to be present by implication. If "Reason alone" is not a sufficient guide for man, seen as a creature of mixed nature: if the good human beings are examples of a particular kind of virtue, which is not to be defined in purely rational terms: then Swift's position is opposed to Deism and neo-Stoicism, and this would in itself suggest, even without the Biblical associations which surround the Yahoos, that definition of man's nature which Christian tradition has handed down. The conclusion is as natural as for Montaigne, who at the close of the *Apologie of Raymond Sebond* places Stoic pride in a firmly Christian context with his comment on the mingled nobility and absurdity of the heathen cry, "Oh what a vile and abject thing is man unless he raise himselfe above humanity!"

Observe here a notable speech, and a profitable desire; but likewise absurd. For to make the handfull greater then the hand, and the embraced greater then the arme; and to hope to straddle more then our legs length; is impossible and monstrous: nor that man should mount over and above himselfe or humanity; for he cannot see but with his owne eyes, nor take hold but with his owne armes. He shall raise himselfe up, if it please God extraordinarily to lend him his helping hand. He may elevate himselfe by forsaking and renouncing his owne meanes, and suffering himselfe to be elevated and raised by meere heavenly meanes. It is for our Christian faith, not for his Stoicke vertue to pretend or aspire to this divine Metamorphosis, or miraculous transmutation.[86]

To assert the dual nature of man was still, in the early eighteenth century, the traditional defense against the partial truths of philosophical systems: Pascal's *Entretien avec Saci* appeared in 1728, and its argument that the notions both of Epictetus and of Montaigne were incomplete because they regarded only one aspect of our nature—"l'un la grandeur de l'homme, l'autre la foiblesse"— and that these can only be reconciled in the Christian faith, was followed in 1734 by John Arbuthnot's one serious poem, "Know Yourself," based on Pascal's theme. Arbuthnot contrasts, more topically, the theories of the Stoics and the Epicureans, both of which had their modern counterparts, and shows that while the former recognizes only man's strength, and ignores the instincts and passions which hamper it, the latter commits the opposite error of ignoring human possibilities for good. It is only to be expected, however, in the circumstances and particular dangers of the time, that Arbuthnot's comments on the nature of man, like those of his friends Pope and Swift, seem to stress human weakness rather than human strength, senses and instincts more than reason:

> These Godlike Thoughts while eager I pursue,
> Some glitt'ring Trifle offer'd to my view,
> A Gnat, an Insect of the meanest kind,

> Erase the new-born Image from my Mind,
> Some beastly Want, craving, importunate,
> Vile as the grinning Mastiffs at my Gate,
> Calls off from heav'nly Truth this reas'ning Me,
> And tells me I'm a Brute as much as He . . .
> So Man, amongst his Fellow-Brutes expos'd
> Sees he's a King, but 'tis a King depos'd:
> Pity him, Beasts! you by no Law confin'd,
> Are barr'd from devious Paths, by being blind;
> Whilst Man, through op'ning Views of various Ways
> Confounded by the Aid of Knowledge, strays.

One creed calls man a god, one a "two-legg'd Beast," and revelation alone can reconcile such "wide Extremes":

> Marks of my Birth, which I had worn in vain,
> Too hard for worldly Sages to explain:
> Zeno's were vain, vain Epicurus' Schemes,
> Their systems false, delusive were their Dreams;
> Unskill'd my two-fold Nature to divide,
> One nurs'd my Pleasure, and one nurs'd my Pride;
> Those jarring Truths which Human Art beguile,
> Thy sacred Page thus bids me reconcile.

For these traditional writers, whether divines like Butler and Swift or laymen like Pope and Arbuthnot, it is only in the Christian positive that the contradictions in man can be reconciled, his strength and weakness, his reason and passion, so that the whole of his nature, even his self-love, can be turned to affection and an active desire for the good of others. Anything simpler than this, any neater system, can be attained only by omission: compromise alone will avoid the opposed errors of *Gulliver's Travels* and *A Tale of a Tub,* and lead from delusion and death to a full, inclusive, and vital truth, to the fruitful life of Don Pedro and the Brobdingnagian king, and of Martin, who has best sustained the tradition of the primitive church. As Pascal believed, and as Swift demonstrates in the story of Gulliver, any one-sided account of the nature of man, any scheme that denies the paradoxical reality in favor of simplicity, will lead to disastrous practical results, to pride or despair or cynicism; and in its view of humanity Christianity approximates to a middle way between contemporary "wide Extremes," "jarring Truths which Human Art beguile." Swift's careful selecting and adjusting among opposing systems brings him, time and again, to his one certainty in the traditional teachings of his church and the morality which they support. Only thus can chaos be organized without loss, and the dangers of life surmounted. The words of Joseph Glanvill, sceptic follower of the middle way, form an apt comment on the task which faced Swift and his contemporaries: "Every Truth is near an Errour; for it lies between two Falsehoods: and he that goes far from One is apt to slip into the other; and while he flies from a Bear, a Lyon meets him. So that the best way to avoid the danger is to steer the middle Course; in which way we may be sure there is Charity and Peace, and very probably, Truth in their company." For only by countering one extreme opinion with another, "bending a crooked stick as much the other way, to straighten it," setting Yahoo against Houyhnhnm, can we reach that "discreet modest aequipoize of Judgment, that becomes the sons of Adam."[87]

CONCLUSION

The late seventeenth and early eighteenth centuries constitute our great age of satire, the period when irony and obliquity seemed to many writers the most appropriate way of presenting their views on the subjects important to them, and it was appropriate because of certain conditions prevailing in the various spheres of life with which writers were concerned. Inheriting the Renaissance positives of nature and reason, the absolute standards of goodness and truth, which their predecessors had confidently celebrated, they found their positives inadequately interpreted and their beliefs assailed from all sides. In this situation a firm presentation of positive values was a hazardous undertaking, and difficult to achieve on any but a small scale. The most profound and inclusive statements of value to be found in the literature of the time are satiric: the close of *The Dunciad,* "Of the Use of Riches," "Of the Characters of Women," the fourth book of *Gulliver's Travels.* Traditional acceptances can now be best supported and expressed by attacking what is hostile to them, and by a shifting process of adjustment, compromise, balance. The single truth can be neither grasped in thought nor embodied in words; singleness and simplicity now only exist in the false abstractions of modern thinking. But a modest approximation to truth, a modest certainty, can be achieved and expressed by that strenuous and agile effort which issues in the serious Augustan wit. Positive truth is now best presented by implication, through the deployment of negative materials.

Among the great Augustans who looked to the integral life of the past and strove to protect and to adapt what still survived against the inroads of the Enlightenment, Swift is the most indirect, most shifting, yet most inexorable, of all. He is deeply conscious of the disturbing tendencies of the age and very earnest in carrying out the task that seems so urgent to him as the moralist he always—and rightly—claimed to be and as a man whose personal need to feel himself in control of experience is peculiarly strong. His materials and their organization, the form and content of the satires, are his response to a particular situation at a time when, within man and without, chaos constantly threatened. Defense was essential, yet it could be achieved only by vigilant attack, sustained simultaneously on many fronts. Our first impression, in Swift's work, is of the elusive brilliance of the attack; a glancing, dazzling mind appears to be concerned solely with the presentation of absurdity or of evil, shifting its point of view constantly the better to perform its task. But as we grow accustomed to his ways of thinking and feeling we become aware that at the heart of Swift's work are unity and consistency, and we see that the attack is also a defense, that tools of destruction are being employed for a positive and constructive purpose. The inventiveness and resourcefulness of his satiric method is seen as arising directly out of the necessities of his mind and of his age; the changing complications of his irony are the necessary expression of an untiring devotion to the few certainties that life affords. For all his elusiveness and indirection, his readiness to compromise or to change his ground, few writers have been more essentially consistent than Swift, but for him consistency could be sustained only by such methods as these. Balance in the state or in the individual mind could be kept only by an agile shifting of weights.

Because Swift's indirections are governed always by a firm central purpose, it can be particularly misleading in his case to isolate one example or one aspect of his work. Letters, sermons, poems, sets of stray "Thoughts," political pamphlets, are all governed by the same attitudes and the same basic beliefs; technical satiric devices are never arbitrarily chosen, simply as the most devastating weapons available, but perform a more positive task and so are never merely attack. The stock terms in which simpler satires can be criticized are of little use for Swift. In him, parody of the style of a period or of a writer becomes a moral comment on mental habits and on wrong beliefs; a "device" which may serve a lesser writer for satiric distance and force must present in itself Swift's vision of those deeper ills in man which underlie our particular failings. That the device of relative size, in Books I and II of *Gulliver's Travels,* enables man to be seen from a startling angle is the least of its effects, for the relation

211

of giant, pygmy, and man contributes not only to satiric attack but to the presentation of humanity and its predicament. Through relativity we are shown man's insecurity and insignificance, his dependence on physical circumstance. The Lilliputians in their fragility perfectly display the temptations of man as a political animal, efficiently but ruthlessly organized for his own defense and too ready to see morality in terms of the state; the Brobdingnagians show us the goodness of man who sees the state in terms of morality, and whose energies are devoted to the simplest and truest of human values. These figures do more than attack; they are symbols, as much embodiments of individual insight as are the images of a poet, and the same is true of the Yahoos and Houyhnhnms and the terrible immortals of Luggnagg. Behind them all is a constant view of life in which intellectual conviction and personal necessity coincide; passion as well as thought has contributed to Swift's power of imaginative realization.

Since method in Swift arises from the center of his deeply and sometimes desperately held convictions, the more fully we explore those convictions, becoming famliar with them from his writings both public and private, the more deeply we can respond to the great satires themselves. For what we see in *Gulliver's Travels* is the culmination of a long process visible everywhere in Swift, a process of investigation, of moving tentatively among conflicting opinions, testing and trying them against that central conviction which in his satiric writing can be only unobtrusively present. The task that faced him is most clearly to be seen, perhaps, in the early odes, where unattainable order and inescapable chaos are sharply and despairingly opposed, where images of confusion and deceit proliferate to overwhelm the steady light of truth. And in the poems too can be seen Swift's response to the situation which the odes present. Abandoning the attempt to find and to express the single, simple truth, he accepts a less heroic but more painstaking role and plunges into giddy circumstance, working to achieve in the confusion of the world of sense a less ambitious order. When he resolves to end, "with a puff," the delusion of exalted poetry he resolves also to explore the world of sublunary nature, source of all delusions, and to content him-

212

self with those fragments of truth which may with difficulty be related to one another. For though perfection is indeed beyond the Empyreum, and reserved for glory, yet there is a "discreet modest aequipoize of Judgment, that becomes the sons of Adam."

For Swift as much as for Sidney or Milton, true order is moral order, and any "system" which has no relation to moral good and evil is to him a danger. Most dangerous of all are those which falsely claim to have found the single truth, and so appeal in their clarity and simplicity to men weary of the difficulties of their human state and seeking a way of escape. All such schemes, in every sphere, ignore some aspect of reality and so are doomed to failure; no system whether of politics or morality or philosophy can succeed if it fails to reckon with the facts of human nature and human experience, for success to Swift means not theoretic consistency, however intellectually satisfying, but practical moral results. It is this preoccupation which leads him to emphasize so strongly the importance of experience as the basis for all human endeavor. That we should keep close to experience—our own experience gained, as Locke would have it, from the senses and from reflection, and the ordered experience of the past which is traditional wisdom—this is the first step towards reasonable living, for though experience can delude, it is our only basis for reaching such certainty as we can. Christian doctrine as presented by his own church is important to Swift primarily as a "scheme" which, once revealed, can stand the test of experience and indeed is the only way of making sense of our world without omission, since human reason is so involved with our passions and prejudices that our attempts to free it can only lead to a more complete delusion. His attitude to all theoretical constructs of the human mind is a sceptical one, for he sees them, not as honestly ordering experience but as dishonestly ignoring it. Romanticism, sentimental patriotism, reliance on "inner light" or on reason alone, are all delusive because all depend upon a password, a simple magical formula unrelated to the conditions of life. Swift's anti-romantic poems are, like Johnson's later strictures on classical and pre-romantic poeticizing, attacks on a very real danger of the time, the tendency to substitute for hard realistic thinking and feeling a ready-made theory, whether of literature or of conduct.

Swift's dealings with political matters show clearly these central concerns. The state, like everything else, must be set in relation to moral standards before it can be seen in proportion and properly evaluated, but since it has its origins in human needs it must be seen also as part of the muddled life of man. There is no simple answer to political problems, for the state has grown through trial and error, through the pressure of experience, and it is not a planned and consistent thing. To try to impose consistency upon it, cutting through those growths which have developed through necessary adjustment to the vagaries of life, would be dangerous. It would also be a waste of time; for men of Swift's generation the reorganized state of the Commonwealth, which so quickly crumbled under the pressure of chaotic circumstance, was still a vivid lesson. A country may be organized according to the best and most reasonable theory, as the Venetian state had been, but in the end it must stand or fall by the people who compose it, and what is theoretically perfect is not likely to work well in practice, since clarity is usually achieved only by evading some of the facts. Swift will go no further towards a theory of government than to suggest that the Gothic system works best in England—a suggestion which is itself based on a consideration of the country's past experience—and the Gothic system is the most flexible of all, since it depends on the sensitive interrelation of the three sources of power. The modern state has developed in the way that events and persons compelled it, and in doing so it has not followed moral and Christian principles, so that its schemes of wealth and power are, in the last analysis, wrong. But the task of the good man in the modern commercial state is not the easy negative one of condemnation; he can still behave morally and charitably and try to persuade governments to undertake the positive encouragement of virtue. The state can never be a perfect embodiment of moral truth, but it can and should be constantly aware that within the limits laid down by human weakness it can contribute to good. Individual corruption can wreck the best theory of government, but equally virtue in individuals, both governing and governed, can produce moral and physical well-being, provided that the state is seen for what it is, a collection not of economic units nor of disinterested rational beings, but of fallible men and women, to deal with whose passions and prejudices continual flexibility, adjustment, and compromise are essential.

Thus in the political sphere is visible Swift's characteristic approach to the problems of human activity. He does not lose sight of his central principles, but he finds that in practice these principles are best sustained through adaptability, for they can never be fruitfully considered except in relation to "John, Peter, Thomas, and so forth," to the way human beings really act, think, and feel. The actuality against which all systems must finally strike is that of human nature, and, set against one another, theories and individuals present only the barren opposition of the early poems, that between unreal order and real confusion. The only remedy is to build a tentative and approximate order from confusion itself, one which will allow for human oddity. This is always Swift's compromise solution, the only way in which something like moral order can be attained, for man, being incalculable, will break out of any system and can only be accounted for by the most flexible, inclusive, and empirical of methods. The conception of man as a creature ruled by self-love was the most adaptable of contemporary approaches to a definition, for it allows for degrees of goodness and, handled as Swift handles it, can form a basis for improvement without departing from a realistic interpretation of human possibilities. It can be reconciled not only with Swift's experience of individual men but with Christian tradition, and so is a firmer basis for morality than those schemes which, in striving to avoid sin by an appeal to the dignity of human nature, fall into the greatest sin of all, the pride which is displayed, at the end of his story, by Lemuel Gulliver. Like so many of Swift's inventions, the philosophers and Aeolists of *A Tale of a Tub,* the Laputans and the sorry heroes of the anti-romantic poems, Gulliver in trying to avoid the deceiving senses and passions has fallen further into matter. Swift's fear and hatred of the mindless, the merely material, is every-

215

where apparent, but if surrender to matter is evil so is the attempt to escape from it by whatever means. Both attitudes must end in deceit and death, for both deny the uniqueness of man, the "mingled Mass of Good and Bad" whose function is to wrest meaning and goodness from the chaotic "matter" of his own nature and of the world he lives in. Nothing could be further from the truth than to see Swift as a destructive and negative satirist; his purpose in destroying false and unrealistic simplifications is to show us the only conditions upon which life can be fully and creatively lived. As he himself claims in his letters to Pope, his is a constructive approach to his fellow-man, in the long run kinder and more helpful than the optimistic enthusiasm of those who expect him to be not *animal rationis capax* but *animal rationale,* interpreting the ancient definition to imply that man can be summed up in terms of reason as a beast is summed up in terms of instinct. For in fact much of the goodness man is capable of arises not from reason but from feeling, if that feeling is guided by a reason and a conscience subject to religion. Swift never believed that rational benevolence or action for the good of the species was possible for fallen humanity; in Shaftesbury's terms he is, he admits by implication, a "compleat Timon or man-hater": "principally I hate and destest that animal called man." But he did believe we are capable of something that he considered to be a sounder basis for goodness; he believed in tolerance, compassion, responsiveness to one another's individual needs. His examples of such goodness are necessarily, in the terms of his satire, unobtrusive and quiet, since they represent all that is left after the destruction of mistaken aims and unrealizable ambitions, the humble endeavors of men content with the common forms, with unrefined reason and traditional wisdom, who recognize that a radical removal of prejudice may end in the loss of all that makes us human. But for all their unobtrusiveness they can be recognized as embodiments of a consistent and positive view, from the wise bee and the wise ancients and the modest sensible Martin to the giant and human figures of the *Travels,* so attractive in their touching concern for the increasingly graceless Gulliver. In *The Battle of the Books* Swift's ordering of chaos is made

216

on the limited scale which is all he can, so far, honestly achieve; he moves among the comparative simplicities of literary and scientific argument. In *A Tale of a Tub* the emphasis is on the "uncreating word," on the sterility and inhumanity of all philosophic or religious movements which turn away from the center, from sense and experience interpreted by a humble reason. The *Tale* is Swift's own modern cobweb, fastened precariously to reality at one point only, at the figure of Martin, and through it he explores the dilemma of the odes. This is the fairyland of dreams and deceit, where for all the busy spinning of Peter and Jack, the Author and his philosophers, "the animating mind is fled," and with it moral standards; as in *The Dunciad*, "unawares Morality expires."

If this were Swift's last word his message would be incomplete, his work unsatisfying in the last resort for all its brilliance, for though his solution is present here it is lacking in force and inevitability, and it is felt as a conditional acceptance, a hypothesis rather than a conviction. But in *Gulliver's Travels* conviction is reached after a long testing of the hypothesis against experience, and is given complete expression. The madness of *A Tale of a Tub,* which is the madness of all of us, is set into place, seen in due proportion by a mature and tolerant mind. In three books human absurdities and failings are shown, but so, in Brobdingnag, are human possibilities, and in the voyage of Houyhnhnm-land the kind of moral order possible and desirable for man is more precisely displayed. Two extremes, two false simplifications, are set into relation, and the contrast between clarity and confusion is at last resolved. Between the opposed half-truths of Houyhnhnm and Yahoo, of mind and matter, stand Swift's examples of fulfilled humanity, embodying an order reached not by omission but by acceptance of complexity. The full meaning of this last book is not in any one figure but in the interrelation of them all, and its form is a perfect expression of the process of balance and inclusion by which Swift's solution is attained. Here he is successfully at grips with that problem which underlies the difficulties of politics and philosophy, science and morality, the problem of man himself, and in solving it he has produced one of the greatest, sanest, and wisest of the serious comedies of the age of compromise.

NOTES

The following abbreviations are used:

Works *Prose Works of Jonathan Swift,* ed. Herbert Davis (Basil Black-well, 1937) (in progress).

T.S. *Prose Works of Jonathan Swift,* ed. Temple Scott (George Bell, 1898-1908).

Corr. *The Correspondence of Jonathan Swift,* ed. F. Elrington Ball (George Bell, 1910-1914).

Poems *The Poems of Jonathan Swift,* ed. Harold Williams (Clarendon Press, 1937).

T.T. *A Tale of a Tub to which is added The Battle of the Books and The Mechanical Operation of the Spirit,* ed. A. C. Guthkelch and D. Nichol Smith (Clarendon Press, 1920).

Journal *Journal to Stella,* ed. Harold Williams (Clarendon Press, 1948).

CHAPTER I

1. See Sandor Ferenczi, "Gulliver Fantasies," *Final Contributions to the Problems and Methods of Psycho-Analysis,* London, 1955, pp. 41-60.
2. *T.S.,* XI, 367-82.
3. *Corr.,* IV, 76.
4. *Journal,* I, 110.
5. *Corr.,* IV, 366.
6. *Corr.,* III, 315.
7. *Corr.,* V, 306.
8. *Corr.,* IV, 195.
9. *Corr.,* II, 153.
10. *T.S.,* I, 280.
11. *Corr.,* I, 4.
12. *Poems,* I, 55.
13. *Corr.,* I, 367.
14. *Journal,* I, 229.
15. *Journal,* I, 229-30.
16. *Journal,* I, 231.
17. *Corr.,* IV, 78.
18. *Corr.,* IV, 217.
19. *Corr.,* III, 436.
20. *Corr.,* IV, 330.
21. *Poems,* I, 170.
22. *Corr.,* III, 157.
23. *Corr.,* III, 277.
24. *Corr.,* IV, 167.
25. *Poems,* II, 498.
26. The recognition of the importance of the "mask," or assumed identity, in Augustan satire has been one of the most vital of modern contributions to the criticism of Swift. Among those who have written on the

subject are Robert C. Elliott, "Swift's *Tale of a Tub:* an Essay in Problems of Structure," *PMLA,* LXVI, 1951, and "Gulliver as Literary Artist," *ELH,* XIX, no. 1, 1952; John M. Bullitt, *Jonathan Swift and the Anatomy of Satire,* Cambridge, Mass., 1953; William B. Ewald, *The Masks of Jonathan Swift,* Oxford, 1954.

27. *An Essay on Man,* I, 87-90, and III, 19-20.

28. *The Memoirs of Martinus Scriblerus,* ed. C. Kerby-Miller, Yale University Press, 1950, Preface, p. 32.

29. Herbert Davis, *The Satire of Jonathan Swift,* New York, 1947, p. 42.

30. *T.T.,* p. 157.

Chapter II

1. Prologue to *Aureng-Zebe,* ll. 21-22.

2. *Essays,* ed. W. P. Ker, Oxford, 1900, I, 14-15. See also T. S. Eliot, "The Age of Dryden," *The Use of Poetry and the Use of Criticism,* London, 1933, pp. 54-58.

3. "To My Honored Friend Sir Robert Howard," ll. 25-34.

4. "An Hymne of Heavenly Beautie," ll. 295-96.

5. *The Faerie Queene,* VII, 58.

6. *An Essay on Man,* I, 289-90.

7. *The Countess of Pembroke's Arcadia,* ed. A. Feuillerat, Cambridge, 1912, III, 10, v.

8. *Essays,* ed. Ker, II, 123.

9. *Of Human Understanding,* II, i, 24.

10. *The English Works of Thomas Hobbes,* ed. W. Molesworth, London, 1840, IV, 22.

11. *Of Human Understanding,* III, iii, 11.

12. *T.S.,* III, 193.

13. This concern is of course by no means confined to Dryden and Swift. Shaftesbury and John Dennis among others recognized and tried to deal with the problem, Shaftesbury being concerned chiefly with its moral, Dennis with its literary, aspects. But Shaftesbury's attempt was suspect in its religious unorthodoxy, Dennis's in its religious enthusiasm and its hostility to the literature of wit, which included all the greatest writing of the period.

14. Meyrick Carré, *Phases of Thought in England,* Oxford, 1949, p. 258.

15. *English Works,* ed. Molesworth, IV, 449.

16. *Poems,* I, 19-20.

17. *Poems,* I, 25.

18. *Poems,* I, 34.

19. *Poems,* I, 35.

20. It is frequent in the "Ode to Mr. Congreve," where the image of the obscured sun of wit approaches the use made of it by Pope, though Swift's handling of the figure never achieves the density of Pope's

> Spin all your Cobwebs o'er the Eye of Day!
> The Muse's wing shall brush you all away.
>
> ("Epilogue to the Satires," II, 222-23.)

NOTES (pp. 27-37)

21. "Preface to Shakespeare," *Works,* London, 1825, V, 109.

22. See Gordon McKenzie, "Swift and Reason," *Five Studies in Literature,* University of California Publications in English, VIII, No. 1, 101-28. John Toland, who was very alert to the religious and philosophical problems of the day, remarks: "But we find by Experience, that the word Reason is become as equivocal and ambiguous as any other" (*Christianity Not Mysterious,* London, 1702, p. 8). The clergy, he says, often "preach against Human Reason" (p. 109). Toland's own definition of reason follows that of Locke.

23. *Religio Laici,* 62-67, 78-79.

24. *An Essay on Man,* III, 229-32; I, 293-94.

25. *The True Intellectual System of the Universe,* London, 1734, Preface, p. xxxvii.

26. Whichcote, *Aphorisms,* ed. Salter, 1753, No. 460.

27. John Tulloch, *Rational Theology and Christian Philosophy in England in the Seventeenth Century,* 1874, II, 68.

28. John Smith, *Select Discourses,* ed. H. G. Williams, 1859, p. 14.

29. *Works,* IX, 261-62.

30. *T.S.,* III, 178.

31. *Christianity Not Mysterious,* London, 1702, pp. vii-viii.

32. *Of Human Understanding,* IV, xviii, 8.

33. *Works,* IX, 262.

34. *Works,* I, 243.

35. *Works,* IX, 261.

36. *T.S.,* III, 194.

37. This is of course an ancient and orthodox argument, but in the climate of the eighteenth century the choice of arguments from the fathers of the church becomes significant. The doctrine of the Trinity was the focal point at this time of the controversy between the orthodox and the Deists and rationalists of various kinds.

38. *Christianity Not Mysterious,* London, 1702, p. 6.

39. *Of Human Understanding,* IV, xvii, 23.

40. Locke's position in *The Reasonableness of Christianity* is similar.

41. *Orthodox Paradoxes,* London, 1657, First Part, I, i.

42. *Works,* IX, 161-62. For an examination of the sermon "On the Trinity" as a deliberate marshaling of contemporary arguments against Deism (and of course against the Socinians) see Louis A. Landa, "Swift, the Mysteries, and Deism," *University of Texas Studies in English,* 1944, pp. 239-56. It is plain from Toland's *Christianity Not Mysterious* that the Deists recognized the orthodox insistence on the mysteries as above our "corrupt and limited Understandings" as directed against themselves.

43. *Works,* IX, 77.

44. *Works,* IX, 264.

45. *Works,* II, 15. Compare Hobbes: "When a man reasoneth he does nothing else but conceive a sum total, from addition of parcels; or conceive a remainder, from subtraction of one sum from another. . . . For REASON, in this sense, is nothing but reckoning, that is adding and subtracting, of

221

the consequences of general names agreed upon for the marking and sig-
nifying of our thoughts" (*English Works*, ed. Molesworth, III, 29-30).
Also: "When from his conclusion a man may, by good ratiocination, derive
that which is contradictory to any evident truth whatsoever, then he is said
to have concluded against reason: and such a conclusion is called absurdity"
(IV, 24).

46. *Works*, IX, 164.

47. *Works*, IX, 166.

48. *Poems*, I, 34-35.

49. That the senses are the source of all knowledge available to man
was a respectable doctrine long before the new philosophy of the seventeenth
century; Aquinas accepts the Aristotelian "nihil est in intellectu quod non
prius fuerit in sensu." But whereas for him the reason which operated
upon this lowly material enabled man to reach knowledge beyond the
senses, already by Montaigne's time the situation looked different: "The
senses are the beginning *and end* of humane knowledge." (My italics.)
The lowered status of reason forced many writers of the seventeenth century to insist on the activity of the mind in intellection, and on the independence of the "Act of Intellection." Richard Baxter, Charron, and many
others, as well as the Cambridge school, were concerned in this.

50. This familiar example was known to the ancient sceptics and used
for various purposes through the centuries, e.g., by Duns Scotus and by
Montaigne. It was still in regular use in the seventeenth century, e.g., by
Joseph Glanvill.

51. Spenser uses "th' eternall lampes, wherewith high Jove Doth light
the lower world" (*The Faerie Queene*, III, i, 57) for contrast with the
vanity and fickleness of sinful humanity, and Montaigne compares weak
man with "the incorruptible life of the celestiall bodies, their beauty,
greatnesse, and agitation, continued with so just and regular a course"
(*Essays*, trans. Florio, 1908, II, 169).

52. *Poems*, I, 39.

53. *Aphorisms*, ed. Salter, No. 76.

54. *Works*, IX, 262.

CHAPTER III

1. *Works*, IX, 263.

2. *T.S.*, I, 278. Presumably on the grounds that Tillotson had put
forward at length in his sermon, "The Wisdom of Being Religious," where
he points out that religion serves our eternal interest, not the transitory
pleasures of the world, and that "upon consideration of the whole, and
casting up all things together, it does advise and lead us to our best interest"
(*Works*, London, 1743, I, 13). Shaftesbury would have agreed that self-love
can be a motive, though a mercenary and servile one, for religious ob-
servance, but he disapproves of the church's appeal to it because this
strengthens self-love by constant exercise and spreads it through all the
parts of life (*An Inquiry concerning Virtue and Merit*, I, 3, iii; *Characteristicks*, 1723, II, 58).

3. *T.S.,* I, 278, and *Works,* I, 242. Such ideas may readily be paralleled by references to the passions as necessary to produce movement and action in man, as a wind is necessary to a ship, in *An Essay on Man,* in Montaigne (*Essays,* trans. Florio, London, 1908, II, 347), and Fontenelle (*Œuvres,* Paris, 1790, I, 298), and in part by William Wollaston's reference to the passions as disposing us to action "when there are no arguments of a higher nature to move us" (i.e., arguments of reason) (*Religion of Nature Delineated,* London, 1726, p. 174).

4. *An Essay on Man,* II, 53-54, and 107-08.

5. *Upon Compassion, Works,* ed. Gladstone, Oxford, 1896, II, 98.

6. *An Essay on Man,* II, 101-06.

7. *Works,* IX, 145-46.

8. *Works,* IX, 73.

9. *Works,* IX, 242.

10. *Works,* IX, 247.

11. *Works,* I, 244.

12. W. K. Wimsatt, "The Augustan Mode in English Poetry," *Journal of English Literary History,* XX, 14.

13. *Scepsis Scientifica,* London, 1885, p. 163.

14. For a discussion of the role of scepticism in the seventeenth century see Louis I. Bredvold, *The Intellectual Milieu of John Dryden,* Ann Arbor, 1934.

15. Montaigne was much read in the later seventeenth century, apparently as a result of Charles Cotton's new translation in 1685. Four editions of this had appeared by 1711.

16. *Corr.,* IV, 98.

17. R. P. Blackmur, *Language as Gesture,* New York, 1952, p. 375.

18. *Essays,* trans. Florio, London, 1908, II, 254.

19. *Essays,* II, 166.

20. *Essays on Several Important Subjects in Philosophy and Religion,* 1676, "The Agreement of Reason and Religion," p. 11. Compare Swift's sermon "On the Trinity."

21. *The Weakness of Human Understanding,* trans. Edward Combe, London, 1725, pp. 129, 143.

22. *Works,* IX, 241.

23. *The Hind and the Panther,* I, 72-79, II, 529-32, I, 68-69.

24. Descartes too is well acquainted with these proofs of the weakness of the senses, which were truisms in the seventeenth century, "those matters of ancient lore," as Hobbes calls them in his set of *Objections* to Descartes's *Meditations.* But Descartes, knowing that "general doubts of this kind lead us straight to the ignorance of Socrates, or the uncertainty of the Pyrrhonists," who "seem never to have worked for anything but learning to doubt" (*Philosophical Works,* trans. Haldane and Ross, Cambridge, 1911, I, 314, 320) and supported by a belief in certain ideas, such as those of God and the soul, which are "imprinted on our souls by nature," uses the ancient proofs not to undermine reason but to support it by showing how necessary

it is to correct the falsity of the senses. Duns Scotus had made similar use of the sceptic examples.

25. *Against Confidence in Philosophy*, p. 17.
26. "Agreement of Reason and Religion," p. 17.
27. *Orthodox Paradoxes*, 1657, Second Part, Third Century, No. 282. Swift often stresses the inconsistency of man, and his dogmatic assertion of constantly changing opinions: e.g., in *Thoughts on Various Subjects*.
28. *Scepsis Scientifica*, p. 183.
29. *Against Confidence in Philosophy*, p. 22.
30. *The Weakness of Human Understanding*, 1725, p. 131.
31. *Against Confidence in Philosophy*, pp. 21-22.
32. *English Works*, ed. Molesworth, IV, 57.
33. *Entretiens sur la Métaphysique*, Cinquième Entretien, XIII. The sharp distinction between mind and bodily "prejudice" is stressed throughout the Fifth, Sixth, and Seventh Dialogues. See also Descartes, e.g., *Principles of Philosophy*, I, xlvii (*Works*, trans. Haldane and Ross, I, 237): "Indeed in our early years, our mind was so immersed in the body, that it knew nothing distinctly, although it perceived much sufficiently clearly; and because it even then formed many judgments, numerous prejudices were contracted from which the majority of us can hardly ever hope to become free."
34. *Scepsis Scientifica*, p. 99.
35. *Works*, I, 240.
36. *T.T.*, pp. 167, 171.
37. *T.T.*, p. 161.
38. *T.T.*, p. 4.
39. *Christianity Not Mysterious*, 1702, p. 127.
40. *Works*, III, 56, 79.
41. *Works*, II, 29, 33.
42. *Works*, I, 243.
43. *Works*, VII, 106.
44. *Works*, II, 27.
45. *Works*, I, 244.
46. *Free Thoughts on Religion, the Church, and National Happiness*, 1720, p. 65.

CHAPTER IV

1. *Works*, IX, 263.
2. *Corr.*, V, 246.
3. *Corr.*, III, 267.
4. *Corr.*, III, 293.
5. "The Difficulty of Knowing One's Self." This sermon is not fully authenticated as being Swift's, and is "printed in the Appendix as doubtful" in *Works*, IX, 349-62. For the arguments for and against its authenticity see, in that volume, the Introduction to the Sermons, by Louis Landa. Though the arrangement of the sermon is more formal, and the style less clear and fluent, than is usual with Swift, the content is often reminiscent of his way

of thinking, and it is quoted here not as an illustration of, but as a well-turned comment upon, an attitude to be felt everywhere in his work.

6. *Corr.,* III, 292-93.

7. *Poems,* II, 553.

8. La Rochefoucauld, *Maximes,* ed. F. C. Green, Cambridge, 1946, p. 29.

9. *Maximes,* 81, 305.

10. *Corr.,* III, 436.

11. *An Essay on Man,* II, 93, 197.

12. *An Essay on Man,* III, 317-18.

13. Bolingbroke, *Philosophical Works,* London, 1754, IV, 389.

14. *Journal,* II, 401.

15. *Corr.,* II, 153.

16. *Corr.,* II, 233.

17. *Corr.,* V, 251. In the context of the letters this remark probably has specific reference to the political situation, but Pope had never shown much pleasure in Hanoverian rule, and the reference to "philosophy" suggests that Swift's satisfaction has a wider basis.

18. *Corr.,* III, 296-97. Objecting to Swift's definition, he refers to a similar conception attributed to Cotta; it is clear from another reference to Cotta in his own writings that what he dislikes in the definition is its implied distrust of human reason. In *Works,* 1754, IV, 390, he attacks those who, like Cotta, question reason on the grounds that it has brought mankind more harm than good.

19. *Corr.,* III, 359.

20. *Works,* 1754, IV, 314.

21. *Corr.,* IV, 98-99. Bolingbroke believed that self-love is "the original spring of human actions" but that it is under the direction of reason and is, in effect, transformed (*Works,* 1754, IV, 2).

22. *Corr.,* III, 208.

23. *The Moralists,* II, ii: *Characteristicks,* 1723, II, 256. See also Shaftesbury's Preface to the sermons of Benjamin Whichcote.

24. *The Moralists,* I, ii: *Characteristicks,* 1723, II, 197, 192.

25. *Corr.,* III, 293, 277.

26. *Characteristicks,* 1723, II, 243; *Characteristicks,* II, 110.

27. *Poems,* II, 659.

28. *Corr.,* III, 277.

29. *Characteristicks,* 1723, II, 153.

30. *Characteristicks,* 1723, I, 118.

31. *Characteristicks,* 1723, II, 25.

32. *The Fable of the Bees,* ed. F. B. Kaye, Oxford, 1924, I, 324.

33. *The Fable of the Bees,* Introduction, p. lxxiii.

34. *The Fable of the Bees,* I, 323-24.

35. *An Enquiry into the Origin of Honour, and the Usefulness of Christianity in War,* 1732, p. 31.

36. *The Fable of the Bees,* I, 325.

37. Mandeville's editor, F. B. Kaye, uses the word to denote the "blend of asceticism and rationalism" in his author's definition.

38. *The Fable of the Bees*, I, 48.

39. *The Fable of the Bees*, I, 323.

40. *T.S.*, I, 278.

41. E.g., the acceptance of mysteries as "contrary to common Reason" and the tendency to see them as trials of our faith and obedience, in "On the Trinity."

42. *Works*, II, 15.

43. *Works*, IX, 244.

44. *The Fable of the Bees*, ed. F. B. Kaye, Oxford, 1924, I, 343.

45. *Works*, IX, 166, 164.

46. *Works*, IX, 247, 246.

47. "On the Testimony of Conscience," *Works*, IX, 154.

48. "An Inquiry concerning Virtue and Merit," II, ii, 1: *Characteristicks*, 1723, II, 119.

49. *Works*, IX, 152.

50. *Works*, IX, 154.

51. *Epistles to Several Persons*, III, 293, *Epistle to Dr. Arbuthnot*, line 319, *The Dunciad*, IV, 653-56.

52. *Works*, IX, 73. This is a common enough example for the necessity of revelation: it is put forward, for example, by Locke, in *The Reasonableness of Christianity*, and by Daniel Whitby in *A Discourse of the Necessity and Usefulness of the Christian Revelation*. But Swift adopts it not as a handy current argument but as a necessity of his nature; revelation offers the only certainty.

53. *Works*, IX, 248.

54. *Corr.*, V, 106-07.

55. R. Crawfurd, *Plague and Pestilence in Literature and Art*, 1914, p. 204. Quoted in *The Poems of Alexander Pope*, Twickenham edition, London, 1950, III, i, 138 n.

56. *Essays*, tr. Florio, London, 1908, II, 402.

57. *The Poems of Alexander Pope*, Twickenham edition, III, i, 7. For a discussion of the "doctrines seemingly opposite" and of Pope's method of steering between them, see the Introduction to this volume.

58. *Epistles to Several Persons*, II, 277-78.

59. *An Essay on Man*, II, 3-18.

60. *Works*, IX, 262.

CHAPTER V

1. *Imitations of Horace*, I, i, 65-70, 77-82.

2. *Epistles to Several Persons*, III, 351-52, 370-74, 47-48.

3. *Epistles to Several Persons*, IV, 169-71.

4. *Scepsis Scientifica*, London, 1885, p. 207.

5. Certainly Berkeley appears to have thought so. In his reduction to absurdity of Mandevillian theory in *Alciphron* he makes Lysicles say that the notion that vice is pernicious to the public, and that men cannot be kept from vice but by the fear of God, has done much mischief, "being in truth

the cause of religious establishments" (*Works,* ed. A. A. Luce and T. E. Jessop, 1950, III, 65).

6. Now presumably best represented by the beliefs and practices of Anglicanism, as in "primitive Sancroft" ("To Dr. William Sancroft") or as in Dr. Sacheverell's famous sermon, in which the primitive worship of the church is sharply opposed to Whiggism, Latitudinarianism, Deism, Socinianism.

7. *Works,* II, 28.

8. *Works,* II, 27.

9. *Works,* III, 91-92.

10. Herbert Davis, *The Satire of Jonathan Swift,* New York, 1947, p. 51.

11. *Works,* II, 62.

12. *Works,* II, 45.

13. *Works,* II, 47.

14. *Works,* II, 57.

15. *Works,* IX, 157.

16. *Works,* III, 92.

17. *Works,* IX, 261.

18. *The Moralists,* II, iv: *Characteristicks,* 1723, II, 321.

19. *Works,* XI, 183.

20. *Works,* II, 2.

21. *Works,* X, 102.

22. *Corr.,* II, 348-49.

23. *Corr.,* II, 39.

24. *Corr.,* IV, 377.

25. *Corr.,* V, 65.

26. *Corr.,* V, 143.

27. Quoted by Rae Blanchard, *The Englishman, A Political Journal by Richard Steele,* Oxford, 1955, p. 427.

28. *Works,* II, 25.

29. *Works,* XI, 173.

30. *Works,* IX, 230-31.

31. *Corr.,* III, 120.

32. *Works,* IX, 229. Compare *Examiner* 33, *Works,* III, 114.

33. *Boswell's Life of Johnson,* ed. G. Birkbeck Hill, Oxford, 1934, I, 424.

34. *Corr.,* III, 120.

35. *Works,* IX, 224.

36. *Works,* II, 17, 18.

37. Forms of mixed government other than this "Gothic" form had, however, existed in the ancient world, as Swift takes care to point out in *Contests and Dissensions, Works,* I, 199.

38. Swift seems to interpret the term "balance of power" quite literally; in *Contests and Dissensions* he considers "what the Nature of a ballance is," and shows that balance in a state is as finely adjusted as a pair of scales, requiring in practice the same tiny adjustments between one side and another (*Works,* I, 197).

227

39. *Works,* IX, 221, 222, 224.

40. *Works,* II, 14-15.

41. Compare the Drapier's *Humble Address to Both Houses of Parliament,* which asserts that in modern Ireland "the highest Points of Interest and Liberty, have been often sacrificed to the Avarice and Ambition of particular Persons" (*Works,* X, 121).

42. *Works,* IX, 234-35.

43. *Works,* IX, 232-33.

44. "On Mutual Subjection," *Works,* IX, 142, 144.

45. *Works,* IX, 206-07.

46. See Louis A. Landa, "*A Modest Proposal* and Populousness," *Modern Philology,* XL, November 1942, 161-70.

47. *Works,* XII, 6.

48. *Works,* XII, 89-90.

49. Louis A. Landa, *Swift and the Church of Ireland,* Oxford, 1954, p. 155.

50. *Works,* XII, 89. See also *An Answer to a Paper, Called A Memorial, Works,* XII, 19, 22.

51. Quoted by Landa, *Swift and the Church of Ireland,* p. 157.

52. *Works,* XII, 112, 111.

53. *Works,* XII, 135-36.

54. *Works,* XII, 116, 115.

55. *Works,* XI, 42.

56. *Works,* XI, 43.

57. *Works,* XI, 119-20.

58. *Works,* XI, 122.

59. *Works,* XI, 254.

60. *Works,* XI, 243.

61. *Works,* XI, 276.

Chapter VI

1. *Works,* I, 244.

2. *Corr.,* IV, 329.

3. *T.T.,* p. 224.

4. *T.T.,* p. 219.

5. See R. F. Jones, *Ancients and Moderns, a Study of the Background of the Battle of the Books,* St. Louis, 1936.

6. *T.T.,* p. 244.

7. *An Examination of Dr. Burnet's Theory of the Earth,* quoted by Ernest Tuveson, "Swift and the World Makers," *Journal of the History of Ideas,* XI, 1950, 63.

8. *T.T.,* p. 232.

9. *T.T.,* p. 235.

10. *Novum Organum,* trans. Johnson, London, 1859, p. 91 (Axiom xcv). Bacon's and Temple's use of these emblematic insects is noticed in Herbert Davis, *The Satire of Jonathan Swift,* New York, 1947, p. 23.

11. *T.T.,* p. 239.

12. See Ernest Tuveson, "Swift and the World-Makers," *Journal of the History of Ideas*, XI, 65.

13. *The Garden*, ll. 67-70.

14. *Works*, II, 29, 32.

15. *Works*, XI, 117.

16. *Works*, XII, 117-18.

17. *T.T.*, p. 209.

18. W. K. Wimsatt, "The Augustan Mode in English Poetry," *Journal of English Literary History*, XX, 9.

19. *T.T.*, p. 83.

20. *T.T.*, pp. 136-37.

21. No doubt Swift had in mind that "moderns" of various kinds, as well as the dissenters, were anxious to simplify religion. It was often the cloak for Deism and so was regarded with double suspicion. Fontenelle remarks with some regret, in *The History of Oracles:* "Meantime these Prejudices that have got into the true Religion are, as I may say, so closely interwoven with it, that they have attracted a Respect to themselves, which is only due to the true Religion; and we dare not censure the One for fear of attacking at the same time something that is sacred in the Other." This is precisely Martin's problem, and Swift himself has a worried comment on the question in his *Thoughts on Religion*.

22. *Works*, IX, 226.

23. *T.T.*, pp. 30, 210.

24. See Miriam K. Starkman, *Swift's Satire on Learning in 'A Tale of a Tub,'* Princeton, 1950.

25. *T.T.*, pp. 78, 79-80.

26. *T.T.*, p. 169.

27. *T.T.*, p. 62.

28. *T.T.*, p. 68.

29. This could presumably be deduced from Hobbes's opinion that imagination and memory are but one thing, the only difference being that memory "supposeth the time past" (*English Works*, ed. Molesworth, I, 398).

30. *T.T.*, p. 174.

31. *T.T.*, p. 173.

32. *T.T.*, p. 172.

33. *T.T.*, p. 173.

34. *Essays*, trans. Florio, 1908, II, 399.

35. This doubleness of reference is one of the many indications that the "Author," though conveniently spoken of as a person, is really only an embodiment of various aberrations from reality and good sense, a rag-bag of qualities, some complementary but some flatly contradictory.

36. *T.T.*, p. 123.

37. *T.T.*, p. 193. Henry More uses a similar figure when he compares those who abandon reason for "the Spirit" as their guide to men who should put out their torches and lanterns in the dark and run the hazard of "knocking their noses against the next tree they meet, and tumbling into the next ditch" (*Enthusiasmus Triumphatus*, section 54). That Swift's

emphasis is not on reason but on the senses which provide the materials reason has to work upon, and the limits within which it can function, is the measure of the difference between him and the Cambridge school.

38. *T.T.*, p. 271.

39. *A Discourse concerning the Mechanical Operation of the Spirit,* *T.T.*, p. 291. This philosopher is a familiar figure in the seventeenth century and earlier. In Montaigne's *Apologie of Raymond Sebond* (*Essays,* trans. Florio, 1908, II, 303) he appears as an illustration of the "dreames, and mad follies" of presumptuous reason, and he is indeed part of that attack on human pride of which Swift's work is a late example.

40. *T.T.*, p. 171.

41. Miriam K. Starkman, *Swift's Satire on Learning in 'A Tale of a Tub,'* p. 49.

42. *Works*, I, 240.

43. *Poems*, I, 32.

44. *Poems*, I, 54, 55.

45. *Poems*, I, 224, 223, 225.

46. *Poems*, I, 226.

47. *Poems*, II, 583.

48. *Essays,* trans. Florio, 1908, II, 222-23. I have omitted supporting quotations from Ovid and Lucretius.

49. *Poems,* II, 586, 585, 590, 591.

50. *Poems*, I, 321.

51. *T.S.*, XI, 74.

52. *Poems*, I, 42.

CHAPTER VII

1. See especially Marjorie Hope Nicolson and Nora M. Mohler, "The Scientific Background of Swift's *Voyage to Laputa*," and "Swift's Flying Island in the *Voyage to Laputa*," *Annals of Science,* Vol. II, Nos. 3 and 4, 1937.

2. *Works*, XI, 91.

3. *Works*, XI, 116.

4. *Works*, XI, 41.

5. *Works*, XI, 71, 74, 106.

6. *Works*, XI, 41.

7. Ingratitude was a capital crime in the original institutions of Lilliput, but many "scandalous corruptions" had occurred by the time of Gulliver's visit. In *Gulliver's Travels,* countries, as much as individual persons, have to perform subsidiary tasks of specific satiric purpose as well as their general one. The same thing is true of conditions in Brobdingnag.

8. *Works*, XI, 57.

9. *Works*, XI, 107-08.

10. *Works*, XI, 121. The same truth is put forward by the Houyhnhnms of Book IV, though they do not, any more than Gulliver, draw correct conclusions from it.

11. *Works*, XI, 91.

12. *Works*, XI, 97.
13. *Works*, XI, 120.
14. *Works*, XI, 119.
15. *Works*, XI, 111.
16. *Works*, XI, 116.
17. *Works*, XI, 118-19.
18. *Works*, XI, 117.
19. *Works*, XI, 276.
20. *Works*, XI, 49-50.
21. *Works*, XI, 279.
22. Nicolson and Mohler, *Annals of Science,* Vol. II, Nos. 3 and 4.
23. *Works*, XI, 156.
24. *Works*, XI, 154.
25. *Works*, XI, 143.
26. *Works*, XI, 144.
27. *Works*, XI, 147.
28. *Works*, XI, 145.
29. *Works*, XI, 147.
30. *Works*, XI, 150.
31. *Works*, XI, 159.
32. *Works*, XI, 161.
33. *Idler,* 88, *Works,* London, 1825, II, 640.
34. *Works*, XI, 161.
35. *The Dunciad,* IV, 465-68.
36. *Works*, XI, 164.
37. *Works*, XI, 166. Swift always hated, as did Pope, any use of words that suggested the mechanical: another example in Lagado is the scheme, in the School of Language, for carrying "Things" about to converse with, since "Words are only Names for Things" (XI, 169), a hit at the scientific view of words as mere labels for objects. At the other extreme there is the argument from words alone, in effect just as mechanical, which irritates him in Tindal's conclusion that the "body-politic" must be dealt with in the same way as the "body-natural." Upon this argument his comment is, "What, because it is called a Body, and is a Simile, must it hold in all Circumstances!" (*Works*, II, 94). Peter's hunting of syllables and letters is of the same mindless, mechanical nature, and several of Swift's mouth-pieces parody what Locke calls using words without a signification, "only as sounds, which usually served instead of reasons on the like occasions" (*Of Human Understanding,* III, xi, 8).
38. *Works*, XI, 192.
39. *Works*, XI, 196.
40. *Works*, XI, 198.
41. *Works*, XI, 175.
42. *Works*, XI, 111.
43. See, for various approaches to Book IV of *Gulliver's Travels,* John F. Ross, "The Final Comedy of Lemuel Gulliver," *Studies in the Comic* (University of California Publications in English, VIII, no. 2, 1941); May-

nard Mack (ed.), *The Augustans,* 1950 (V of *English Masterpieces: An Anthology of Imaginative Literature from Chaucer to T. S. Eliot*); Kathleen Williams, "Gulliver's Voyage to the Houyhnhnms," *ELH,* XVIII, no. 4, 1951; Harold D. Kelling, *"Gulliver's Travels,* A Comedy of Humours," *University of Toronto Quarterly,* XXI, no. 4, 1952; John M. Bullitt, *Jonathan Swift and the Anatomy of Satire,* Cambridge, Mass., 1953; Martin Price, *Swift's Rhetorical Art, a Study in Structure and Meaning,* New Haven, 1953; R. Quintana, *Swift: an Introduction,* Oxford, 1955; Ellen Douglass Leyburn, *Satiric Allegory: Mirror of Man* (New Haven, 1956); Irvin Ehrenpreis, "The Origins of *Gulliver's Travels," PMLA,* LXXII, no. 5, 1957.

44. *Works,* IX, 242.

45. *Histoire de Caléjava, ou de l'Isle des hommes raisonnables, avec le parallèle de leur Morale et du Christianisme,* Dijon, 1700.

46. Frédéric Lachèvre, *Les Successeurs de Cyrano de Bergerac,* Paris, 1922, p. 210.

47. Gabriel de Foigny, *La Terre Australe Connue,* printed from the edition of 1676 (Geneva) with variants from the edition of 1692 (Paris) in Lachèvre, *Les Successeurs de Cyrano de Bergerac,* Paris, 1922, p. 104.

48. Lachèvre, p. 102.

49. Lachèvre, p. 95.

50. Lachèvre, p. 105. In the 1676 version; the passage was omitted later.

51. It is used in the seventeenth century, for example, by Godfrey Goodman, in *The Fall of Man, or the Corruption of Nature* (1616) and is one of the *Orthodox Paradoxes* of Ralph Venning (London, 1657, Second Part, First Century, 77): "He believes that it is a shame for any man or woman to go naked, and yet he believes that the very clothes which cover our nakedness are a shame to us: For Adam and his wife were naked, and were not ashamed."

52. *Works,* XI, 251.

53. *Works,* XI, 224, 228.

54. *Works,* XI, 252-53.

55. *Works,* XI, 258.

56. *Works,* XI, 251.

57. *Works,* XI, 219, 243, 232.

58. Lachèvre, p. 106.

59. *Works,* XI, 220-21.

60. *Works,* XI, 237.

61. *The Fable of the Bees,* I, 323.

62. *Philosophical Works,* London, 1754, VI, 315-16, IV, 388. These terms are frequently reiterated; e.g., *Works,* II, 289; IV, 98, 187.

63. *Corr.,* III, 208-09.

64. See Gordon McKenzie, *Five Studies in Literature,* University of California Publications in English, VIII, No. 1, 104.

65. *Corr.,* IV, 208.

66. D. G. James, *The Life of Reason,* London, 1949, p. 260.

67. *Works,* XI, 222.

68. *Works,* XI, 264.
69. *Works,* XI, 267.
70. "Swift's Yahoos and the Christian Symbols for Sin," *Journal of the History of Ideas,* XV, 1954, 201-17.
71. "On the Philosophical Background of *Gulliver's Travels,*" *Studies in Philology,* XXIII, October 1926, 434-50, a most valuable study.
72. *Works,* XI, 256.
73. *Works,* XI, 234.
74. *Works,* XI, 226.
75. *Works,* XI, 226, 244.
76. *Works,* XI, 238-39, 242-43.
77. *Works,* XI, 242.
78. *Works,* XI, 273-74.
79. *Works,* XI, 280.
80. *Works,* XI, 270, 271, 272.
81. *Works,* XI, xxxvi, xxxv.
82. *Works,* XI, 270.
83. *Works,* IX, 248.
84. *Works,* XI, 273, 272, 276.
85. *Works,* IX, 207.
86. *Essays,* trans. Florio, London, 1908, II, 403.
87. *Catholick Charity Recommended,* p. 28; *Scepsis Scientifica,* London, 1885, p. 193.

Index

For the reader's convenience, all titles are put in italics, whether or not italicized in the text.